SO-BJK-238

Unanticipated Gains

Unanticipated Gains

Origins of Network Inequality in
Everyday Life

Mario Luis Small

Montante Family Library
D'Youville College

OXFORD
UNIVERSITY PRESS

2009

MAR 0 3 2010

OXFORD
UNIVERSITY PRESS

Oxford University Press, Inc., publishes works that further
Oxford University's objective of excellence
in research, scholarship, and education.

Oxford   New York
Auckland   Cape Town   Dar es Salaam   Hong Kong   Karachi
Kuala Lumpur   Madrid   Melbourne   Mexico City   Nairobi
New Delhi   Shanghai   Taipei   Toronto

With offices in
Argentina   Austria   Brazil   Chile   Czech Republic   France   Greece
Guatemala   Hungary   Italy   Japan   Poland   Portugal   Singapore
South Korea   Switzerland   Thailand   Turkey   Ukraine   Vietnam

Copyright © 2009 by Oxford University Press, Inc.

Published by Oxford University Press, Inc.
198 Madison Avenue, New York, New York 10016

www.oup.com

Oxford is a registered trademark of Oxford University Press.

All rights reserved. No part of this publication may be reproduced,
stored in a retrieval system, or transmitted, in any form or by any means,
electronic, mechanical, photocopying, recording, or otherwise,
without the prior permission of Oxford University Press.

Library of Congress Cataloging-in-Publication Data
Small, Mario Luis.
Unanticipated gains : origins of network inequality in everyday life / Mario Luis Small.
  p.   cm.
Includes bibliographical references and index.
ISBN 978-0-19-538435-2
1. Social networks.   2. Social capital (Sociology)   3. Day care centers—Case studies.
I. Title.
HM741.S585 2009
302.3082—dc22   2008041902

Montante Family Library
D'Youville College

9 8 7 6 5 4 3 2 1
Printed in the United States of America
on acid-free paper

Hm
741
.5585
2009
Preface

How well people do depends on the range and quality of their connections. The thousands of books and articles spawned by social capital theory have probably convinced even the toughest skeptics that better connected people enjoy better health, faster access to information, stronger social support, and greater ease in dealing with crises or everyday problems. It has convinced many that to understand inequality in well-being we must understand something about the structure of people's connections. And it has inspired hundreds to study the formal structure of these networks, to uncover the patterns in the systems of nodes (people) and ties (relations) that constitute an actor's network.

But networks do not arise out of thin air. People's networks emerge over the course of their routine activities, in the everyday organizations where those activities take place. Every day, women and men drop off their children in childcare centers, head to work in office buildings, eat lunch in cafeterias, pick up food in grocery stores, get manicures in beauty salons, and attend PTA meetings in schools. They kneel down to pray in churches among other believers, play sports in gyms with other sports fans, and discuss politics in neighborhood associations with other concerned residents. Networks do not exist in a vacuum; they are formed and sustained in offices, schools, churches, country clubs, barber shops, gyms, community centers, universities, political clubs, YMCAs, childcare centers, and countless other everyday organizations where people encounter others.

This book's point of departure is the proposition that these everyday organizations matter to not merely the size but also the nature, quality, and usefulness of people's networks. Routine organizations are not merely places, sites where clusters of nodes and ties happen to exist. Instead, they constitute sets of institutional rules, norms, and practices that to lesser or greater extent affect how their members or participants interact, form personal connections, think of one another, build trust, develop obligations, and share information and other resources. In some organizations, patrons routinely encounter many other people; in others, they meet few. In some, they are subject to formal and informal rules that affect the obligations they feel toward members; in others, they are not. These and many other dynamics affect the nature of the ensuing social relations. That is, the organizations shape, in varying degrees, their patrons' social capital.

This book introduces a perspective on inequality in well-being that considers how people's social capital responds to organizational conditions. Rather than conceiving of networks primarily as nodes and the ties between them, it conceives them mostly as sets of context-dependent relations resulting from routine processes in organizational contexts. Prioritizing context over structure, the book proposes that how much people gain from their networks depends fundamentally on the organizations in which those networks are *embedded*. It also proposes that individuals receive distinct advantages from being embedded in effective *brokers*—organizations that, both intentionally and unintentionally, connect people to other people, organizations, and their resources. This book, following the tradition of studying the unanticipated consequences of social action, documents the network advantages that people may gain from doing little more than participating in the organizations that structure their day-to-day lives. In so doing, it identifies many of the often hidden mechanisms that sustain social inequality.

The book illustrates and develops this model through what might appear to be an unlikely case: a study of the experiences of scores of mothers whose children were enrolled in New York City childcare centers. These mothers varied in race, class, education, and lifestyle; most of them worked, but they had little else in common. The book documents that, because of the conditions of their centers, many of these mothers expanded both the size of their networks and the resources available through them. At the same time, the book reveals that how much, if anything, mothers gained depended on the institutional practices of their respective centers. And it shows that the practices of the centers often resulted from larger factors such as policies of the state, something far removed from the mothers' everyday lives. To help assess these mothers' experiences, the book also analyzes a national survey of 3,500 urban mothers and a New York City survey of nearly 300 centers. To help assess whether the experiences of these mothers were unique, the book compares its findings to published studies on how colleges, churches, beauty salons, and many other organizations affect various aspects of the networks of their members. The results make clear that the experiences of the mothers are not unique, suggesting that differences in well-being arise, in part, because of differences in the organizations in which people's networks are embedded.

Writing this book would have been impossible without the help of many people and institutions. I received invaluable course relief from Princeton University and the University of Chicago during the research and writing of the book. Semester-long leaves taken at Columbia University and at New

York University were instrumental. I thank Irwin Garfinkel at Columbia and Dalton Conley at New York University for making the leaves possible. Parts of this study were funded by grants from Princeton University and from National Institute of Child Health and Human Development (grant 3 R01 HD039135–03S1; Christina Paxson, principal investigator). Sara McLanahan provided invaluable help early on, including the opportunity to add questions to her national survey of mothers of newborns. Christina Paxson allowed me to join one of her grants, and to make this possible did more than anyone could ask. Without Sally Waltman's expert assistance, the survey of New York City childcare centers would not have been successful. Jean Knab and Kevin Bradway provided expertise assistance on the intricacies of the Fragile Families data set. Emily Art, Martha Biondi, Kate Cagney, Cathy Cohen, Michael Dawson, Edward Laumann, Jennifer Lee, Devah Pager, Nicole Marwell, Omar McRoberts, Yasmina McCarty, Jamila Michener, Sabrina Placeres, Sandra Smith, Celeste Watkins-Hayes, and Chris Winship read several early chapters, and in some cases entire drafts. Several anonymous reviewers provided invaluable feedback. Several research assistants were instrumental to the completion of the work. Laura Stark worked diligently on this project when it was nothing more than a hunch. Erin Jacobs and Rebekah Massengill were hard-working, astute, and thoughtful researchers. My original plan, when I still entertained the fantasy that the book would be finished in two years, was to coauthor the book with the two of them. The changes in the book and the shifts in their interests did not make this possible. However, I am happy that at least one coauthored paper resulted from our collaboration. That paper was published in the September 2008 issue of *Social Forces* and is reproduced (with some changes) in Chapter 7 with permission. At Oxford University Press, James Cook was a pleasure to work with, and Stephanie Attia was a patient and constructive production editor. Finally, and most important, I thank the many women and men who agreed to give us their time for this project. I gained much more from their openness than I ever anticipated.

Contents

Part I

PERSONAL TIES IN ORGANIZATIONAL SETTINGS

1

Social Capital and Organizational Embeddedness

Imagine two women, Jane and Victoria, both single mothers of a young child who earn $18,000 a year as cashiers in a department store. While Jane's education ended after high school, Victoria's has continued, and she is currently a sophomore in college. What is Victoria's advantage over Jane?

An economist might expect Victoria to have better prospects because of her investment in human capital, the skills and education she is accumulating in college.[1] This human capital would include not only the knowledge of specific subject matters such as English literature or engineering, but also the general skills that students tend to acquire through their classes, such as how to write clearly, how to investigate a topic using libraries and the Internet, and how to make convincing arguments. This human capital would improve Victoria's future prospects and also her current circumstances, since her research and communication skills would probably help her when meeting immediate needs such as finding a doctor, a babysitter, or subsidized health care.

A sociologist might expect Victoria to reap additional gains from her investment in social capital, the resources inherent in the social networks she is acquiring in college.[2] These resources, which include the information these networks provide and the informal and reciprocal obligations their members may feel toward her, would motivate her to invest in meeting others, such as students and professors. Some students would provide social support; others would connect her to people beyond her socioeconomic background; and her professors would likely guide and advise her, inform her about job and educational opportunities, and recommend Victoria to potential employers. Social capital theory would alert us to the fact that the college is a place not merely to acquire skills but also to make connections.

The theory ignores, however, that the magnitude of Victoria's social capital advantage would depend substantially on the conditions of the college. A college is not merely a place; it is a formal organization with norms, rules, and practices that, by guiding the behavior and interactions of its participants, inevitably shapes their networks. Victoria's network

3

advantage, I suggest, might be either much greater or greatly diminished, depending on conditions of this organization.

First, these conditions would strongly affect the size and composition of her new network. Social capital theorists such as Pierre Bourdieu and Nan Lin, when explaining why people made connections, used the term "investment" to emphasize that people made ties because they recognized, or believed, that connections offer advantages. (This helps explain the term "social *capital*.") In doing so, however, they implicitly prioritized, in the process of tie formation, the role of people's choices over that of their environments. While some people certainly make connections because they know it may help them later on, others are shy, reluctant to approach strangers, or uncomfortable with thinking of relations in instrumental terms. The less of a social investor Victoria is, the more her new friendships will depend on how the college structures her interactions with others—for example, on its professors' rules with respect to group projects, on its deans' support of sports teams or student clubs, and on its available cafés, lounges, socials, festivals, and the like. In fact, Victoria may be least likely to make friends with some of the students who, from an investment perspective, might be the most useful. Seniors, being more experienced, knowledgeable, and locally connected, are for many purposes more useful social ties than are underclassmen and women. But Victoria, if she resembles most sophomores, will tend to make friends among sophomores, if for no other reason than colleges tend to structure courses, and therefore opportunities to meet, around cohorts—with seminars reserved for juniors and seniors and introductory lectures intended for first-years and sophomores. Victoria's new social ties would be made not merely *in* the college, but in many ways *by* it.

Second, the organizational conditions of the college would shape the nature of these social networks, including the obligations they carry. James Coleman and other social capital theorists emphasized that the obligations that people feel toward each other tend to emerge informally from within their networks, a process easy to imagine in Victoria's situation.[3] For example, if Victoria resembles most students, then over time she will probably develop informal relationships with some of her professors, who will in turn feel inclined to provide some form of guidance. But not all obligations bubble up naturally from interpersonal relations. Depending on her college, many professors who feel no personal inclination to help Victoria will provide some guidance anyway, because many colleges institute *formal* obligations under which professors are supposed to guide students. Under these obligations, faculty must become available to students for meetings, advise direction in the course of study, provide insight into a future career, write letters of recommendation, and generally provide access to the resources characteristic of their roles. If her college strongly enforced such obligations, then Victoria's advantage over Jane would be significantly greater.

Third, the conditions of the college would determine whether, in addition to ties to other people, Victoria also formed ties to other organizations. Colleges can maintain ties to many organizations, and many types of resources may travel across them. Sometimes, these connections might produce little more than access to information from other organizations. The college might make Victoria's job search much easier than Jane's if it provided a "career services" office with a small library with file folders listing contact information for area employers and graduate programs. This targeted, ready-collected, presorted information would be available to Victoria as needed. Other times, the connections might be more engaged, such that the college effectively *mobilized* these connections for its students. If the college cooperated with those management and finance firms that visit campuses each spring to recruit graduating seniors, Victoria's advantage over Jane in finding a well-paying job would be immeasurably greater. Finally, some connections to other organizations would be not so much mobilized as institutionalized, providing access to resources useful to her day-to-day well-being. Victoria might now be indirectly associated with a loose network of organizations that target resources toward those who share membership in organizations such as hers—that is, toward formally enrolled college students. By virtue of her student identification card, Victoria could receive automatic discounts on museum, theater, musical entertainment, and even train and airplane tickets.

In short, Victoria's network advantage over Jane would depend strongly on her college, which might, intentionally or not, either increase it dramatically or diminish it substantially. Colleges are unique organizations, ones that can be as close to a "total institution" as an average citizen is likely to encounter in contemporary industrialized societies.[4] But with respect to their impact on networks, colleges are often little more than especially effective *brokers*, organizations that, through multiple mechanisms, tie people to other people, to other organizations, and to the resources of both.

This book argues that people's social capital depends fundamentally on the organizations in which they participate routinely, and that, through multiple mechanisms, organizations can create and reproduce network advantages in ways their members may not expect or even have to work for. Some organizations are more effective than others, and others are not effective at all. But understanding people's connections—and how much connections generate social inequality—requires understanding the organizations in which those connections are embedded. It requires conceiving of people as organizationally embedded actors, as actors whose social *and* organizational ties—and the resources both available and mobilized through them—respond to institutional constraints, imperatives, and opportunities. The book proposes a model to understand these processes and illustrates this model by applying it to the case of mothers whose children are enrolled in childcare centers. I believe the childcare center represents an ideal place to examine these questions, because centers tend to be effective brokers while nonetheless differing dramatically in their effectiveness, and because they exhibit a remarkably wide array of mechanisms by which both social and organizational ties are brokered.

The present chapter makes the case that the mechanisms by which organizations broker social and organizational ties can be studied systematically, and that childcare centers represent an ideal site in which to identify many of these mechanisms. The chapter proceeds in four parts. First, it briefly reviews and critiques the social capital perspective, identifying the questions the theory has failed to answer and explaining the consequences of this neglect. Second, it identifies the three basic assumptions on which this book's alternative, the organizational embeddedness perspective, rests.[5] Third, it briefly summarizes the implications of these assumptions, specifying *what* aspects of people's networks are affected by organizational conditions, *how* they are affected, and *why*. Finally, the chapter explains why childcare centers, and the experience of mothers within them, constitute an ideal case to examine these questions.

SOCIAL CAPITAL THEORY

The Theory

Social capital theory argues that people do better when they are connected to others because of the goods inherent in social relationships. These goods— the social capital—include the obligations that people who are connected may feel toward each other, the sense of solidarity they may call upon, the information they are willing to share, and the services they are willing to perform. People who are socially connected therefore have recourse to a stock of "capital" they can employ when needed. The term "social capital" was first used in this sense by economist Glenn Loury. However, the intellectual roots of the theory lie more firmly in the works of Bourdieu and Coleman. In recent years, Lin has worked harder than anyone to develop a formal theory of social capital. These three authors, Bourdieu, Coleman, and, Lin, define social capital in somewhat different ways, but they all conceive it as the resources that inhere in social relations.[6]

Bourdieu defined social capital as "the aggregate of the actual or potential resources which are linked to possession of a durable network of more or less institutionalized relationships of mutual acquaintance and recognition"—that is, as the resources one derives from belonging to a network.[7] Bourdieu believed that people possessed varying amounts of different kinds of "capital," such as cultural capital (knowledge of high art) and economic capital (possession of financial resources). As a result, he argued that social capital included any type of resource available through one's social ties: the "volume of the social capital possessed by a given agent thus depends on the size of the network of connections he can effectively mobilize and on the volume of the capital (economic, cultural, or symbolic) possessed in his own right by each of those to whom he is connected."[8]

Coleman defined social capital as the obligations, norms, and information available to a person from her or his network. To understand Coleman's definition, it helps to know that his intellectual mission was to develop a model of social behavior that was both sociologically compelling and rooted in the idea that actors are rational.[9] Thus, he explained, "If we begin with a theory of rational actor, in which each actor has control over certain resources and interests in certain resources and events, then social capital constitutes a particular kind of resource available to an actor."[10] The first of these resources was the set of obligations a relation might feel: "If A does something for B and trusts B to reciprocate in the future, this establishes an expectation in A and an obligation on the part of B."[11] This obligation becomes a resource that actor A can employ in the future. A second resource was the presence of norms that encourage people to help each other: "A prescriptive norm within a collectivity that constitutes an especially important form of social capital is the norm that one should forgo self-interest and act in the interests of the collectivity."[12] If a group has a norm that people should forgo their self-interest, then an actor within it can reliably turn to others in the group for help when needed. A third resource was information, the knowledge that people to whom an actor is connected possess.

Lin defined social capital as the "resources embedded in a social structure that are accessed and/or mobilized in purposive actions."[13] Lin's objective was both to synthesize the work of earlier theorists and to fit the theory formally into social network analysis, something Bourdieu never did and Coleman only began to do. In fulfilling this objective, Lin assumed that actions are not only purposive but also rational. Lin, following Coleman and Bourdieu, argued that four types of resources constitute social capital: information, the influence that networks have over people, the social credentials that networks can impart, and the personal reinforcements, essential for mental health, that networks provide actors. Lin has contributed to a large body of work showing that people who have access to these resources have better mental health and reach higher positions in the occupational ladder.[14]

In sum, while the authors differed in the specific resources they included under the rubric of social capital, they all agreed that social capital referred to resources people derived directly from their social ties.

The Missing Question: How Do People Make Social Ties?

These researchers have spawned a massive literature on the benefits of social capital.[15] But the researchers devoted little time to an important question: how do people make the social ties that provide access to these resources? Coleman sidestepped this question; Bourdieu devoted but a few paragraphs to it; and Lin, who wrote perhaps more, ultimately did not answer it.[16]

Lin did not explain how people made social ties because his model, in which networks result from investments, made the question irrelevant. Lin believed that people act rationally, motivated by both instrumental and expressive needs. For either reason, actors invest in social relations with an eye to the returns: "[The] theory . . . suggests that actors . . . are motivated by instrumental or expressive needs to engage other actors *in order to* access these other actors' resources for the purpose of gaining better outcomes."[17] That is, the model explicitly proposed that people make connections because of the gains they anticipate. However, the model did not *show* this to be the case—the proposition followed naturally from Lin's assumptions that actors tend to behave purposely and that social capital is an effective investment. From this perspective, asking why people make ties inspires as much curiosity as asking why they make money; people do it because they know it is good for them, which is to say that rational actors do what is rational. And since the *why* question was answered in rational terms, the *how* question became trivial, resulting in a programmatic neglect of the processes by which people form useful ties.

Bourdieu also wrote about how people form ties and stated that networks result from investments. However, what he meant by "investments" was ambiguous, so why he did not say more about how people form ties remains unclear. In his most extensive comments on social capital, Bourdieu argued that the "existence of a network of connections is not a natural given, or even a social given."[18] Instead, it results from people's deliberate efforts. "In other words," he explained, "the network of relationships is the product of *investment strategies*, individual or collective, consciously or unconsciously aimed at establishing or reproducing social relationships that are directly usable in the short or long term."[19] By one reading, Bourdieu is arguing that people strategically enter into social relationships because these will be useful in the future. This is not only consistent with Lin's argument; it is Lin's reading of Bourdieu. In fact, Lin argues that an "investment" perspective is the common thread across *all* major social capital theorists.[20] By a different reading, Bourdieu is arguing that, regardless of how they are formed, new ties effectively end up being an investment. This second reading, which is considerably more generous to the author, can be justified by noting that in other works Bourdieu has argued that many actions tend to be habitual, rather than purposive.[21] Nevertheless, I do not believe Bourdieu resolved this tension.[22] So, whether his model made the question irrelevant or he simply never came to address it, Bourdieu did not articulate the mechanisms by which people make connections. At most, he explained that it requires "unceasing effort."[23]

The assumption that social ties result from investments was abandoned by many later social capital researchers, especially those whose research did not involve formal mathematical modeling. Today, authors differ in how much emphasis they place on this assumption, as Charles Kadushin noted when evaluating the idea of investment in social capital theory.[24] Nonetheless, the theoretical lacunae it generated persist in most of the later works: in their devotion to studying the *consequences* of social ties, many researchers have taken for granted the processes from which ties arise. As a result, recent reviews of research on social capital have found little to report about how actors form ties (despite the fact that recent research by formal network analysts and experimental psychologists provides tools with which to answer this question).[25]

Why the Missing Question Matters

Not asking how people form ties creates important problems. First, it leaves unanswered a critical question in the study of network inequality: what mechanisms account for it? A theory of network inequality cannot be content with demonstrating that social ties are useful: if some do better because they have more ties than others, then it certainly seems important to understand why they have more ties. For example, recent studies have tried to determine, using advanced statistical techniques, whether having connections helps people find jobs.[26] Researchers increasingly acknowledge, to their credit, that to properly answer this question they must take into account unobserved differences among people that determine who is well connected in the first place. As a result, researchers have examined ways of statistically controlling for these differences. This solution, however, addresses only half the problem: how people make ties is not merely a statistical nuisance to "control away"; it is a substantive process to understand. Knowledge comes about not only from demonstrating associations but, more important, as Peter Hedstrom and Richard Swedberg maintain, from explaining the mechanisms that give rise to them.[27]

Consider that, without knowing how network inequality arises, developing the means to reduce it becomes impossible. Some believe that social capital theory "blames the victims" for their problems, since it could lead one to the conclusion that if only people bothered to network more effectively, then social inequality might be lowered. More important, critics maintain that the theory's focus on personal networks comes at the expense of the study of larger structural forces. In fact, the theory can be faulted for leaving practitioners at a loss, since one remains unclear about how to decrease differences in the number of useful connections to which people have access.[28]

Second, while this book's concern is the social capital of individuals, this question also informs our knowledge of the social capital of neighborhoods and of nations. At the neighborhood level, Robert Sampson and his colleagues have argued that collective efficacy, the willingness of neighbors to get involved in local problems on behalf of the common good, reduces neighborhood delinquency.[29] When neighbors are willing to call the police if they see something suspicious or scold young people they witness vandalizing street corners, they make it difficult for people to perpetrate street crimes. Sampson and colleagues have found that collective efficacy rises when neighbors tend to know one another. How do neighbors come to know one another? Why do people know more of their neighbors in some areas than others? Unpacking this process is critical to understand what gives rise to collective efficacy. A similar concern motivates this question at the national level. Political scientist Robert Putnam has argued that over the last several decades the United States witnessed a decline in civic participation and collective social capital, as people spend less time in the company others, even when conducting recreational activities such as bowling. To know why people are more likely to bowl alone, it is important to know how people normally make friends with whom to bowl, and why some have more such friends than others.[30]

Third, as I discuss in this book, how a person forms and sustains a tie can affect the social capital to which she has access. That is, many of the obligations people feel and the resources they feel willing to provide others derive from the contexts that gave rise to and sustain their relationships. Of these contexts, none is more important than the organizational context.[31]

ASSUMPTIONS UNDERLYING THIS BOOK

This book proposes an alternative model that first asks how people make connections and argues that a major part of the answer lies in those organizations in which people participate routinely.[32] The book examines how the resulting social capital is affected by these organizational contexts. And it argues that participating in organizations that effectively broker social capital improves people's well-being. The model rests on three assumptions, each of which I discuss with some care: first, that actors may form ties either purposely or nonpurposely; second, that forming ties either purposely or nonpurposely depends on the context of social interaction; and third, that the context of interaction can be shaped significantly by organizations.[33]

Actors May Form Ties Either Purposely or Nonpurposely

Earlier, I described the proposition by social capital theorists that actors invest in networks with an eye to their gains. That proposition suggests that people make ties as a result of purposive actions geared toward the benefits of acquiring social capital. However, people may form new ties through at least three other types of action. To understand what these are, we must distinguish purposive from nonpurposive acts, and global from local action.

Theorists such as Robert Merton refer to an act as purposive if the perpetrator was motivated by an objective, such as requesting an application (act) in order to apply for a job (purpose). Often, the objective motivating an act is rational; in fact, rational choice theory assumes that actors tend to act in pursuit of rational objectives.[34] However, the objective may be rational or irrational, self-interested or altruistic, individual or collective, psychological or cultural.[35] Consider, for example, that people can deliberately act in ways that harm them. All that is required is some purpose. By contrast, a nonpurposive act has no conscious objective. An example is the act of laughing.[36]

An act may be defined either *globally* or *locally*, depending on how narrowly we draw the boundaries around it. A global purposive act, for example, is to attend college with the objective of obtaining a diploma; a very local one is to sign the registration card containing a semester's list of courses. Global acts constitute bundles of local acts; consequently, they may result from multiple or even contradictory motivations, even when they are guided by one overarching purpose. The overarching purpose of college attendance may be to obtain a diploma, but other, subsidiary purposes may include escaping from home, feeling good about oneself, yearning for new experiences, or finding someone to marry.

Depending on their purpose or lack thereof, people may form ties as a result of at least four types of action. First, an actor may form a tie when the purpose of her action is to make a tie. That is, an individual may introduce herself to another to either have more connections or gain access to his or her resources. This idea, the core of the investment perspective, reflects the common usage of "network" as a verb.[37]

Second, an actor may form a tie when the purpose of her action is to accomplish some other objective. That is, making a tie may be a by-product of the pursuit of another aim. Consider a local example: in a grocery store a man waiting in a long checkout line asks the one standing before him for the time. The other responds and starts a conversation that finishes with an exchange of phone numbers and an invitation to have coffee. In this case, the time-seeker formed a tie even though "networking" was not his purpose; the relationship was triggered by an act whose (local) purpose was to learn the time.[38] Consider a global example, which might illustrate more common circumstances: a churchgoer volunteers at a summer block party that serves as a fund-raiser, and consequently meets several of her neighbors. Her (global) purpose was to raise funds for her church; meeting her neighbors was a by-product.

Third, an actor may form a tie when her action had no purpose other than itself. Sociologists have defined an act as *expressive* when it is perpetrated for its intrinsic value, when conducted for its own sake rather than in pursuit of an objective. Many of the actions that we consider emotional, such as laughing, sighing, or crying—when they have no ulterior purpose—are expressive. And they can lead to new ties in informal social situations. Consider an example: a teenager awaiting his turn at a barbershop overhears a barber crack a joke, to the client whose hair he is trimming, about the presidential election; the teenager laughs, prompting a reply from the barber that leads to a conversation and an informal relationship. The teenager's laughter had no purpose; it was strictly an expression that triggered a conversation and relationship.[39] While this teenager's act was locally expressive, globally expressive acts also often form and sustain social relations, according to sociologist Georg Simmel. Simmel believed that much of what makes us human is our practice of "sociability," the state of associating with others for the sake of association, a state in which "talk is a legitimate end in itself."[40] Just as we cry for the sake of crying, Simmel would argue, we often talk for the sake of talking, not in pursuit of some other objective or even for the sake of making ties.

Fourth, an actor may form a tie when her action had neither a true purpose nor even itself (expressively) as a purpose. In these actions, purpose plays no role whatsoever, because they result from preexisting dispositions. Such an act may be defined as *habitual*. While Bourdieu's writings on social capital relied on a model of purposive action, his books on cultural capital examined what he called the "habitus," the set of cultural dispositions to act, accumulated over an actor's lifetime, that embody both a person's own history and that of the group, class, or society of which she formed part. In this model, people act as a result of their customary predispositions.[41] These often operate locally. Consider an example: a woman at a bus stop sees a man bring his forearm to his face and sneeze. She instinctively blurts, "Bless you"; he thanks her, and a conversation ensues. Her act did not, properly speaking, have a purpose (even if later, when prompted, she might explain that her blessing was the polite reaction). Nor was it expressive, the way laughing or crying are intended to express a feeling. Instead, her "Bless you" was blurted out of habit(us). Predispositions also (and perhaps more commonly) operate globally, since global actions that result from habitual tendencies may either place or not place people in situations where meeting others is likely. For example, in the crowded grocery store, suppose that two shoppers see an opportunity to cut the long checkout lines, as one cashier is about to open a register. One cuts; the other does not even think about it—cutting was not his predisposition. Only the second man is likely to meet other shoppers, as they commiserate over the perils of rush-hour shopping.[42] When acts are habitual, expressive, and perpetrated for other purposes, forming ties is often unexpected, resulting from social interactions in the presence of strangers. In these three types of action, forming ties, by definition, is a by-product.

In sum, people can make ties when it was their purpose, when they had a purpose other than making ties, when their purpose was nothing but the act itself, and when they had no purpose at all at the time of social interaction. These four circumstances must form part of any model of tie formation that considers the motivations of the actor.[43]

Forming Social Ties Either Purposely or Nonpurposely Depends on the Context of Social Interaction

The fact that people may form ties when doing so was not necessarily their intention makes clear that understanding how their actions lead to new connections requires knowing something about the context of social interaction. And the less purposely actors pursue social connections, the more we must know about their context. Specifically, we must know whether, how, and under what conditions they interact with others.[44]

First, forming social ties depends on *whether* actors interact at all—that is, on the availability of opportunities to interact with strangers. Among the first researchers to make this point explicitly were Paul Lazarsfeld and Robert Merton, who argued that the root of friendship formation lay in the opportunities people had to interact.[45] Since then, this idea has been proposed and demonstrated many times, perhaps most systematically by Peter Blau and Joseph Schwartz, who relied on it to ground their network theory of contemporary society.[46] For example, sociologist Ray Oldenburg argued that people will find it difficult to meet more than just a few of their neighbors in the absence of informal gathering places such as cafés and neighborhood bars. And Maureen Hallinan has found that elementary and junior high school students tend to have more friends if they are enrolled in larger classes. In fact, opportunities to interact may be critical even for purposive social investors. For example, William J. Wilson argued that people in poor neighborhoods looking for jobs will find it difficult to develop middle-class networks because they lack opportunities to interact with them informally, an argument consistent with the evidence.[47]

Second, making ties depends on *how* actors interact with others: how long they interact, how frequently, how intensely, and while performing what activity. Two of these modes of interaction have been shown to be especially important: how frequently and while performing what activity.

The consequences of frequent interaction have been the foundation of several lines of research, especially those inspired by Richard Emerson's exchange theory and by George Homans's theory of the group. Emerson believed that repeated exchange between people reduced their mutual uncertainty, while Homans believed that repeated interaction between two parties heightened their mutual affection.[48] In support of these ideas, social psychologists have shown in controlled experiments that the more frequently two people interact, the closer they become and the more they trust each other.[49] I suggest that when strangers, for whatever reason, encounter each other repeatedly, they become increasingly likely to develop a friendship. For example, if two neighborhood residents repeatedly see each other at a local diner, with each successive encounter they are more and more likely to become friends, as sociologist Mitchell Duneier chronicles in his study of men's friendships in a Chicago restaurant.[50]

Equally important is the activity being performed. People may form ties when engaged in many activities, as the earlier examples of the shoppers and the passengers at the bus stop illustrate; but not all activities produce new ties in equal measure. Sociologist Scott Feld has defended the significance of "focus," which he defined as "any social, psychological, or physical entity around which joint activities of individuals are organized."[51] A "focus of activity" may result from a common concern, such as when two mothers in a childcare center start a conversation about their children's progress, or two black men waiting at a barbershop begin to debate the best means to avoid razor bumps. The common focus—childcare or grooming—provided each pair a topic around which to start a conversation, a natural entry point to the relationship. Relationships often arise around a common object of attention.[52]

Third, forming social ties also depends on the conditions under which people interact. I refer specifically to the degree of *competitiveness* and the degree of *cooperation*. When interaction is competitive, the parties are struggling over a particular good or resource, such that one will acquire it, or acquire most of it, or acquire it first. Competition makes opponents out of actors, undermining trust and the formation of friendships. As the stakes increase, the chances of tie formation decrease quickly. Consider two job applicants waiting at a small lobby for their respective job interviews. While they might strike up a friendship as they wait to be summoned, the probability that they will do so becomes lower if each of them knows why the other waits; even lower if the firm will offer only one position; and lower still if, in the current job market, no other openings have emerged in many months.[53]

The dynamics of cooperation differ substantially. In cooperative interaction, the parties work jointly to accomplish a collective goal. Cooperating with strangers, I suggest, tends to produce friendships. In experimental settings, social psychologist Edward Lawler has shown that when people successfully accomplish joint tasks, the cohesion of the group increases.[54] For example, when two new mothers at a childcare center are asked to collaborate on a fund-raiser, their need to coordinate and find a way to work together should increase the chances that they become friends.

In sum, independent of their own intentions, people are more likely to form ties when they have opportunities to interact, when they do so frequently, when they are focused on some activity, when they are not competitors, and when they have reason to cooperate.

The Context of Interaction Is Shaped Significantly by Organizations

Finally, I assume that these elements of interaction—whether, how, and under what conditions people interact—react to the organizations in which people participate.[55] This book defines an organization as a loosely coupled set of people and institutional practices, organized around a global purpose, and connected, both formally and informally, to other organizations.[56] It considers routine organizations in which people, whether patrons or employees, have opportunities to interact with others, such as childcare centers, barbershops, diners, Internet cafés, colleges, firms, synagogues, YWCAs, bowling alleys, and recreation centers. Three issues in this definition demand attention.

First, an organization refers to both the actors who compose it and the institutional practices that organize their behavior. A childcare center is composed of teachers, directors, parents, children, and janitors and institutional practices such as teaching, pickup and drop-off, play time, after-lunch napping, and PTA meetings. An organization's *actors* influence tie formation to the extent that they determine how people interact, such as when a center director asks parents to introduce themselves to one another at a PTA meeting.[57] An organization's *institutional practices* also influence tie formation to the extent that they shape social interaction. Practices, however, may be "institutional" in two different senses, one normative and one cognitive.

An institution in the normative sense may be defined, following Victor Nee and Paul Ingram, as "a web of interrelated norms—formal and informal—governing social relationships."[58] That is, an organization may enforce rules and norms that its actors feel compelled to follow, such as a requirement that all new college students participate in first-year orientation or the norm that congregation members should fund-raise for the church. Since organizations can enforce compliance under the threat of lost membership, they can motivate participants effectively. An institution in the cognitive sense may be defined, following John Meyer and Brian Rowan, as "classifications built into society as reciprocated typifications and interpretations."[59] These institutions are not mandates but categories, generally taken for granted, through which actors interpret their world and social interactions. Whereas normative institutions tell actors how they ought to behave, cognitive institutions shape their perception of their circumstances. Such cognitive understandings shape, for example, whether coworkers perceive one another primarily as competitors or, instead, as members of the same team. For example, while some clothing retailers do not pay their workers on commission, others do, implicitly encouraging competition even though there is no "rule" or "norm" mandating competitiveness. Either normatively or cognitively, organizations may institutionally encourage social interaction that is limited or frequent, competitive or cooperative.[60]

Second, while organizations may have a global purpose, the people who compose them may be motivated by separate or additional objectives and beliefs, resulting in a collection of actors with multiple purposes. In this sense, the various actors and activities of an organization constitute a loosely coupled entity.[61] Consequently, understanding what motivates people in an organization is more complex than simply knowing its purported objective or function. A childcare center may be more than a place for childcare; a mosque, more than a site for prayer. For example, while a beauty salon might pursue the global objective of earning profits by setting hair and decorating fingernails, a given beautician might be motivated, on a daily basis, by the wish to spend time in the company of others or to sustain an informal support group among neighborhood women.[62]

Third, organizations may be tied to other organizations through multiple arrangements that vary in many elements, such as their complexity, stability, authority, and formality.[63] I assume that these organizational ties will affect the attitudes and behavior of actors within the organization. Particularly, external organizations that possess strong authority may motivate people within an organization to institute practices that build or sustain social ties among its members. For example, a philanthropic agency may donate a large sum to a community college provided that part of it is used to build a gathering place for students.[64] In this respect, the community college was externally motivated to establish a place likely to build social capital.

In sum, the context under which people interact can be shaped by both the actors and the institutional practices that constitute an organization, which may be motivated by internal and external factors.

OTHER ASPECTS OF PERSONAL TIES

The preceding assumptions make clear why organizations may affect whether and how people *form* ties. But they also provide a way to understand how and why organizations may affect other aspects of social capital. First, people may not just form but also sustain, strengthen, or weaken their relations to others either purposely or nonpurposely. For example, globally habitual actions that repeatedly place people in the company of others may sustain their relations even when the actors fail to make "unceasing efforts" to do so. People sustain friendships at gyms with others whom they only see at gyms, because they patronize gyms repeatedly. Second, the context of social interaction—whether it is frequent or infrequent, focused or unfocused, competitive or noncompetitive, and cooperative or noncooperative—is likely to affect the *quality* of the ensuing relations: how strong or weak ties are, how much the parties trust each other, and what resources, services, information, or support the parties are willing to provide. For example, people may more willingly trust and help others when their interaction takes place in noncompetitive contexts. Third, both the actors and institutions that compose an organization may not only regulate activity but also impose obligations, enforce pro-social norms, and encourage organizational members to share resources. For example, if a church encourages cooperative interaction, it helps build pro-social norms (a form of social capital), as researchers have documented in recent years.[65]

Fourth, what is true about organizations' motivations to form social ties is likely true about their motivation to form *organizational* ties. That is, just as a center director might be motivated to form connections among mothers, she might be motivated to form connections between mothers and external organizations. Such ties rarely form part of social capital analyses, but they may constitute, I suggest, a major source of goods and information.

In short, I argue that (1) organizational contexts affect most aspects of social capital, including whether a person makes ties, what kind of ties she makes, whether the goods in those ties are available to the person, and how those goods are acquired; (2) organizations may affect social capital either purposely or nonpurposely, and through the influence of either actors or institutional practices; and (3) organizations, or their members, may be motivated to affect social capital by either internal or external pressures. The three arguments represent answers to three questions on the impact of organizational embeddedness on people's ties: *what* is affected, *how*, and *why*. I briefly summarize these implications, before turning to the case study, the childcare center.

What Organizational Contexts Affect

Social and Organizational Ties

By shaping their participants' interactions and activities, organizations can shape the extent to which they form either social or organizational ties. Organizational ties, such as Victoria's ties to external libraries and employment firms, have formed little part of social capital theory, but they represent an important advantage potentially available through an organization. In addition, organizations can shape the nature of the ensuing relationships, including their strength or weakness, and the resources available through them.[66]

Resources, Access, and Mobilization

We have seen that social capital can refer to different kinds of resources embedded in social networks. Bourdieu, Coleman, Lin, and others included the following: information, services, material goods, trust, obligations, and pro-social norms. Organizational contexts may affect not only ties but also these resources—specifically, whether a person has access to them and whether she makes use of them, which scholars have called, respectively, *access to* and *mobilization of* social capital.[67] Organizations affect the former by influencing whether people form ties to the people or organizations that possess the goods; they contribute to the latter to the extent that they enact, enforce, or encourage trust, pro-social norms, supportive services, information sharing, the provision of services, and the distribution of material goods. One must not neglect the importance of people's agency: some actors mobilize connections more effectively than others, and some will take greater advantage of the network resources available in a given organization. However, I suggest that mobilization does not depend solely on how willing a person is to use her ties; mobilization is mediated, and sometimes perpetrated, by organizations.[68]

Organizational context may also affect what scholars have called negative social capital.[69] For example, scholars have noted that group solidarity may restrict individual freedoms or place stringent demands on members, such as when religious institutions forbid their members from marrying outsiders. Through mechanisms such as the threat of lost membership, organizations may enforce norms or practices that result in such consequences.

How They Do So

Brokerage

To capture the many ways organizations can shape social ties, an effective umbrella term is *brokerage*. The notion of brokerage enjoys a distinguished lineage in sociology; a broker is generally defined as the actor who brings two previously unconnected actors together. In recent years, Ronald Burt has demonstrated convincingly the importance of brokers in organizational contexts.[70] In this book, brokerage is *the general process by which an organization connects an individual to another individual, to another organization, or to the resources they contain.* Since here the broker is an organization, and since brokerage involves connecting people both to other people and organizations and to their resources, the process of brokerage may be significantly more complex than in person-to-person situations. Yet the term succinctly captures the heterogeneous set of practices by which organizations function as connectors. Organizations broker connections in many different ways; however, these may be categorized as either actor driven or institution driven and either purposive or nonpurposive.[71]

Actor-Driven and Institution-Driven Brokerage

Actor-driven brokerage is the process by which a person in the organization connects people to other people, to other organizations, or to the resources of either; institution-driven brokerage is the process by which an institution, in the normative or cognitive sense, brokers any of these connections. For example, when a college professor (actor) teaching a seminar requests that students introduce themselves to one another, she is connecting persons to other persons; when a librarian (actor) obtains for a student a difficult-to-find book from another library, he is connecting a person to the resources of another organization. These constitute forms of actor-driven brokerage. But when an STD clinic automatically refers a client testing positive to a social support agency, it is institutionally connecting a person to another organization.

Purposive and Nonpurposive Brokerage

The act of brokerage may be purposive or nonpurposive, depending on whether the broker intended to connect people or to attain some other objective. The professor who asked students to introduce themselves certainly acted purposely. Other instances are neighborhood association meetings where participants, sitting in a circle, are asked to introduce themselves to the group, or office parties where employees are asked to affix name tags to their clothing. While such strategies vary in their effectiveness, they do not differ in their purpose: to form connections among participants. I emphasize that personal motivations may operate independently of global organizational purposes and that brokerage may involve other types of connections. While a Dominican botanical drugstore might pursue the global objective of earning profits by dispensing ethnically specific medication, a given pharmacist might be motivated, on a daily basis, to help new immigrants transition to American society by tying them to resource agencies—that is, to connect people to the resources of another organization.[72]

Much of this book explores the interesting and important nature of nonpurposive brokerage, whereby an organization had no intention of forming ties among participants or patrons. In the sociology of complex organizations, several researchers have studied related ideas, including Charles Perrow, whose concept of "normal accidents" suggests that organizational systems may unwittingly be designed such that accidents are inevitable, and Diane Vaughan, whose idea of "normalization of deviance" captures how small, daily acts over time result in mistakes an external observer might find to be rationally avoidable.[73] Both authors believe that institutionalized practices produce unexpected consequences. In the present context, nonpurposive brokerage may occur in multiple ways. For example, many neighborhood laundries, to ensure that washers and driers are continuously available, do not permit their patrons to leave clothing unattended, forcing them to spend hours sitting and waiting in the company of others. The laundry's purpose was efficiency; an unintended consequence, socialization among neighbors. In a study of dormitories for returning World War II veterans at MIT, researchers found that simple architectural design decisions, such as how many apartments to place on one floor or how far apart to situate the staircases, affected friendship formation, with the strongest ties forming among those living close enough that unplanned encounters were frequent.[74] Many circumstances or practices common across organizations, such as waiting lobbies or collective tasks, create similar possibilities of unintentionally brokered connections.[75]

In sum, organizations may broker ties through mechanisms that may be either actor or institution driven, and either purposive or nonpurposive.

Why They Do So

The discussion to this point should make clear that organizations may broker connections for multiple reasons, depending on who does the brokering and whether it is purposive. This discussion nonetheless benefits from distinguishing motivations *internal* to the organizations from those *external* to it. Internal motivations include the personal goals of the members, as in the case of the Dominican pharmacist, and the institutional imperatives necessary for organizational survival, such as a struggling church's thirst for cash from fund-raisers. External motivations may derive from funders, professional associations, and the state, which may encourage or mandate practices that in the end contribute to local social capital. For example, a philanthropic organization may grant several hundred thousand to a not-for-profit childcare center, provided it institutes a parent association or collaborates with a neighborhood agency aimed at helping women with domestic abuse.

One important implication is that few external entities are able to exert stronger influence than the state, which can impose regulations with the threat of fines, penalties, decertification, or incarceration. As a result, it is possible that state pressures may be so powerful that they increase social capital in measurable ways. This book suggests that such pressures do, in fact, produce some forms of social capital under some circumstances.

EFFECTIVE BROKERS

We have seen that when people participate in organizations, they encounter a set of actors and institutions that, through varying mechanisms, may alter their social capital in ways that could be beneficial to their well-being. The sheer number of factors at play would seem to suggest a rather haphazard process, one in which the accumulation of social capital remains an unwieldy amalgam of practices, institutions, and motivations impossible to study systematically. On the contrary, I submit that organizations exhibit regular patterns that would lead us to expect some of them to be systematically effective brokers—so effective that, through their effects on social capital, they can measurably improve the well-being of their participants.

What such patterns are depends on the types of ties being brokered, whether social or organizational. With respect to social ties, effective brokers are likely to exhibit, among other traits, (a) many opportunities for (b) regular and (c) long-lasting interaction, (d) minimally competitive and (e) maximally cooperative institutional environments, and both (f) internal and (g) external motivations to maintain those opportunities and sustain those environments—particularly such practices that would likely contribute to organizational survival. With respect to organizational ties, effective brokers will likely demonstrate (a) resource rich and (b) diverse organizational networks in which (c) transferring resources fulfills the objectives of multiple constituencies. Among effective brokers, these newly acquired ties and the resources gained therein would observably, even if unexpectedly, benefit participants. One organization that, on average, is a remarkably effective broker is the childcare center.

CASE STUDY: MOTHERS AND CHILDCARE CENTERS

Childcare centers are often thought of as the impersonal alternative to family care, as the place where formal rules overwhelm informal relations. Yet for a study of how people make and use the connections that matter to their well-being, few cases are more appropriate than that of mothers of children in daycare centers. Childcare centers are strategic study sites, ones that, because of their uniqueness, allow us to observe processes that would be difficult to examine in other settings.[76] They are ideal for theoretical, substantive, and methodological reasons.

Why Centers?

First, childcare centers, as described throughout this book, tend to be remarkably effective brokers for the mothers whose children they service. They broker both social and organizational ties, and their brokerage is associated with greater material and mental well-being, bringing to light the concrete implications of organizationally embedded networks.

Second, childcare centers provide an important methodological advantage, the analytical leverage to unravel why some organizations are more effective brokers than others. Even though the *average* center is a rather effective broker, the variance is high, and many centers are terribly ineffective at connecting mothers either socially or organizationally. This wide range is due in part to the diverse array of organizational forms that centers can take: childcare centers may be for-profit or nonprofit, privately or publicly funded, corporate or family run, and secular or religious, yielding a rich variety of configurations and institutional practices. This organizational heterogeneity is matched by few other organizations in which one might conduct such a study. Churches, probably the most commonly studied organization among urban sociologists, are always religious nonprofit entities; firms, the most commonly studied entity among organizational sociologists, are always profit-oriented businesses. Childcare centers allow us the analytical leverage to observe the role of multiple sets of pressures while holding the type of organization constant. A different type of methodological advantage is that centers provide a unique opportunity to study tie formation as it happens. Since a new cohort of families enrolls in childcare centers every year, it is possible to study the formation of new networks just as it is happening, something difficult to accomplish in other settings.

People in churches, for example, have often known each other for years, making it difficult to examine how participants think about people they are just beginning to meet.

Third, mothers of young children remain one of the most important populations in the study of well-being and networks, as evidenced by classic studies such as Elizabeth Bott's *Family and Social Network,* Carol Stack's *All Our Kin,* and Kathryn Edin and Laura Lein's *Making Ends Meet.*[77] Mothers of young children have more to gain from supportive or resourceful ties than do people at almost any other point in the life cycle, since having a new child undercuts parents' free time, increases their household costs, and introduces the many unpredictable events, crises, illnesses, and accidents to which young children are prone. While fathers are increasingly affected, it still remains the case that mothers bear most of the burden of caring for young children. At the same time, most mothers of young children today either work or actively are looking for work, as I document in chapter 2. Consequently, at the moment when new friends might be most useful, mothers have the least time to make them.

In fact, the childcare center has become an increasingly important organization because births to unmarried mothers have reached historic highs, at 36% in 2004 for all unmarried mothers. Among Latinas the rate is 46%; among African-Americans, 69%.[78] It has become especially important to low-income mothers since the Personal Responsibility and Work Opportunity Reconciliation Act of 1996, which eliminated the old welfare system, instituted a work requirement, forcing mothers to find childcare arrangements. Among organizations relevant to unmarried mothers, the childcare center is one of the most crucial.

Data Sources

This project is based primarily on four data sources (see table 1.1). This multilevel, multimethod project employed both qualitative and quantitative data sources collected from both individuals and organizations. The integrated nature of the design provides the means to untangle the mecha-

Table 1.1. Principal data sources for the study

	Quantitative	Qualitative
Individual level	Fragile Families and child well-being study ($n \sim 3{,}500$ mothers)	In-depth interviews (67 mothers and some fathers)
Organizational level	Childcare Centers and Families Survey ($n \sim 300$ centers)	Center case studies (23 centers)

nisms through which centers broker mothers' social and organizational ties while identifying how prevalent and how distributed at least some of these mechanisms are. I describe each data source briefly below. For details, see appendices B and C.

The quantitative, individual-level data set is a national panel survey of approximately 3,500 mothers of children born between 1998 and 2000 in 20 large U.S. cities. The survey, named the Fragile Families and Child Wellbeing Study, or Fragile Families, is representative of all mothers of newborns in U.S. cities larger than 200,000. Mothers were interviewed at the time of their child's birth and when the child was one, three, and five years old; the study described in this book employs the last two waves of the survey. Mothers were asked questions regarding their demographic characteristics, their use of formal childcare centers or alternatives, and their friendships in and out of childcare centers. The Fragile Families survey allows us to compare basic network characteristics of mothers who use childcare centers and those who do not and to test a few of the ideas developed from the qualitative studies about the factors affecting tie formation.[79]

The quantitative, organization-level data set is my Childcare Centers and Families Survey, an original study of approximately 300 centers randomly sampled in New York City in 2004.[80] The survey, which I commissioned after conducting preliminary fieldwork, contains data on the organizational structure of childcare centers, basic institutional practices, opportunities available for parents to network, services provided other than childcare, referrals to other organizations, ties to other organizations providing resources, the characteristics of those organizations, and other organizational variables. The survey, which I will refer to as the Childcare Centers survey, allows me to paint a basic picture of the average characteristics of childcare centers in a major city, to observe the level of heterogeneity, and to test several of the hypotheses developed from the qualitative studies.

The qualitative data consist of case studies. For the qualitative, organization-level data, two research assistants and I interviewed the directors or other supervising personnel of 23 childcare centers in New York City. The centers were selected to exhibit a range of income and racial characteristics, particularly among blacks, whites, and Latinos. In 11 of the centers, a plurality of children was white; in five, it was black; in seven, it was Latino. Nine of the 23 centers were publicly funded by either Head Start or New York City's Administration for Children's Services. We interviewed directors and other center staff on their motivations for establishing interorganizational ties, the nature of those ties, opportunities available to network, basic institutional practices, and the general resources available to parents. We also observed parent meetings, field trips, and other practices and center characteristics. The case studies allow us to detail the particular mechanisms by which centers broker connections, adding subtlety to the basic pictures painted by the quantitative data sets and generating the core hypotheses about the nature of organizational brokerage.

The qualitative, individual-level data set consists of 67 in-depth interviews conducted by my research assistants and me with parents, most of whom were mothers, in a subset of the case study centers. Our objective was to understand, from the parents' perspective, whether and how they had formed ties in the center, how they understood these relations, and under what circumstances they mobilized these ties. The interviews yielded the richest data of all, providing a clear window into how ties are formed, what types of ties these are, how trust and obligations operate, and how useful the connections truly are for those purported to benefit from them.

This book stands with the sociological tradition in which the key to understanding social processes is uncovering the mechanisms that give rise to them—in this case, the mechanisms producing and reproducing inequality in personal networks.[81] I use the quantitative survey of mothers to frame the findings in New York City and to empirically assess whether childcare center participation is associated with larger networks and greater well-being. The three remaining data sources I use to examine the mechanisms that give rise to this association. To the extent it uncovers how brokerage operates in centers, the book will have met its empirical objectives.

WHAT FOLLOWS

The chapters of the book are arranged in four parts. Chapter 2 concludes part I by making the case, using the national survey of urban mothers (Fragile Families survey), that childcare centers tend to be effective brokers for the average mother, generating personal connections strongly associated with greater well-being. Parts II and III, which constitute the core of the book, answer the core empirical question: how did childcare centers shape the mothers' social and organizational ties?

The chapters in part II examine how centers affected mothers' *social ties.* Chapter 3, "Opportunities and Inducements," asks why mothers so frequently made new friends in their childcare centers, given the demands on their time that most of them reported. Chapter 4, "Weak and Strong Ties," asks whether the friends mothers made in centers were typically close friends, acquaintances, or something else. Chapter 5, "Trust and Obligations," explains why some mothers' support networks in the center were, in fact, larger than their friendship networks. It shows that participating in the center built trust even among mothers who did not know each other personally, revealing how trust and obligations respond to formal imperatives sustained in organizational contexts such as centers.

The chapters in part III examine how centers shaped mothers' *organizational ties*. Chapter 6, "Ties to Other Organizations," examines why mothers' most useful ties were not always social. Shifting the focus from the mother to the center and its relationships, the chapter reveals that many centers were formally tied to other organizations—nonprofit entities, businesses, and government agencies—that provided material and nonmaterial resources to center parents. Chapter 7, "Organizational Ties and Neighborhood Effects," asks why centers bothered to establish these relationships with other organizations and what role location played in this process. Examining one aspect of the persistent "neighborhood effects" question, the chapter examines whether childcare centers in poor neighborhoods were less well connected than those in nonpoor neighborhoods, as would be expected by standard theories about organizational capacity in poor areas.

Part IV extends the discussion beyond the confines of the childcare center. Chapter 8, "Extensions and Implications," documents the presence of several mechanisms uncovered in this book—such as repeated and durable interaction, the assignment of cooperative tasks, the institutionalization of trust, and the application of validation, storage, referral, and collaboration—among churches, diners, bathhouses, beauty salons, colleges, and other routine organizations. In so doing, it makes a case for the importance of organizational embeddedness in the study of personal networks. The chapter concludes by suggesting that the *organizational embeddedness perspective* points to different kinds of questions in the current study of social inequality.

I conclude this introduction by clarifying what this book does and does not purport to accomplish. This book probes personal networks as understood by the people who form and sustain them, and in the day-to-day organizational contexts in which these processes take place. The book does not constitute a standard social network analysis of the mothers' personal networks, a project in which relationships are conceived mainly as nodes and the ties between them. The focus is not structure but interaction, thus revealing those elements of social capital that formal structural analysis largely sets aside. In addition, this book is not a study of children or child-*care*, issues that have been studied many times before.[82] It is also not, finally, a study in the organization of centers—an examination of how centers balance their books, hire and fire staff, select managers, develop curricula, or strive to meet government regulations. Organizational sociologists will learn little from this book about the issues that have traditionally concerned them—in fact, I employ their concepts, and those of formal network analysis, to inform and enrich our discussion.

Instead, this book examines one aspect of the relationship between the center and the mother: how the former shapes the social and organizational ties of the latter. It makes a case for a revaluation of social capital theory, and offers a related but alternative perspective on personal ties, one concerned less with choices than with contexts, less with "unceasing efforts" than with structured interaction, less with purposive action than with unexpected gains. It uncovers how the manifold advantages that people gain from their networks may derive from little more than those organizations in which they happen to participate routinely.

2

Childcare Centers and Mothers' Well-Being

Whether Mothers Did Better When Their Children Were in Daycare

Effective brokers connect people to useful others. They not only enlarge social networks but also produce those particular connections that yield concrete benefits, such as well-paying jobs, better health, discounts on services, or lesser material difficulty. Consequently, being embedded in the right organizations can either lift an actor to a higher rung on the socioeconomic ladder or, as explored in this book, improve her current well-being. That is, it represents a significant advantage. I have suggested that childcare centers, though they differ dramatically from one to the other, nonetheless tend to be effective brokers for the mothers of enrolled children, because they tend to generate useful connections. Do they? And if so, then do mothers enrolled in centers thereby experience greater well-being?[1]

The present chapter addresses those two questions. Based on the national survey of urban mothers of young children (Fragile Families), it tests whether mothers who enrolled their children in centers improved their circumstances when compared to those who did not.[2] The chapter begins by grounding the analysis of the national data. Relying mostly on the in-depth interviews with New York City parents, it examines how and why parents decide to employ childcare centers in the first place. Then, based on the Fragile Families survey data, it assesses whether mothers who employed centers thereby enlarged their social networks, particularly the number of friends they reported. The third section asks whether these networks improved mothers' well-being, specifically, their ability to avoid material and mental hardship. The results are consistent with expectations: (a) most mothers who patronized childcare centers made new friends therein, and (b) making friends in centers was strongly and robustly associated with lower material and mental hardship.

CHOOSING CHILDCARE

While experts, journalists, and politicians continue to debate the merits of placing children in centers, parents have decided to do so at rapidly rising rates. Figure 2.1 exhibits the percentage of 3- and 4-year-olds in the United States enrolled in nursery, preschool, or kindergarten from 1965 to 2005. The figure reveals that centers have become an increasingly common choice over the past generation. In 1965, only 11% of children 3 to 4 years of age were enrolled in nursery, preschool, or kindergarten; by 2000, more than 50% were.[3]

Figure 2.1 suggests that practical considerations may be driving this trend. Today, many more mothers of children under six participate in the labor force.[4] In 1965, less than a quarter of all such mothers were either employed or searching for work; by 2005, the figure was 60%.[5]

To examine how the parents we interviewed arrived at the decision to employ center-based care, I begin by identifying the options available in New York City. I then examine how they weighed priorities and ultimately made a choice. The trends in figure 2.1 hint at what I found: for most parents, higher order worries, such as the quality of care provided, were

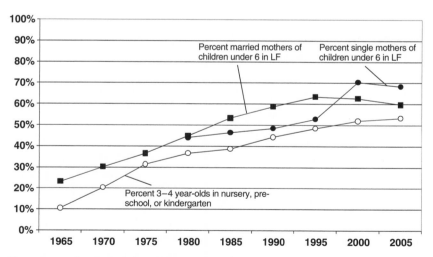

Figure 2.1. Labor force (LF) participation of mothers of young children and enrollment of young children in daycares, 1965–2005.
Sources: Historical Tables, Table A-2. Census Bureau, census.gov/population/www/socdemo/school.html (accessed 2/7/07) and Statistical Abstracts of the United States, various years, census.gov/compendia/statab/ (accessed 4/20/07).

surpassed by practical considerations, such as the need to find care quickly in order to return to work. For many mothers, childcare centers were the most affordable or practical option.

Diverse Options

Parents searching for childcare today face many options. These options may be categorized into three general alternatives: (1) childcare centers, which are formally licensed organizations—such as Head Start centers, prekindergartens, and nurseries—in which more than five children are cared for, usually in age-sorted classrooms, by teachers and staff; (2) family daycare services, which are licensed or unlicensed homes in which one adult cares for up to five children if licensed or more than that (though rarely much more) otherwise; and (3) paid or unpaid informal care arrangements, by which relatives, friends, babysitters, or nannies care for children in their or the child's home.

Formally licensed childcare centers vary widely in form and orientation; consequently, they defy categorization. For the present purposes, I categorize them by their primary funding source: government-funded nonprofit, privately funded nonprofit, and for-profit centers.[6] Those in the government-funded category include Head Start centers, part of the federal program designed to improve the social and cognitive development of low-income children and integrate the family into the education of the child; and locally funded centers, such as New York City's Administration for Children's Services centers, aimed at providing subsidized care to low-income and working-class families, under principles consistent with those of Head Start.[7] Other government-funded centers specialize in care for particular populations, such as children with physical disabilities. Centers funded primarily by the government are usually either free or deeply discounted based on household income.

Privately funded nonprofit centers exist in many forms and styles of operation. Some are run by large nonprofit organizations aimed at child well-being. For example, the Children's Aid Society, a 150-year-old organization with operating expenses of more than $70 million, runs a half dozen childcare centers, many in low-income areas, with active education programs and no charge or nominal fees for income-qualifying families.[8] Many nonprofit centers are run by religious organizations, such as churches and synagogues, as part of their community service operations, or with the explicit purpose of providing religious instruction. Still others are operated by ethnic organizations (e.g., Puerto Rican, Dominican, or Jewish nonprofit organizations) and provide group-specific services, such as bilingual instruction and the celebration of religious holidays.

Among nonprofit centers, fees vary widely, and nonprofit status by no means implies low cost. Some nonprofit centers are free; the rest of them range, for a child 2 or 3 years of age, from about $75 to about $1,800 a month.[9]

For-profit centers also vary widely. Some are corporate centers with multiple branches, others are private centers reserved for employees of large companies, and others are small, family-run businesses. Most for-profit centers in New York depend on private fees for funding; the least expensive cost about $340 a month for a child 2 or 3 years of age. However, for-profit centers also serve low-income clients. The federal and local governments provide childcare vouchers to a number of populations, including women enrolled in Temporary Assistance for Needy Families and foster parents, and some for-profit centers rely heavily on these vouchers to run their operations (which illustrates the difficulty in categorizing centers by funding source). One for-profit center in our field study accepted government vouchers from more than half of its clients.

A Decision Governed by Practical Concerns

How do parents decide among these options? Empirical studies suggest that price and location may be the primary motivating factors. For example, in a study based on the 1985 wave of the National Longitudinal Survey of Youth, Sandra Hofferth and Douglas Wissoker found that center-based care was often cheaper than other paid options and that price was a critical variable in predicting which form of childcare families employed.[10] In a survey of parents in Maryland, about 80% preferred a childcare center near their homes, and proximity was the most important factor associated with use of center-based care, surpassing even cost, quality, or hours of operation.[11] When we asked New York mothers and fathers what factors weighed on their decisions, they also expressed concern about price and location, but they reported numerous other worries as well. Many mothers declared the difficulty of facing what Sharon Hays called an inherent contradiction in motherhood, by which mothers are both expected to devote themselves to raising their children and yet implicitly berated for doing house and care work instead of "real" paid work.[12] Others worried about the center's hours of operation, the availability of slots in their neighborhood, the safety of the environment, the level of caring they *felt* during their visit to the site, the amount of leave from work the mother could appropriate, the number of different alternatives they would have to employ, and the available time they had to search for options.

In spite of their diversity, their answers revealed two tendencies. For many, finding care proved a difficult and exhausting process, drawn out over months and complicated by the pull of multiple criteria; for most, the decision to employ centers was governed not by philosophical but by practical concerns. When deciding among childcare options, parents might, in theory, make two separate decisions: first, which type of childcare to employ (whether center care, family care, or informal care); and second, which particular center or family care provider or babysitter to employ among the alternatives. In practice, however, the decisions were often made jointly, as parents shifted and balanced preferences nonstop until cost or convenience won out. Finding childcare in a city such as New York required flexibility, hard work, some luck, either affluence or sacrifice, and, often, the willingness to satisfice rather than maximize—that is, to opt for the first available among the good-enough alternatives over the best of the best, including settling on a center when one preferred a sitter. In this process, having access to financial resources helped dramatically, but did not guarantee an easy task.[13]

Consider Iris, a thin, petite, blond lawyer whose husband worked full time for pay while she worked pro bono, from home, until she was ready to return to paid employment.[14] Not returning to work was economically infeasible. Her only daughter, an infant, was enrolled in Little Friends Day Care, a center in an upper middle-class neighborhood in the city, even though Iris and her husband first preferred an at-home nanny. She explained why: "[I]nitially I started looking for a nanny because my husband and I had discussed it and we just thought that the flexibility that a nanny gives is probably better suited to our needs. Unfortunately after interviewing about ten candidates [we came] to the conclusion that we weren't comfortable with any of [them]." As she explained later in the interview, the nannies had not met her standards.

> There's just, you know some of them barely spoke enough English to have a conversation with us. Which doesn't mean they're not good and loving but our concern is that if anything, God forbid, happened, I wasn't sure that . . . they mastered enough English to be able to call an ambulance, or call the police . . . which was a huge issue for us. Also [for] a lot of them . . . we don't know anything about them . . . [since so] . . . many of them are illegal immigrants and you have no recourse [if something bad were to happen]. . . . Also, I think having taken some time off before I started studying for the bar I spent a great deal of time in the park and in the neighborhood. And there are things about some of the nannies that just bothered me. . . . I've seen so many children strapped to their strollers for long extended periods of time while their nannies are either chatting with their friends on their cell phone or they're doing their own shopping. And that's just not the . . . sort of childcare that I consider adequate.

In spite of her impressions, one candidate met their expectations. But the reality of the cost quickly set in.

IRIS: There might have been one candidate with whom we would have been comfortable.... Because she had a background in child development and she spoke very good English and all of that. [But] she actually got a competing offer which was much out of our league [economically]. So, we had to sort of scramble and in talking to another mother in the park she suggested that I look into the Little Friends Day Care....

INTERVIEWER: So you just met this parent in the park?

IRIS: That's right. Someone, actually she was someone from the neighborhood and since we had just moved into the neighborhood she knew of the place. But she had said, "Well you can call them but usually it's quite difficult because there's a long waiting list." And I just happened to be very lucky that [my daughter, at seven months] was at the age [that] she fit into the slot that was open. 'Cause I actually have friends who have a little boy her age who applied six months later and were on the waiting list for a year and a half.

While Iris and her husband worried about quality, English-speaking abilities, accountability, and the full attention that a nanny could provide, cost and the opportune opening of a slot near their home ultimately settled their decision.

In fact, it was not uncommon for parents to jump from alternative to alternative during the process. Naomi, a white mid-level manager, placed her name on a waiting list at a center near her home while she was pregnant, since, given that her job had provided only three months of leave, she wanted a backup plan. However, having grown up in a family daycare setting, she wanted the same for her young daughter, believing it provided the type of warmth and attention Naomi treasured. For this reason, she searched for and located an organization that provided a list of licensed family daycare providers, by Zip code:

I looked up my home Zip code, my work Zip code and everything in between, figuring I could drop [my daughter] off on my way.... Many of them...I didn't even call because I knew the block they lived on and it was not an acceptable neighborhood for me to take my child to. One I called and she was full.... And my last resort [was] this woman who sounded nice on the phone [and] invited me to come to her home, interview with her.

Naomi's last resort had given her hope. However, she soon realized what she would not settle for, when she visited the home with her husband:

It was so horrible. It was...[in] the projects down on [another neighborhood] and we got to outside the building and I was like, "Oh this is it? I'm not going in here," and [my husband] was like, "You've got your cell phone, call her and cancel the appointment." I [thought it would be rude to cancel, so]...we went in and there were...broken needles on the steps outside and little crack vials and all kinds of sort of signage in this very dim and filthy lobby that made me nervous. Oh, things about "Rat poison" and "Danger" and "Don't touch these wires; they're live" and ... this woman's apartment was so ... dark and dirty and had no air and no light. And she'd done the best she could with it ... [and] ... she was the loveliest woman ... and already had one little baby she was taking care of and we conducted the interview as though we were serious about it.... [But in the end, I told my husband] "I'm not taking my baby to the projects everyday." And even for that, that was going to cost me $300 a week. I mean, childcare's expensive.

Naomi began to worry, because her backup plan, enrolling her child in a center, was not materializing as she expected: "I had huge anxiety about solving the daycare problem.... [W]hile I was still pregnant ... I got on the wait list, and the plan was [my daughter] was supposed to have gone to them at three months old when I came back to work." However, a space was not available when she was ready to return to work.

I found out I had maybe two or three weeks before I was coming back to work and I panicked. Nannies can cost, I'd say probably going rate for a nanny in Manhattan is $500 a week. I also got quotes as high as $800 a week which I thought was insane. Through the friend of a friend I found an amazing woman who came to me for $400 a week. She was somebody else's family nanny ... but they were going on vacation for two months and she had some down time. And it was exactly the eight weeks that I needed until [the slot at the center was available]. So, that was like somebody smiled on me.

In the end, she considered herself fortunate. "Yeah, I totally lucked out."

The experiences of Iris and Naomi were made more difficult by the fact that both their children were infants (for whom there are fewer slots) but also easier by the fact that they could afford $400 a week in childcare. But Irina, a second-generation Latina mother of two in her late twenties who worked as a staff assistant in a government office, could not. While she had strong preferences for center-based care, her only practical options were the four childcare centers near her apartment in a predominantly Latino neighborhood with a high poverty rate. One of them, a church-based center, was not only open too few hours but also in a general state of disrepair:

[The church] has a daycare center now but it's only [open] from like 9:00 to 12:00. That wasn't working for me. They opened that up not too long ago, but I wasn't interested.... It was not ... perhaps they've done renovations now, but a few years ago it was not up to par. I was not pleased. A lot of the information was outdated; a lot of their supplies were ruined. It was ... it just looked really bad.

Another center, by a local college, had recently opened: "I did have my eye on [that] one.... [B]ut they wanted $275 a week and I couldn't hack it. And then ... they did take [subsidized housing vouchers for low-income families in the city], but I guess some parents were like starting to get involved. So, by the time I did come around, they weren't accepting it no more."

A third center, costing $375 a week, was even more out of reach. The final center, Alegre, was an organization funded by the Administration for Children's Services in which parents paid on a sliding scale according to income. When her first son, whom she had as a teenager, was almost two, she tried enrolling him in the center, only to be met by a daunting wait list: "[My first son] never had the privilege of going to daycare because [the waiting list was] backlogged. Everybody was on waiting lists. And at the time, I was a working parent. My income wasn't enough to go in privately." She had to use ad hoc arrangements with family and friends to get herself through her first son's early years. She learned her lesson: "So, when Samuel [, my second son, was born,] the second time around, you can say I did it smart and I put him on the waiting list while I was pregnant. Not a lot of daycare centers around here, I mean, ours is one of the most affordable."

In sum, our interviews confirm and expand on the findings of the existing literature: when parents enroll their children in centers, they do so after a great deal of trial and error in which practical concerns have won out.

MOTHERS' NETWORKS AND WELL-BEING

Many mothers felt fortunate to have found center-based care. Yet perhaps they were more fortunate than they realized. The rest of the chapter carefully engages the quantitative data to answer two questions—did mothers make new ties as a result of enrolling their children in centers? And was enrolling their children in centers associated with greater well-being?

To answer these questions, I estimated statistical models based on the last two waves of the Fragile Families survey, the national survey of urban mothers identified in chapter 1 (for details, see appendix B). The survey was first conducted immediately after mothers had given birth (wave 1), and mothers were then reinterviewed when their child was one, three, and five (waves 2–4). I refer to this child as the "focal child." For simplicity, if the focal child is enrolled in a center I refer to the *mother* as "enrolled."[15] Of the two waves employed in this study (waves 3 and 4), only the latest (conducted around the year 2004) contained information about mothers' experiences in childcare centers needed to answer all the questions posed here. Wave 3, however, allowed me to take mothers' prior circumstances into account.[16] The survey has an important limitation: it does not provide informative data on the alternatives to childcare that parents employed. For example, enrolling in family care may benefit or constrain mothers just as much as enrolling in a childcare center.[17] I cannot assess this possibility because of how the survey was administered; I can only compare mothers with children in centers to all other mothers.[18] The details behind the survey design and all of the statistical models estimated in this chapter are described in appendix B. Here, I mainly summarize the results and discuss the most important aspects of the basic rationale behind my analysis.

Table 2.1 exhibits the basic characteristics of enrolled and non enrolled mothers in the survey. The statistics in table 2.1 are weighted to account for the design of the survey; numbers represent the characteristics of urban mothers of children who were newborns 5 years earlier in cities with populations of at least 200,000. In table 2.1, a "center" is any formal organization providing care, whether it is referred to as a Head Start, preschool, prekindergarten, kindergarten, nursery, or any other type of center-based care.[19] (Later chapters examine which differences among centers affect the networks of parents.)

Table 2.1 makes clear that enrolled and non enrolled mothers differ in important ways. Enrolled mothers have slightly fewer children and higher probabilities of being married, college educated, and employed or in school full time. Notably, the number of adults in the household, which is a standard indicator of social support, does not differ among the sets of mothers. But perhaps the greatest difference is income, with the average childcare center mother making more than twice as much (>$62,000) as one

Table 2.1. Characteristics of urban mothers of 5-year-olds with children in centers and not in centers

Characteristic	Focal child not in center	Focal child in center
Married	41%	53%
Cohabiting	11%	9%
Number of children [mean (SD)]	2.86 (2.86)	2.61 (1.51)
Worked or school 40 hr	58%	68%
High school degree only	61%	79%
College degree or more	13%	29%
Household income [mean (SD)]	28,661.06 (58,653.42)	62,163.45 (87,614.88)
Age [mean (SD)]	30.61 (11.96)	32.60 (7.31)
Number of adults in household [mean (SD)]	2.00 (1.61)	2.00 (0.83)
Black	29%	36%
Latina	39%	26%
White	25%	30%

Source: Fragile Families Study. Results are weighted.

not in a childcare center. These numbers do exhibit large standard deviations; there is considerable overlap between the income distributions of the two sets of mothers.[20] Nevertheless, these differences must be taken into account statistically when comparing the networks or well-being of enrolled and non enrolled mothers.

DID MOTHERS MAKE NEW FRIENDS IN CENTERS?

Before assessing the impact of center participation on well-being, I examined mothers' acquisition of new friendships. The survey specifically asked enrolled mothers, "Do you currently have any friends whom you've met through your child's center?" If they answered "yes," they were asked how many. The results are exhibited in figure 2.2.

Figure 2.2 makes clear that most enrolled mothers made friends in centers. About 60% made at least one friend, and more than 40% made three or more friends in centers. Given the prevalence of friendship formation, we should not be surprised if enrolled mothers had larger social networks than non enrolled mothers.

We shall see that they do, suggesting that centers increased enrolled mothers' total friendship network size. To be clear, the Fragile Families survey cannot be used to state definitively that these mothers would not have made new friends had they not enrolled in centers. Since wave 3 of the survey did not ask how many friends mothers had *before* enrolling in centers,

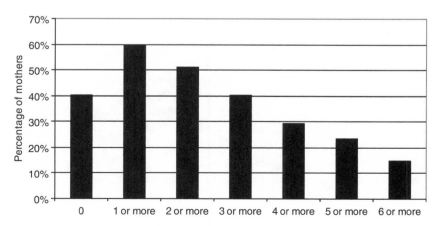

Figure 2.2. Number of friends met in center: Mothers with child in childcare center. Source: Fragile Families Study.

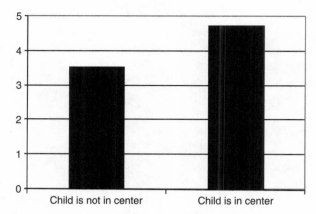

Figure 2.3. Predicted number of close friends for a statistically average mother of a 5-year-old.
Source: Fragile Families survey. Negative binomial regression model; includes controls for income, race, age, education, number of children, number of adults in household, employment, and marital and cohabiting status. Robust standard errors account for city clustering.

we do not know whether friendly mothers were more likely to enroll in centers in the first place.[21] Nevertheless, since we know for certain that mothers made new friends *through* their centers, it is informative to compare the networks of enrolled and non enrolled mothers before and after taking into account center-made friends.

Figure 2.3 and table 2.2 present these results. All mothers in the survey were asked how many close friends they had. They averaged 5.4 friends, and 8.4% of them described themselves as having no close friends whatsoever, the worst type of social isolation.[22] I ran separate statistical regressions estimating the relationship between enrolling in a center and both (a) the number of close friends and (b) the probability of having no close friends at all. To ensure the mothers were as comparable as possible, I adjusted for variables affecting whether mothers enroll their children in centers: income, race, age, education, number of children, number of adults in the household, employment status, and marital and cohabiting status. The estimates also adjust statistically for several important elements of the survey design. (The first model is a negative binomial regression; the second, a logistic regression model. The details and technical justifications behind all models in this chapter are discussed in appendix B. The coefficients for figure 2.3 and table 2.2 are presented in appendix B, tables B.1 and B.2, respectively.)[23]

Figure 2.3 presents the results for the relationship between center enroll-ment and total number of friends. For ease of interpretation, instead of presenting regression coefficients, figure 2.3 exhibits the predicted number of close friends separately for statistically average enrolled and non enrolled mothers. Statistically average enrolled mothers have about 4.7 close friends; non enrolled mothers have about 3.5 close friends. This difference of 1.2 friends is statistically significant. To assess whether those friends made in centers could account for the difference, I reestimated the model reported in figure 2.3 after adjusting for whether the mother had specifically made friends *in* the center. After these friends were taken into account, the difference was reduced to 0.2 friends and no longer statistically significant. This is consistent with the idea that enrolled mothers have more friends specifically because of the friends they made in centers.

Table 2.2 exhibits the results for the relationship between center enroll-ment and the probability of having no close friends. Fewer than 10% of mothers in the sample are this radically isolated, so the question is whether enrolling in a center reduces that probability even further. As shown in table 2.2, this appears to be the case. The predicted probability of having no close friends is about 8% for a non enrolled mother, and 6% for an enrolled mother. The difference of about 2 percentage points (or about a fourth of the baseline probability) is statistically significant. As I did in the earlier estimates, I separately assessed whether the friends mothers made *in* centers could account for the difference in probability of being isolated. The differ-ence was reduced to 1.3 percentage points and was no longer statistically significant.

In sum, most mothers in childcare centers made friends there; as a result, enrolling in a center is statistically associated with both having more friends and being less likely to be isolated. We now turn to our broader question, whether enrolling their children in centers, and making friends there, con-

Table 2.2. Predicted probability of being socially isolated: Urban mothers of 5-year-olds (after controls)

Enrollment Status	%
In center	5.8%
Not in center	7.7%

Difference statistically significant at 0.05 level.

Source: Fragile Families Survey. Logistic regression model; includes controls for income, race, age, education, no. children, no. adults in household, employment, and marital and cohabiting status. Robust standard errors account for city clustering.

ↄ

stituted an advantage with respect to mothers' well-being—specifically, whether it was associated with lower material and mental hardship.

WAS ENROLLMENT ASSOCIATED WITH LOWER MATERIAL HARDSHIP?

Probably the most fundamental indicator of well-being is the experience, or avoidance, of material hardship.[24] Social scientists interested in poverty have argued for years that the poverty rate is too crude a measure of the true material hardship that individuals face, such as their inability to obtain food or housing. We have inherited the commonly used poverty rate from an attempt by Margaret Orshanski during the 1960s to estimate how much income a family would need to avoid hunger and other difficulties.[25] Orshanski obtained the cost of the basic food basket and, knowing that at the time a typical family spent a third of its income on food, multiplied this number by three and proposed it as a poverty threshold. Since then, this number has been adjusted for inflation every year. Having a single poverty rate simplifies the task of examining shifts over time in the number of people at the bottom of the economic ladder; however, it also masks important problems. For example, the value of real estate has risen dramatically over the past 50 years, and especially over the 1990s and the early 2000, outpacing inflation. Consequently, buying a house today is more difficult than it was 50 years ago, something that the poverty rate would not account for. A solution to this problem is to examine specifically the experience of material hardship, such as the inability to pay rent, eat, or obtain health care.

We would expect center enrollment to reduce the material hardship of mothers if the average center brokered social connections effectively. The reason is that acquiring the resources needed to avoid or reduce material hardship is not simply a matter of having enough income. In fact, there are many ways to acquire such resources. Susan Mayer and Christopher Jencks found that, for the Chicago families they surveyed, income accounted for only about a quarter of the variation in material hardship (measured by food, housing, and health care insecurity).[26] Food banks and soup kitchens provide food, the Medicaid program provides health insurance, and emergency utility coverage in many cities covers heating during the winter—and all these resources are for free. However, people have to know of their existence and the means to obtain them, and networks are effective means to acquire such knowledge—as well as for acquiring other goods. The question is whether centers provide access to resources that on average result in lesser hardship for mothers who enroll their children in them.

Assessing Material Hardship among Enrolled and Nonenrolled Mothers

Material hardship is not rare among mothers of young children. Table 2.3 exhibits the weighted percentages of mothers who experienced each of eight different measures of material hardship in the year roughly encompassing the focal child's 5th year (age 4 to age 5). The first four measures identify home-related hardship. Eleven percent of mothers, for example, did not pay the full amount of rent at least once. Small percentages of mothers—fewer than 10%—were forced to move in with others or into a shelter. A very small percentage needed but were unable to receive the care of a doctor. The larger percentages are in the subsequent measures, which indicate whether the mother did not pay the utility bills or had to borrow money from friends or family to pay such bills. While the percentage that was forced to borrow in order to pay bills is relatively high at about 22%, the percentage that had their gas or electricity cut off is relatively low, probably due to protections in many local laws against cutting some utilities, as well as emergency utility coverage provided by governments.

My basic approach was to use regression techniques to estimate hardship level as a function of enrollment status and other confounding factors. The technical details are discussed in appendix B. I stress that this analysis does not purport to be a definitive statement on whether centers causally improve

Table 2.3. Experience of hardship over the previous 12 months among urban mothers of 5-year-olds

Measure of hardship	Percentage of mothers
1. Did not pay the full amount of rent or mortgage payments	11.3%
2. Was evicted from home or apartment for not paying the rent or mortgage	2.2%
3. Moved in with other people even for a little while because of financial problems	6.5%
4. Stayed in a shelter, abandoned building, automobile, or other place not meant for regular housing, even for one night	2.8%
5. Needed to see a doctor or go to the hospital but couldn't go because of cost (anyone in household)	3.3%
6. Did not pay the full amount of a gas, oil, or electricity bill	17.5%
7. Borrowed money from family or friends to help pay the bills	21.9%
8. Had gas or electricity cut off, or heating oil not delivered by company, because there wasn't enough money to pay the bills	3.9%
9. Was hungry but didn't eat because couldn't afford enough food	5.0%

Source: Fragile Families survey.

well-being. To make such a statement with certainty, an omnipotent social scientist with no moral constraints would select a representative sample of parents of young children, assign some of them at random to centers and others to alternative arrangements, and track their progress over time. Only this experimental process would ensure that any observed differences between the two sets of parents result from the fact that one of them participated in centers, rather than to other factors. That approach is in many ways impracticable.[27] Instead, the present chapter seeks to determine whether there is a robust association, which would help motivate the search, in the rest of the book, for the mechanisms or processes that might account for it.[28]

To determine whether there is a robust association, it is important to take into account the possibility of "selection bias" from unobserved factors. For example, suppose that some mothers are more resourceful than others. It is not difficult to imagine that resourceful mothers are more effective at getting their children into a center *and* making sure they do not go hungry or that their telephone is not cut off. If so, then failing to take into account "resourcefulness" would overstate how much a mother is helped by having her child in a center. Since we cannot observe resourcefulness, this and other unobserved differences ought to be accounted for through other means.

There are several alternatives with different strengths and weaknesses to deal with this problem; none of them is perfect.[29] However, having longitudinal data provides a distinct advantage. I followed a strategy that requires minimal assumptions, produces naturally interpretable results, and yields robust estimates. When testing for the effect of enrollment on the mother's current well-being, I statistically controlled not only for demographic variables known to matter but also for the mother's well-being *prior* to enrolling in the center.[30] This approach greatly increases confidence that the effect is not biased due to selection, since it explicitly takes into account how well mothers were doing before the time for enrollment, thereby accounting for fundamental but unobserved differences such as resourcefulness.[31]

Finally, the estimates consider the role of center networks—specifically, whether making friends in centers helps account for any relationship between enrollment and lesser hardship. In doing so, we must consider differences in people's basic propensity to make friends. For all mothers in a given center, the friendlier ones will be more likely expand their network, if for no reason than their greater likelihood of being purposive social investors. To determine whether, among center mothers, making friends has some impact on well-being, we must somehow take account of mothers' differences in friendliness or sociability. It is difficult to observe a person's basic propensity to make friends, but the survey did ask respondents how many close friends they had in general (regardless of whether they made them at the center). I use this variable as a rough proxy in the equations.[32]

Effects of Enrollment on Mothers' Overall Experience of Hardship

To examine mothers' overall hardship, I used the indicators of hardship in table 2.3 to create a standard hardship scale in which each indicator was worth one point.[33] In order to include the "lagged" measure of hardship from the earlier wave, I had to restrict the indicators of hardship to those questions included in both waves of the survey, and only measures 1–7 in table 2.3 fit this criterion. Sixty-six percent of the mothers (by weighted estimates) had experienced none of the seven measures; 16% experienced one; 10%, two, and about 7%, three or more.

I first estimated this model for all mothers, and then separately for poor and non poor mothers, since experiencing material hardship is more common at the bottom end of the income distribution (I still controlled for income within each group). Based on the model, I computed separate predicted hardship scores for non enrolled mothers, for enrolled mothers who did not make friends in centers, and for enrolled mothers who did—after controlling for income, race, age, education, number of children, number of adults in the household, employment status, and marital and cohabiting status; for a proxy for propensity to make friends; and for prior hardship. Figure 2.4 presents the results. (Coefficients are shown in appendix B, table B.3.)

The results for all mothers (poor and non poor pooled) in figure 2.4 show how much lower the enrolled mothers' predicted hardship score is compared to non enrolled mothers. Enrolled mothers who did not make friends in centers have predicted scores about 11% lower than non enrolled mothers; those who did make friends had scores about 36% lower than non enrolled mothers. Both effects are significantly different from the baseline. The figures suggest that being in a center helps lessen hardship, but making friends there lessens it even more.

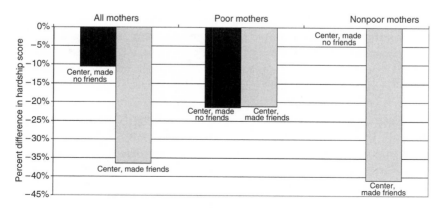

Figure 2.4. Predicted hardship score: Enrolled compared to nonenrolled mother's.

The separate results for poor and non poor mothers in figure 2.4 suggest that the consequences of being in a center depend on the poverty of the mothers. For poor mothers, enrolling a child in a center reduces the predicted hardship score, regardless of whether they made a friend. This difference is marginally significant.[34] Why do poor mothers experience lower hardship even if they did not make friends? In subsequent chapters, I examine this question further, but there are probably at least two factors. First, the childcare centers that poor mothers attend often provide access to resources through *organizational* ties, and some of these resources are likely to significantly ameliorate hardship (chapters 6 and 7). Second, what the respondents understood by "friend" probably does not capture what social scientists believe is captured by that term. Consequently, some people whom a respondent may not consider a "friend" probably provide the benefits the social scientists argue tend to come only from friends (chapter 4).

The predicted hardship scores for non poor mothers in figure 2.4 are revealing. The absence of a left bar indicates that, for non poor mothers, enrolling in a center but not making friends there does not provide even a marginally significant buffer against hardship. For non poor mothers, it is the friends made in centers that make a difference, and a large one, resulting in a 41% lower hardship score. The importance of center-made friends is explored in the chapters 3–5.

Probing Further on Hardship

Employing a general measure of material hardship allows us to paint a overarching picture. However, some of the indicators on table 2.3 may measure hardship imperfectly. For example, the first measure asks whether the mother did not pay the rent or mortgage at least once during the previous 12 months. In any given month, many people do not pay their rent or mortgage because they do not have the money to do so. But others simply forget. Still others decide to withhold payment, such as renters who want to punish the landlord for not fixing the radiator, or those generally exercising their legal rights in the face of neglectful management. Therefore, while some measures of hardship indicate material *difficulty*, others confound material difficulty with other conditions.[35]

It is impossible to measure a concept as abstract as material hardship perfectly well, but we can focus on those measures of hardship that seem to capture material difficulty as purely as possible. We can follow this procedure with respect to housing.[36] I constructed a purer measure of housing hardship indicating whether the mother had experienced any of the three purest indicators (measures 2–4) over the previous 3 months. Four percent of non poor mothers and 16% of poor mothers had done so.

Table 2.4 exhibits the predicted probabilities of experiencing at least one of the three measures of housing hardship, after controlling for the previous covariates. Given the association between housing hardship and poverty, it focuses only on poor mothers. As in figure 2.4, table 2.4 also controls for the total number of friends and for prior housing-related hardship. As figure 2.4 makes clear, the probability of being evicted, having to move in with friends or family, or having to move to a shelter or sleep in an abandoned building or in a car is lower for a statistically average enrolled poor mother than for one not enrolled, even after taking into account for *prior* experience of these difficulties.

A purer measure of hardship can also be developed with respect to utilities. In table 2.3, measures 6–8 are related to the payment of utilities.[37] Table 2.4 also presents results of a model estimating the probability of experiencing either of the two purest forms of utilities hardship for a statistically average poor mother. All previous controls are included, including prior utilities-related hardship.[38]

As table 2.4 makes clear, the statistically average urban poor mother has a 25–35% probability of experiencing material hardship with regard to her utilities. This probability is lower if her child is in a childcare center, and even lower if she made friends there. Nevertheless, the effect of being enrolled does not attain the level of statistical significance if the mother made no friends in the center; if she did, the difference is marginally significant at the 0.09 level. Chapters 6 and 7 show that this difference is probably due to the organizational ties poor mothers access and mobilize through their centers.[39]

Table 2.4. Predicted probability of experiencing housing or utilities-related hardship for a statistically average urban poor mother of a 5-year-old

Enrollment status	Percent
Housing-related hardship	
Not in center	8.8%
In center, mother made no friends	3.9%
In center, mother made friends	4.0%
Utilities-related hardship	
Not in center	33.3%
In center, mother made no friends	30.5%
In center, mother made friends	26.8%

Source: Fragile Families survey. Logistic regression model; includes all previous controls plus total number of close friends and lagged version of the dependent variable. Robust standard errors account for city clustering.

WAS ENROLLMENT ASSOCIATED WITH LOWER MENTAL HARDSHIP?

A final important measure of well-being, and also a condition associated with a host of other problems, is mental hardship. The most straightforward measure of mental hardship is depression. Depression and networks are related, given that people who are more socially connected appear to experience less long-term depression. Clinical psychologists have developed a few agreed-upon indicators of depression. The Fragile Families survey asked respondents a series of eight diagnostic questions to ascertain the experience of a major depressive episode over the previous 12 months. These questions were derived from the Composite International Diagnostic Interview, Short Form, Section A.[40] Psychologists are currently debating how to assess depression given this test. By one measure, respondents who reported seven symptoms for half a day or reported taking depression medication were counted as depressed; by another, respondents who reported seven symptoms for *most* of the day or reported taking medication were counted as depressed. The second measure sets a higher bar.

Based on these measures, I assessed whether the probability of being depressed is affected by childcare center enrollment and by the networks formed there. I estimated the probability for poor and non poor mothers, controlling for prior depression and for friendliness, as before. By the more conservative indicator of depression, being in a childcare center had *no* effect on the outcome. By the less conservative indicator, it did. Figure 2.5 exhibits the latter results.

The effect of enrolling in the center and not making friends was not statistically significant for either poor or non poor mothers. As shown, the benefits of enrolling a child in a center, for both poor and non poor mothers,

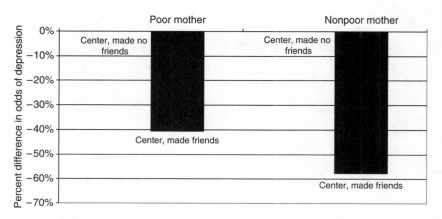

Figure 2.5. Odds of being depressed: Enrolled compared to nonenrolled.

results from the friends made there, and the friends made in centers help non poor mothers more than they do poor ones. The difference between the conclusions based on different ways of measuring depression suggest that there are limits to what social networks, including those made in childcare centers, can do. For a person who is severely depressed (i.e., depressed by the most stringent measure), making friends in childcare centers appears to make no difference; for those who are not quite severely depressed, the networks made in centers appear to matter. Social capital has its limits.

GREATER WELL-BEING, GREATER NETWORKS

Based on nationally representative data, this chapter has shown that enrolling a child in a childcare center is statistically associated with lower material and mental hardship, and that much of this association is tied to the friendships made in centers. In so doing, it has shown that, through some set of mechanisms, the social capital acquired in centers was beneficial to these mothers. The question, then, is why: Why would enrolling a child in a center increase the size of a mother's network? Why would it reduce material hardship? Why would it lower the probability of depression? Why would the friends made in centers have a special impact on hardship (are not all friends equally good for a mother's well-being)?

The answer to these questions, I suggest, lies in how centers, as formal organizations, shape the social and organizational ties of their adult patrons. Answering these questions requires probing deeper than large-scale surveys are able to do; it requires understanding what parents experience when they participate in centers, how centers structure their activities, and what parents feel and think about the relationships they form there. Parts II and III of this book are devoted to this task.

Part II

SOCIAL TIES

3

Opportunities and Inducements

Why Mothers So Often Made Friends in Centers

Why do mothers so often make friends in childcare centers? A number of circumstances seem to conspire against this outcome. Mothers with children in centers may well be the demographic group with the least free time to socialize. As indicated in chapter 2, almost 70% of urban mothers whose children were in centers worked 40 hours or more per week (see table 2.1). Their average number of children was 2.61. A working mother juggling a full-time job, two or three children, and household responsibilities seems unlikely to have time for much more in a center than unloading her children in the morning and retrieving them eight hours later, especially if she must then return home to clean, cook, or perform whatever tasks her partner, if there is one, does not perform. The few minutes that constitute "drop-off" and "pickup" hardly seem enough to develop new friendships, especially the friendships likely to protect against hardship or depression. By contrast, mothers whose children are not enrolled in centers, who work fewer hours and rely on informal care from relatives or babysitters, would seem to therefore enjoy the flexibility to fit into their schedules activities for socializing.[1]

This chapter uncovers that enrolled mothers so often make friends because centers generate multiple opportunities and inducements for parents to interact. Through their rules and norms of interaction and their requests that parents help conduct many of their regular tasks and operations—from apparently mundane field trips to logistically complex fund-raisers—centers created opportunities for friendships to form and even induced such networks inadvertently.

Making friends is not so much a choice as a process, and no perspective reveals more about this process than that of the mothers who experienced it. Thus, I begin this chapter by discussing in detail how three of our mothers, Griselda, Denise, and Serena, made their friends in childcare centers. Their radically different stories, consistent with their widely different temperaments, nonetheless reflect an underlying unity of experience, one in which their centers either encouraged new connections (purposely or not) or provided opportunities to network. I then demonstrate, relying on data from the Childcare Centers survey, a study of nearly 300 New York childcare centers, that these mothers' experiences were not unique, but rather part of a citywide pattern in which centers often require parents to be actively engaged. I conclude by discussing how this pattern of active engagement ultimately reconfigured how mothers used their time, such that their leisure and even quality time with their child was increasingly tied to the center.[2]

THREE MOTHERS

Griselda and the Parties

One hour into our interview, it was clear to me that few things pleased Griselda more than her center's holiday festivities. She had attended them for years, because her daughter, now six, and her son, now three, had both been enrolled since they were toddlers at the Alegre Daycare. A black-haired, round-faced, Dominican-born Latina in her early thirties, Griselda had chosen the only neighborhood center that she and her husband could afford. Their income qualified them to pay $56 a week for each child, rather than the standard $125, which included breakfast, lunch, and snacks. At the nearest alternative, a private nonprofit center, the rate was $300 a week. "I said, 'Three hundred a week?'" recalled Griselda. "'What are you giving them?' I mean, 'What kind of education—not only the education; what else are you *feeding* them?'" That rate did not include meals.

About two years before we met, Griselda had been laid off her job as a secretary in a community center forced to reduce its labor force due cuts in government grants. The job loss had been difficult for her not only because she had lost some independence but also because she found sitting at home without work to be dispiriting. Before the layoff, Griselda was already, by her own admission, a rather stressful parent. The layoff had sunk her deep into a depression: "Because I was used to just being on the go and running around here and there. [After I got laid off] I was just sitting at home, ... saying, 'what do I do now?' And I started to become ... depressed. I said, you know, 'I have nothing to do, nowhere to go, no one to talk to'." For Griselda, the center's celebrations were, as we shall see, a welcome respite.

Alegre Daycare, a government-funded center in a poor, predominantly Latino neighborhood, cared for more than 100 children on the ground floor of one of the buildings of a large housing complex. Many of the neighborhood's poorest children were served by Alegre, since the other nearby center was beyond economic reach. Almost 100% of the center's children were

Latino. For the last three years, the facade of the side of building on which Alegre was located had been outfitted with a large scaffold over the sidewalk, part of a renovation project that had apparently stalled. The scaffold cast a dark permanent shadow over the sidewalk, attracting the garbage, graffiti, and urine that semipermanent scaffolds seem to attract throughout the city. Despite its drab exterior, the center's indoor lobby was a sparkling clean area that was obviously mopped daily and probably buffed once a week. The floors of the lobby and all halls and offices were laid in the cream-colored institutional linoleum tiles ubiquitous at childcare centers, elderly care homes, and hospitals. The center's halls were painted off-white, decorated with the children's paper artwork. If the halls were institutional-off white, the classrooms were bright red, green, yellow, and purple—each room a different color—and they served as sites for some of the center's parent meetings. The large events, though, were held in other venues, such as a school auditorium that the large community organization that administered the center made available.

For Griselda, the contrast between the neighborhood she lived in and the events the center put together could not be greater. The center organized magnificent, elaborate holiday celebrations, complete with children's performances—including singing, dancing, acting, and poetry—in miniature costumes. Practically every celebrated holiday, including Easter and Valentine's Day, served as an occasion to orchestrate what Griselda called "the parties." "Oh [they're] *beautiful*," she insisted:

> They have really nice parties here.... [Especially] when they do ... the Mother's Day [party] it's just beautiful because the kids recite poems or they do little shows and I'm always part of that. I always make sure I always tell my boss ahead of time: "Look, the Mother's Day show is coming up, I need at least two hours lunch, an extra hour lunch." So, I would come, or I would tell a boss, "You know what? I'll make the extra hours up because I need to go and watch the show," if it started a little earlier. So, I was always here for their shows. I never missed it. Never.

Different events had slightly different conceits. Graduation Day, for example, was replete with awards—for good behavior, best math, best reading, and so on—that practically guaranteed everyone's child would receive something, and therefore experience a moment in the spotlight. The shows were designed for Kodak moments.

Griselda's favorite memory was of the first Mother's Day performance in which her daughter participated:

> I remember the first Mother's Day that was here she recited a poem. She was about three and it was in Spanish. And I was just hysterical crying because she was so into it and she was looking at me in my eyes and I was just hysterical

crying. All the mothers cried that day. It was a really nice poem in Spanish. I think she still remembers it.

Griselda was especially tickled by the costumes:

They get [the children] dressed sometimes in these different outfits. Like if it's the Mother's Day they make sure all the kids wear red or certain kids wear, like—[as a] matter of fact the Christmas show was beautiful. [My son] was one of the Three Kings . . . and they had the whole costume with the hat and then they had the angel, they had Mary . . . the baby Jesus and Joseph. They had the whole setup—it was beautiful. Beautiful.

Events of this nature can be emotional for parents of young children, and Griselda was no exception. "I used to cry at practically all the shows."

Griselda was enthusiastic that even the fathers, though fewer of them were frequent participants, had become involved in the events. For years, a type of routine event schedule had set in—Mother's Day, Independence Day, Graduation, Christmas Day, Easter, Valentine's Day, with a few country-specific Latino holidays added. But there had been no Father's Day event:

They started doing Father's Day because my husband made a real big stink about it. . . . He said "Wait a minute, you come to me with a bill and then we don't get acknowledged? You know, I don't understand this. Everything is Mother's Day a big hoo-ha. What about the fathers? There's some good fathers. There's some fathers who are into their children. What about a father like me? You know, 'Here's the bill, pay the day care,' but nobody acknowledges me." And then this year . . . they did a Father's Day [event]. That was the first year. . . . I hope they keep on the tradition the Father's Day because it is true there are a lot of fathers who participate.

("A lot," in this case, was a relative term; as was the verb "participate." I had seen several fathers retrieve their children in the afternoons at Alegre. I had also seen a few at the most important mid-year parent meeting, where parents piled anywhere they could into a small room with toddler-sized furniture. But like all centers, this was still a predominantly female institution in both staff and clientele. A generous estimate is that a quarter of the children at Alegre on a given day were picked up by males; this particular meeting—one of the most attended—was no more than 10% male.)

Organizing these events required work. Making the outfits, assembling the stage, quieting the children, cooking the foods, preparing the programs, and setting up the rooms took time and coordination. As Tania, the director, explained to me, with only three teachers per each of its six classrooms, and toddlers and young children requiring heavy supervision, there was not enough staff to mount these productions from center resources alone. So the center sought volunteers among the parents.

Griselda volunteered early and often, even though she empathized with those who could not do much. "Some of them can't because they work. And I understand, because that's how I was even when I was working, but I always took the time out to come to their shows—but sometimes I just couldn't get that involved as I wanted to, like with the costumes and stuff like that." The costumes tended to require a particularly large amount of work, something Griselda took on with relish, one year even asking her mother, a seamstress, to help out. Griselda signed up to volunteer through the center's parents association, a group with a president, vice president, and secretary, whose charge was, among other things, coordinating the holiday celebrations.

It was through these events—the preparation, the anticipation, and then the participation—that Griselda, in a globally nonpurposive way, met the few parents she knew in the center. She described herself as naturally shy, not so much unfriendly as introverted, and her depression did not help. "[I was] not really that involved with the parents," she explained. But "if there was a party [at the center] coming up [I'd ask] . . . what are you going to cook, what are you bringing?" A typical icebreaker was the children, as she explained: "From the children. I mean especially [my son], he's like well known here because he's very active and he loves to become everyone's friend. So the parents used to say 'Oh, my son talks about him or my daughter talks about him.' I'm like 'yeah, that's [Kyle].' And that's how we would start the conversation." Through her participation in the organization of these events Griselda experienced intergenerational closure, James Coleman's term for the state in which parents are acquainted with their children's friends' parents.[3] In later chapters I examine the nature of these relations, especially whether they were strong or weak ties and how parents made use of them. The concern for the moment is their source.

Without the pull of the parties, and the preparation machinery that surrounded them, Griselda would have had little reason to spend time in the center—and, as a rather unsocial person in the midst of a depression, less motivation to approach these strangers. As Griselda explained to me, "I was so depressed I didn't even want to [leave the house]." The parties gave her work, an opportunity to see her children in a different light, and the opportunity to talk to engage in sociability, that form of non-purposive association that represents little more than social expression. For Griselda, the parties were the road out of social isolation.

Denise and the Field Trips

If Alegre gave Griselda the opportunity to celebrate, the Tweed Center afforded Denise a much sought-after chance to escape the confines of the city. Denise, a bespectacled, pony-tailed African-American in her mid-thirties, enrolled her two daughters and son at the Tweed Center, an independent Christian center run by a neighborhood church. As she explained to her interviewer, Denise was attracted to its religious foundation: "[I chose it] because it was Christian-based school, it's close to home . . . and . . . they had space for all three of my children." A lifelong resident of New York, Denise had worked at least 40 hours a week for the city's transportation department for much of her adult life. Her efforts to save enough to buy a home had not borne fruit, even though the center only charged $300 a month for all her girls and even though she received a subsidy, from the city's children's services administration, for her older son's after-school program.

The Tweed Center cared for more than 100 black children in a five-story, prewar brick building in a small lot on a predominantly black neighborhood in the city. A striking all-wood, 15-foot white cross hung just above eye level on the front of the building—and, to reinforce the message, the center's motto was printed on all its literature: "Train up a child the way he should go; and when he is old he will not depart from it. Proverbs 22:6." Founded in the 1970s, the center was born of the efforts of the pastor of a local church to reach out to the community. Today, parents love the center for its strict religious orientation, and for the fact that a little over half of the children are on grade level, which seems to compare favorably to other centers in the neighborhood. The privately funded center relies on fees, government funding, and furious fund-raising to pay the bills.

In addition to Tweed's religious orientation, Denise appreciated the field trips it hosted to venues in and outside of the city throughout the year, which gave her children an opportunity to ice skate, attend museums, and enjoy the circus. She explained that she particularly wanted her children to consider ice skating, given that they had started the sedentary life of many young people today. "My kids don't want to go; they just want to go home, watch TV, [they're] lazy. But this year they going to be into more activities; this year [will be] healthy for our kids. Sports and stuff like that." Geographic isolation is a problem among many New York City low-income households, where children and parents rarely leave their surroundings for either different environments in the city or the fresh air and greenery of suburban and rural parks. William J. Wilson in his discussion of social isolation also effectively described geographic isolation, as he painted a picture of neighborhood poverty in Chicago's racially segregated, predominantly African-American South Side neighborhood, in which many residents lacked access to recreation areas in other parts of the city. Denise hoped to combat her own children's version of this problem, exacerbated by what she saw as her children's natural disinclination toward the outdoors.

Once a year the field trip was out of the city, and the trip for the year of our observations was to the Family Funslides Park, an amusement ride and water slide extravaganza in Pennsylvania. For many geographically isolated low-income children in New York, field trips are one of the few ways to leave the city, and the center considered taking the children through the lush greens of Pennsylvania not only a fun experience but also part of the exposure children require for a healthy development. Such trips, however, produce complications. The number of adults required to supervise young children in a classroom is much smaller than the number required when children are running about a park, asking for sweets, petting animals, or anxious to ride water slides. Under these circumstances, an adult cannot manage well more than a handful of children for an entire afternoon. For this reason—and, of course, for the diversion—center-based field trips at Tweed were family affairs with most parents in tow.

Denise explained that she personally enjoyed the trips because they allowed her to become involved in the center, which she had done more easily in the past, when her work allowed her the flexibility: "I used to be very involved. I say 'used to be'; that was when I didn't work so many hours before. I mean, I still worked 40 hours a week, but I used to work for the school system so I would be home at 4:00. . . . So, I used to be very involved. I'm not as much as I used to." Still, she managed to make time for the field trips. "I try to go to all of them." Her interviewer asked why. "To spend time with my kids and their friends. So, you know, they can have fun. And to have fun with the other parents, too." She enjoyed meeting parents at these events. She noticed, however, that this was often easier to accomplish at the less high-energy activities. At "[m]useums and stuff like that you can go see different exhibits together [with other parents and their children] . . . and . . . it's a little quieter [because] there's not so much going on. So then you get to talk to them more." By contrast, at outdoor field trips, parents tend to fan out with their children. This was not enough reason, however, to miss the Family Funslides event.

On the day of the trip, one of my research assistants joined the group. The two school buses the center had rented were scheduled to leave on a Friday morning at eight o'clock. Fifteen minutes before, parents began gathering inside a church attached to the center, whispering "good mornings" in their predawn voices. The children's chattering and running around the church gave them something to focus on ("Not in the sanctuary!" yelled one parent). One mother walked in wearing a pink shirt down to her knees and a black tank top. "Good morning," she said, in the direction of the parents sitting at the pews. Then, laughing: "No, I'm not going on any of the rides. I'll just stand and watch." She was more talkative than the rest: "Last year I was totally unprepared. The kids kept asking me for things: 'Mommy, I want some water. Mommy, I'm hungry.' So, this year I stopped and got all sorts stuff." Eventually the families filled the buses, said a prayer, and drove off.

The Family Funslides Park, with a large American flag at the front entrance, is a sprawling space with wet and dry slides, four large roller coasters, dozens of swimming pools, multiple eateries and merchandise stores, and live, photo-ready versions of Saturday-morning cartoon characters. There was more to do than could be done in one day, and, as Denise said, families fanned out from the start. The day was scalding hot, and Denise came ready in a bathing suit and Capri pants.

Soon enough, a minor confrontation erupted. Denise and her 4-year-old daughter had finally reached the front of the line atop a 60-foot, enclosed water slide. After placing her child on the slide, an altercation ensued, words were exchanged, and security guards were summoned. Sometime later, Denise saw two other parents she recognized from the bus standing underneath a tree to cool off, and walked up to them to express her frustration. "I almost got thrown out of the park!" she explained. She pointed to the large, imposing slide: "I put [my child] on that ride and I asked the man at the top if there would be someone at the bottom to catch her. He called it down and assured me that there would be someone there. He promised me. And then [after she went on the slide] there was no one there. I told him that she couldn't swim." When she discovered there was no one at the base, she exchanged strong words with the staff member who had made the promise. The altercation had continued long enough to attract security guards to the scene.

The incident later lent the parents a (comical) icebreaker. One of the mothers asked, smiling, "So, you almost got kicked out?" "Well, I was so upset. The guy promised me there would be someone to catch her. And there was no one there! I was a little upset. The cop almost threw me out." The other chimed in: "That's why I just don't bother trusting them with my children." "Yeah," said Denise, smiling; "it's ridiculous."

It was not difficult to understand why Denise appreciated field trips. They represented an opportunity to counter geographic isolation. As much adult affairs as they were to serve the children, the trips generated opportunities to interact informally, and Denise met many of the center parents through field trips such as this one. Given the circumstances under which she has met them, it is not surprising that Denise seemed to like every parent she had met at the center: "The parents there are very nice, very nice. Ran into not one nasty parent yet."

Serena and the Fund-Raisers

Though not exactly friendly, Serena was by no means shy. A black woman in her late thirties, Serena was poor in income but rich in cultural capital, a college-educated dancer with refined tastes who refused to let her inability to pay deprive her only daughter of the cultural upbringing she deserved. "I can't afford [the] Bank Street [center] at twenty thousand a year," she explained. But "I want [children in our center] to have a music teacher and a yoga teacher.... [An] indoor play space for the winter." A stylish dresser with perfect posture and hair neatly set into a bun, Serena betrayed a somewhat formal disposition. During Serena's first month in the Standing in Faith Center, where her daughter is enrolled, she volunteered to be the president of the parents association and immediately began work on what she saw as educating the other members on the importance of fund-raising. A religious center with limited resources, Standing in Faith found it necessary to fund-raise every year. But if the directors wanted to fund-raise for the center to survive, Serena wanted to fund-raise for her daughter to excel.

The Standing in Faith Center serviced an almost all-black clientele. Located in a low-income black neighborhood in the early stages of gentrification, it was housed in a large nineteenth-century townhouse of four stories. The front stoop had been removed, and the center's front door occupied the space that originally would have been the entrance to the servants' quarters of the townhouse. A fading gray sign on the door indicated the name of the center and address. The entire front facade of the townhouse—four stories in which at least the bottom two rose 14 feet—had been skim coated in concrete, removing all vestiges of charm from its appearance. The center survived through the sponsorship of the church, very modest fees, and aggressive, if not always successful, fund-raising. Like Alegre Daycare, Standing in Faith had a parents association; however, as the director explained to me, the association's main charge here was coordinating, along with the nuns running the center, the center's many fund-raising activities.

Serena was on a mission: to bring the center's infrastructure, curriculum, and services up to what she believed were the standards that middle-class New York children enjoyed. She saw several obstacles along the way, beginning with the 12-member parents association. In our interview she explained that, in her mind, some of the issues had to do with the lack of organizational skills.

> My goal is partly organizational.... The PTA is not particularly well organized. The individuals who are there like Tatiana, [are] gung ho, but it requires an overarching vision where people can plug into it.... Whenever we do an event

I ask for a volunteer [among the other members] to be the project manager: "You are the go-to person for this event. . . . You know the information. You're not required to do everything, but you are required to know what all of the steps are, and when there's manpower needed you put out some phone calls to us and we go get [the people to volunteer]."

What she saw as disorganization became clear early on. For a recent holiday-season fund-raiser, parents would obtain requests for cookie dough for a certain required dollar amount from friends, family, or whomever they could coax into giving up a few dollars. The dough was reputed to produce delicious cookies. With the orders (and cash) in hand, one PTA parent would then request from the company the fresh, refrigerated dough. For a delivery in time for Three Kings Day, the deadline to place the order was December 16.

From Serena's perspective, the fund-raiser was "a disaster from the start." She explained:

Because the company we used as our distributor went out of business and never told us. And thank God they didn't have our money before it happened. . . . But the woman who, the two women who are organizing it: one was supposed to take the sheets, make the call, put in the order. She couldn't get through on the phone. Now December 16th was the call-in day. She couldn't get through. She couldn't get through and figured, "Well there's a vacation message on the outgoing machine. I'll just call in after Christmas." Didn't tell any of us that the order didn't go in. Nobody. . . .

She [and the director] were the only ones who knew and they didn't share the information. And they thought, "Well, we didn't think it would be a problem. I mean, it's Christmas." And I'm thinking, "but a big portion of our schedule has now changed." And I keep, they, they didn't get it. I keep saying, "Did you think that when you came back and ordered on December 30th that the three week turnaround would just disappear and they'd deliver it the next week?" We need to know. They just didn't think to tell anybody. And I didn't know I needed to be that up under their feet.

Serena believed that this slip had undermined the reputation of the center— and of all parents who sold orders—in the eyes of all the "customers" who, having paid for their dough, were expecting delivery.

What Serena had begun to call the "cookie dough fiasco" only became more complicated. After identifying a new company, they eventually placed the order. "[The] cookie dough arrived. And we knew it was going to arrive between nine and twelve—big, huge boxes. We had like a ten thousand dollar order of cookie dough. The truck has to be unloaded." On a $10,000 order the center received about $6,000 in net profit. Cookie dough is raw dough, which needs to remain cold, and the company delivers but does not sort it. Destino, the association member in charge of receiving the order, had not requested volunteers, which were required to not only receive the large truckload but also haul it into the building and sort it into individual packages according to buyers' orders. Serena explained how she would have handled it:

> Cookie dough has to be unloaded. We have no way to refrigerate. So it goes in the yard. And then our group has to assemble specific orders according to what family has what. My thing is, you know, the cookie dough is going to be coming Wednesday, Tuesday or Wednesday, but you don't know [which specific day it will come] until Monday. They won't tell you until Monday. So if you're project manager, you organize people who will commit to ... [each specific day] two weeks in advance. When you find out on Monday [on which day the truck is coming], you go "Okay, Tuesday folks are on. Wednesday folk, you're relieved unless you can help." [But] she waited until Monday to try and get people....

Frustrated, Serena volunteered her time: "And unfortunately the packages were assembled, some of them wrong, so [buyers] are calling and saying, 'I don't have any oatmeal but I have extra chocolate chip!' [*She laughs.*] My God. I, I'm not a control freak. I'm all about delegating, and everybody having something that they're in charge of." In the end, all orders were fulfilled. (For her part, Destino thought the whole process had gone swimmingly; Hector, another parent who was helping Destino, was not quite so delighted, but largely took it in stride.)

Running activities such as these requires the ability to communicate effectively, so Serena assembled all members' contact information. "When I have a meeting, I send everybody an agenda, talking points before the meeting. At our last meeting I had emailed everybody two, three days in advance. I had my one printout, and I had the old agendas from the old meeting." She went further, gathering a list of all parents' contact information. "The first thing I did was organize it. It took me over six months because people ah, ah, ah. [*She laughs.*] I put notes in their cubby.... Where the kids' clothes are. I went to the office and I had to ... to go through ... each class looking for familiar names. Oh, she's on the PTA—phone number."

As a result of her ceaseless organizing, Serena had met many of the other parents, most of whom she liked, a few of whom she found exasperating. One of them, Katia, had started to become a good friend, as they shared fund-raising frustrations. "We walk home together sometimes from meetings and things," she said. "I realize that there is friendship potential there because our values are very similar." "Very similar in what respect?" I asked.

> You know, it's funny. It's like a way to behave, [a] kind of code of conduct with other people. Respect. [*Unintelligible*] thinking. [For example:] She's organizing her building to be renovated into co-ops by the city. She's doing it all by herself. She is a liaison between the building and the government. She had

to convince everybody in the building to agree to move out while they come in and renovate the building. They will get to buy, *buy* their apartments, irrespective of size, for two hundred dollars. [*Author's note*: The building, at the time still a rental unit, is in a low-income neighborhood. The city partners with residents taking over buildings from absentee landlords to convert them to cooperative buildings, where tenants become owners, rather than renters, after paying a nominal sum.] And she had to convince some people that this was a good idea! [*She laughs*] . . . You know, we were talking about her difficulty, though, coordinating the effort with people who are reticent, essentially, and it's similar [to what I'm experiencing] with the PTA.

Serena has organized meals at her home for Katia and another set of parents, a couple, with whom she has begun relations. "[They] have come to brunch with their twins. And my daughter bit her son [*she laughs*]. They were totally fine with it but I was like, 'Oh my God.'" Through the fund-raisers, for better or worse, Serena had quickly, and purposely, developed a large network in the center.

OPPORTUNITIES AND INDUCEMENTS

The experiences of Griselda, Denise, and Serena tell us something about parents and something about centers. With regard to the parents, the experiences illustrate the utility but also the limits of focusing on purposive action as the source of tie formation. Serena is a "networker," someone for whom making social connections represents a purposive strategy to attain her goals, epitomizing theorists' arguments that social capital results from actors' investments in social relations: she asks others for their numbers so she can call on them when needed, organizes volunteers to ensure the success of the fund-raisers. But this model does not explain Denise's circumstances. Denise did not seek to make investments in potentially useful contacts; Denise, by all accounts, including her own, is simply friendly. While she was interested in exposing her children to the greenery of Pennsylvania, her social interaction was rarely instrumental. She approached other parents, for example, to express her frustration about the water slide fiasco. In her case, the idea that making social ties is an investment is not enough to explain the *source* of these ties, even if it helps explain their consequences. If this is true in Denise's case, then it is certainly true for introvert Griselda, who largely made friends in the center without intending to do so. Friendship formation depends not just on the actors' motivation but also the opportunities and inducements to interact produced by their social contexts.

The separate experiences of the three mothers suggest that centers may present many opportunities and inducements to interact because centers expect more from parents than first impressions would suggest. For Griselda, Denise, and Serena the childcare center was not a mere pit stop in the daily race to meet the obligations of work and family. It was a means to celebrate, to leave the city, and, in one way or another, to get work done in conjunction with other parents. In fact, due to the multiple activities required to run a contemporary childcare center, a parent can expect to do much more than pick up and drop off her child. Many centers today require *active engagement*. To understand how, consider the expectations of parental participation from the perspective not of a parent but of a center.

A Place Upstairs

A Place Upstairs center, a publicly funded center for 100 children, was located on the second floor of a three-story, postwar red brick building squeezed into a densely populated high-poverty predominantly black neighborhood in New York. The center was laid out in large linoleum tiles, sky blue, scrubbed, waxed, and buffed. The lobby's cinderblock and sheetrock walls were painted bright blue to match the floors, and decorative paper confections showcased the children's construction-paper projects. The director's office, a 10- by 12-foot room, was stuffed with chairs, a large desk, stacks of papers, file cabinets, and bulletin boards with pinned photographs and pictures. On the walls hung pictures of Nefertiti, Martin Luther King, and several black luminaries, and a large bulletin board with three dozen photographs of the director and the children she had cared for in her 30-year career.

Since the center was run by the city's children's agency, much of the policy came from above, and most of the funds, from the city and federal government. A parent wishing to enroll a child in A Place Upstairs added the child's name to a waiting list held at the regional office of the agency. Deirdre, the director, had managed the center since inception. In the past her staff had included family counselors and assistant directors, but budget cuts had eliminated those positions. At the time of our interview she had a bookkeeper, an assistant bookkeeper, one custodian, two "helpers" who cleaned up and assisted teachers in miscellaneous tasks, five (certified) teachers, five assistant teachers, and two teacher aids. An unpaid 10-member board of directors, composed of community members and a few parents, met once a month to discuss curricula, budgets, and staff performance. "I always overspend," Deirdre explained to me. Required to serve neighborhood children, most parents were working poor who paid according to their income, and seven or eight children were on government vouchers.

Deirdre was a chocolate-skinned, African-American in her sixties with dyed red hair and a firm but warm disposition. "We're community based," she insisted, and asserted her belief that childcare was more of "a family place" than schools—as she said this, Deirdre brought her arms to her chest as if she were carrying an infant. In fact, she found childcare "more loving, close-knitted, family oriented" than school. This orientation, however, did not prevent her from enforcing strict rules regarding center operation.

At sign-up, Deirdre met with first-time parents in her office and informed them of the rules of the center and what to expect with regard to their participation. The center opened at 8:00 A.M. and closed at 5:45 P.M., with a 15-minute grace period. "If a parent is late," she complained, "they're supposed to call." For years there had been no formal penalties for failing to pick up children on time, but persistent violations had forced her to impose a fine. The first time a parent or guardian arrived later than 6:10 P.M., the charge was $15; the second time, a warning was issued; the third time, the child was expelled. "That has worked quite well," she explained, and no children had been let go. (Strict pickup rules were common among the centers we observed.)

A parent could expect, early in the fall, to be asked to attend the first of several mandatory "PTCs," or parent-teacher conferences. For a PTC, as Deirdre explained, the parents visited their children's classrooms and were informed about the rules of the center, the activities for the term, and the expectations for their children. PTCs were also question-and-answer sessions for parents to become acquainted with the process and contribute informally to the curriculum. In December and April, the parent would be asked to attend a second and third meetings, for what Deirdre described as a "progress report" about what had taken place in the intervening time and what to expect in the coming months.

A parent at A Place Upstairs would be asked to attend, every 3 months, additional informal meetings. Some of these, normally attended by 40 or so parents, consisted of workshops, such as the one in which a member of the police department delineated the differences between discipline and abuse; others consisted of informational sessions designed to familiarize parents with the school system. Still others were task-oriented meetings to arrange the many field trips and special gatherings the center sprinkled into the calendar throughout the year.

The complexity of the events varied, but all required parental involvement, and every parent could expect to be asked to participate in some activity. Some were straightforward affairs, such as the International Food Day, for which parents—about half of whom were Latino, half African-American, and a handful African—were invited to cook and bring foods traditional to their cultures for a potluck. Others, such as the yearly field trips to the circus, required advance coordination and many parents to chaperone the children. For safety, the center asked six or seven parents in each of its five classrooms to volunteer. Still other trips, such as the yearly trip to Sesame Place—a 16-acre children's theme park with water rides, live Sesame Street characters, and other attractions in Langhorne, Pennsylvania—required months of advance planning. For this trip, the center, rather than requesting volunteers, permitted parents to bring one family member, since "just about *every* parent comes" to this event, explained Deirdre. Since many families flouted the one-person rule, the center rented large buses for the 90-minute drive outside the city.

Deirdre recognized the many demands on parent's times, finding ways, within her meager budget, to provide incentives for them to participate. She explained that "life is so fast" that she has had to get creative. "We say, 'Next time you come to a meeting, bring another parent.'" She keeps the meetings short, turns parent business meetings into pizza parties, and finds as many ways as possible to arrange for children performances. "Everybody wants to see their children perform."

Active Engagement in New York City Childcare Centers

A parent enrolled in A Place Upstairs would be asked for much more than to unload and retrieve her child on time. Some of these requests would present little more than opportunities to interact with other parents, such as the informational session at which the police officer explained the boundaries between discipline and abuse. Others would induce parents to interact, such as the request that they help coordinate field trips and child watching, or the request, at Serena's center, that parents fund-raise. A Place Upstairs, Alegre, Tweed, and Standing in Faith do not merely provide parents with many chances to run into others; they also ask parents to cooperate, even with those they do not know, on focused, joint tasks conducive to friendship formation. They do so through informational meetings and workshops, holiday celebrations, in-town and out-of town field trips, cleanup campaigns, staffing and curricular meetings, and fund-raisers.

The prevalence of field trips, fund-raisers, celebrations, and other events was not unique to the four centers discussed above. Consider the results of the Childcare Centers and Families Survey of nearly 300 randomly sampled New York City centers. Table 3.1 presents the prevalence of field trips such as the one attended by Denise or organized by A Place Upstairs. As exhibited in the first column, the majority of centers organized a trip to a museum or the zoo in the previous 12 months, many held trips to libraries and farms, and about a third assembled the more time-consuming, expensive trips to children's parks such as Sesame Place in Pennsylvania or Land of Make

Table 3.1. Field trips held by New York City childcare centers in previous 12 months.

| | | For centers that held trip | | |
| | | | For centers in which parents attended | |
Type of trip	Center held trip	Parents attended	Mean(SD) no. of parents attending	Mean no. of children enrolled > 1 year of age
Museum or zoo	79%	91%	14 (17)	96
Library	69%	54%	7 (8)	113
Farm	67%	94%	22 (29)	102
Event in large stadium	38%	93%	20 (35)	87
Children's park outside city	30%	98%	35 (30)	95

Source: Childcare Centers and Families survey. n=293 centers.

Believe in New Jersey and to events in large venues such as Madison Square Garden. The second column shows that, with the exception of library trips, parents in the overwhelming majority of centers attended the trip on the last occasion the trip was held. In short, most centers ran trips throughout the year; when they did, most of the time parents attended.

The last two columns (roughly) describe how actively parents participated in these field trips. The first of these exhibits the average number of parents who attended the last trip, with the standard deviation in parentheses; the second, the average number of children older than 1 year enrolled.[4] Not surprisingly, the most popular trips were those outside the city, with 35 parents on average attending the last trip to a children's park (among centers in which parents attended) and 22 attending the last trip to a farm. If we assume only one parent per child attends each trip, then a little more than one-third of parents on average attended the last children's park trip and more than one-fifth attended the last farm trip. As shown in the standard deviations, however, there was a great deal of variability from center to center.

While attending field trips provided an opportunity for parents to interact, many of the other activities required parents not merely to interact but also to *cooperate*. Through these activities, the center became an active, if often inadvertent, partner in the formation of ties among parents. Three of these activities deserve mention: fund-raising, cleaning, and hiring.

Table 3.2. Activities held by New York City childcare centers in previous 12 months

Type of activity	Center held activity	Parent participation at centers that held activity
Fundraising event	72%	98%
Spring cleaning	26%	43%
Teacher or staff hiring	71%	29%

Source: Childcare Centers and Families Survey. $n=293$ centers. Right column indicates whether parents participated during the last time the center held the activity.

None of the activities requiring cooperation was more prevalent than fund-raising. Earlier I described Serena's efforts to improve the effectiveness with which parents cooperated to organize fund-raisers for Standing in Faith. While Serena's proactive personality (and her position as parents association president) played a role in the *form* that fund-raising took at the Standing in Faith Center, it played no role in the fact that the center fund-raised, or that it did so aggressively—the center had been fund-raising for years. In fact, given the high cost of childcare service, most centers, private or public, have to fund-raise. As shown on table 3.2, 72% of centers had organized a fund-raising event at least once over the previous 12 months. In almost every case (98%), parents participated in the fund-raising event the last time it was held. These fund-raisers included the cookie dough sell-a-thons that Serena helped organize, raffles, bake sales, parties, and restaurant outings.

A second major component of the operation of a childcare center is maintenance, given the comparatively high standards of cleanliness, safety, and sanitation imposed by federal and local regulations (standards that many centers fail to maintain). Childcare centers must maintain cleaning standards that resemble those of hospitals, given the propensity for the spread of disease. Yet children spill, spread, and smear food, drink, and worse over center premises daily. In these conditions, spring cleanup or beautification campaigns were not uncommon, whereby parents substituted for the work that would normally be conducted by janitors or painters. In fact, 26% of centers had conducted spring cleanup activities at least once over the previous year, and in 43% of these the last cleanup event involved the participation of parents.

It may appear peculiar that parents would don gloves and old blue jeans to scrub walls and swing sets for organizations in which they are clients. However, both parents and directors repeatedly bemoaned the budget constraints faced by centers while expressing a desire for high quality facilities.[5] Katherine, a white woman in her late thirties who worked as a consultant, recalled the poor conditions of the playground of her son's center when she first enrolled him:

> 'Cause there was a long time—now it's coming back to me—when my son was in the baby room and just getting into the toddler room. [The center] just used the tennis court 'cause the playground was actually just too dangerous. It was just not a great place for them to play so they just ran around the tennis court, got filthy you know. And who wants to run around in a tennis court? It's hot.

It was clear that something needed to be done and that the funds with which to do so were limited. As a result, the director asked parents to offer their skills: "One father was a landscape architect who designed the playground and put in the little path with the letters on it. He really worked hard, 'cause that was hard, you know, to get budgeting and figure out which structure would be the right size and budget for us." Most parents did not have special skills, but raking leaves and cleanup and painting could be done by nearly anyone. So the parents, teachers, and staff spent "weekends sanding the swing set and repainting and bringing in sod to create that little hill. And putting in dirt and then putting on sod, cleaning the little plastic house.... Now they have the tree and they have the protective surface." The center, in effect, provided the means for collective action.

A third major component of the operation of the center is teacher and staff hiring, given the high turnover rate in the industry. For example, a study of childcare teaching staff in California, found that more than half of respondents surveyed in 1996 had left their centers by 2000.[6] As shown in table 3.2, 71% of centers had conducted a teacher or staff search at least once over the previous 12 months, and in 29% of the centers' parents had participated during the last search that had taken place.

Many of these activities required some formal organization on the part of parents, often in the form of a parents association, as Standing in Faith and Alegre Daycare demonstrated. Table 3.3 shows that 74% of the centers we surveyed either currently had a parents association or had had one in the past. These parents associations were not ad hoc entities instituted to solve short-term problems; instead, like the one for which Serena served as president, most were permanent subunits of the center, with a president, vice president, secretary, and treasurer. Of the centers that reported currently having a parents association, 76% had a governing board composed of parents, and in 95% of these cases the board was elected by parents.

These associations helped account for why 85% of centers had held a meeting or workshop for parents over the previous year: the majority of such meetings, 71% were organized specifically by or for the parents association. It is also worth noting that of the 78% of centers overseen by a board of directors, 32% had at least one parent sitting on the board.

Table 3.3. Parents associations (P.A.) among New York City childcare centers

Center has had a P.A.	74%		
Center currently has a P.A.	69%		
If yes: P.A. governed by board of parents	76%	If yes: Board elected by parents	95%

Source: Childcare Centers and Families Survey. $n=293$ centers.

In short, the average New York City childcare center requires active engagement, such that parental participation forms an integral part of much of the organization's functioning. In Scott Feld's terms, the activities of parents are focused, both oriented toward the daycare and the children, and centered on the concrete tasks that constitute the activities of a modern childcare center, such as the orchestration of fund-raisers, the organization of field trips and holiday events, the improvement and maintenance of facilities, and the establishment of curricula.

PARENTS' REACTIONS TO OPPORTUNITIES AND INDUCEMENTS

There is little mystery in the fact that greater opportunities to interact will, all other factors held constant, increase the probability that mothers form ties. Still, we must examine whether mothers believed that the presence or scarcity of opportunities and inducements to interact was important to their friendship formation. Did mothers understand their ties as resulting from their opportunities or, instead, from their interests, purposive actions, motivations, and abilities—from their individual agency? As the examples below illustrate, while mothers by no means undermined the role of their own agency, they repeatedly pointed to the importance of their structured opportunities.

The opportunity to interact with other parents did not emerge naturally from participating in a center; it resulted from centers' norms or policies that, whether deliberately or not, either provided such opportunities or failed to do so. This much is clear when the opportunities stem from activities such as field trips, graduation parties, and Mother's Day events. But it was no less true when they stemmed from ostensibly trivial circumstances, such as the center's policies about pickup and drop-off times. In fact, this was the most common explanation among the parents we interviewed for why they knew or did not know other parents. Centers differed. When a center tended to hold major events, parents referred to them to explain how they had met other parents; when centers did not, parents referred to the only other opportunity to meet others they could think of, pickup and drop-off times.

Centers differed in how strictly they enforced drop-off and retrieval rules. The Bright Colors Center had a strict 6:00 p.m. cutoff time for retrieving children, after which parents were fined. Lorraine, a slight, brown-haired, white doctor in her thirties whose two children were in Bright Colors, explained how she met the parents she knew there:

> [U]sually, when I drop them off there's often another parent there . . . so in terms of getting to know the parents, it's pretty much [that I] chat with them when we drop the kids off . . . or when I pick them up. Usually there's sort of a 6:00 dash where all the parents are trying to get there before 6 because they charge 20 dollars an hour if you [are even] . . . two minutes late. . . . And so almost every [day], a large group of parents are there at 6:00 and people wind up kind of standing around in the lobby and talking after the day or outside.

For Lorraine, this was only the beginning. An equally important source of friendships were the center's field trips to farms in upstate New York ("there [were] pigs and chickens and goats and stuff") and to the Bronx Zoo, for which she switched shifts with a coworker to be able to attend. She explained how she used the time to meet other parents, while watching her son: "More or less on each trip maybe half the parents come. And I usually . . . talk to the other parents about a third of the time and watching [my son] the other two thirds of the time, depending on how distracted he is or if he wants attention or not."

An instructive contrast is Frances, a plain-spoken, white lawyer with straight brown hair whose interviewer described as an easy conversationalist: "She smiled often and spoke in an easy, slow manner. We chatted so easily that [before we began the interview] it almost felt as if we already knew each other." Frances, whose son was enrolled at the Little Friends Day Care, was in many respects a "networker," one who, like many professionals, purposely mobilized her social contacts to solve problems or obtain needed information. Recently, for example, when she revealed she was searching for a nanny for her younger daughter, and her interviewer asked, "How do you go about trying to find a nanny?" she replied, "We're doing it through friends who are recommending people they know."

These friends, however, were not other parents in the center, a natural target for such an inquiry. "Have you talked to the any of the other parents at the center about it?" asked her interviewer. "No." "Do you think that they might be a good source of information for that?" "[T]hey probably, they might be I'm not sure. I never . . . I'm not really very close to them as a whole." In fact, she had met very few of the parents.

Naturally, many factors accounted for this fact, but her explanation centered on the missing opportunities. Instead of the Bright Colors' strict hours, the Little Friends Day Care had generous, extended drop-off hours of 8:00 to 9:15 in the morning, which allowed parents few opportunities to run into one another. Frances alluded to this fact when explaining why she had not met more of the center's parents:

> So I only met, I only started meeting people now [because] I now take my son in the morning three times a week, so I meet some of the parents that way. [Her husband takes him the other two days.] But usually since it's the morning, one, I'm usually rushing off to work so it's not like you have a lot of time to stand around and chat. . . . And also there's a very flexible time at which people drop off their children—they don't all arrive at the same time. So, usually when I drop my son off in the morning there's . . . only one or two children already there. And so it's rare that I run into more than one parent in any given morning dropping off their child.

Later, she explained her budding relationship with one couple: "This one particular [couple] that . . . I was just mentioning, they seem to be on kind of the same time schedule so they're probably the couple—actually I see the husband dropping off his daughter. So, we often run into them walking in so I generally chat with him and his wife more frequently. But the others, very rarely do I, actually." Frances acknowledges that even a friendly, purposive, motivated networker such as herself will fail to make friends if she lacks the opportunities to network. In this sense, she resembles Lorraine, who attributes her success—in her case, at making friendships—largely to her opportunities to do so, rather than her needs, her motivation, her personality, or her friendliness.

My argument for the importance of opportunities and inducements does not imply that motivations are irrelevant. For example, Linda's motivations derived from her daughter. As she explained her approach to the activities center, "You should be . . . active in you child's education. I don't understand parents who are [not]. . . . [Y]ou cannot say anything [negative] about the educational system or how things have gone if you're not doing anything to either improve or correct it." A black woman who wore horn-rimmed glasses and her black hair straightened flat, Linda was a secretary at a local university. As soon as she enrolled her daughter in the Tweed Center, she asked to be involved: "The day I walked in the school I asked the teacher, 'What can I do to help?' . . . That was my [attitude]: 'What do you need me to do, how can I help you?'" At first she volunteered to help coordinate field trips; later she became secretary of the parents association, which during her tenure organized a yearbook, a major annual fund-raiser, and all of the field trips.

Linda knew many of Tweed's parents. When her interviewer asked how she came to know so many of them, she referred to these opportunities: "I'm the secretary of the [parents association] so ... probably at meetings or coming in the mornings to pick up my daughter." The impact of these opportunities was intensified due to the activities she undertook at the center. She explained that she had become "good friends" with several parents in the association. Her interviewer followed on the question: "And were you good friends with [them] before you were on the [association]?" "Eighty percent of them I was already, we were already friends. . . . And being on the [association] just increased it because we had to be in communication with each other." The orientation toward collective problem solving helped. As she explained later,

> Since I am on the [parents association] and connect with all the parents, being on different committees, I get a chance to meet the parents in the older group, too. But if I weren't on the [association] . . . maybe my span of friends would just be in the lower grades [where my daughter is enrolled]. I wouldn't just say necessarily her class but, like, on this floor, . . . on the preschool through second grade because those are the ones who I see at the gate when I drop them off and, you know, you have a tendency to stay a little [and talk].

Linda's account is consistent with the idea that the inducements to interact—imposed by the activities of the parents association—were important reasons for her formation of new friends.

A mother less motivated than Linda, even as a member of the parents association, would probably have made fewer friends. The agency of the actor is the ultimate arbiter. Nevertheless, as Linda, Frances, and Lorraine make clear, to neglect how centers structure the interactions of parents is to ignore that organizations substantially shape the formation of new friends.

A FUND-RAISER MEETING

Few circumstances reveal more about how parents take the first gingerly steps toward friendship formation than the meetings centers held to coordinate fund-raisers. The Standing in Faith center had held the first of such meetings late in the fall, on a frigid December evening, in the cafeteria of a school nearby, in the high poverty, predominantly black neighborhood. The cafeteria, about the size of a basketball court, had a dozen round tables with chairs flipped on top of them. Posted on the walls were computer-printed signs reading "Happy Birthday Jesus" and several wooden crosses.

A 19-inch television was suspended from a bar on the ceiling (and was turned off). The director had assembled a table with a microphone attached to a small black speaker on one side of the room. At five or six tables sat about 35 parents, all but two of them women, almost all black and two or three of Latino origin. Everyone wore their winter coats and hats. It was 6:30 p.m., and since the center had remained opened late to babysit during the meeting, there were only four children in the room.

The four-member parents association had met previously and was here to report on updates and needs. As I walked into the meeting, Serena, the president, was brainstorming creative sources for funds and resources. She reported, as an example to her audience, that Goldman Sachs recycled its computers every three years; she asked, rhetorically, "What do they do with the old computers? Maybe we can have them for the school." She continued, "As another example, suppose we want to raise money to renovate the basement. That costs a hundred thousand dollars." She explained that the center would like to turn the basement into a play area. "Maybe someone can get us on Oprah. I bet someone knows someone who knows someone that could place a call for us. I bet Oprah could get us a hundred thousand dollars!" Though she spoke with enthusiasm her listeners were rather blasé, doing their best to keep warm in the rather cool hall.

Eventually, she asked, "Why don't we go around and introduce ourselves? I think a lot of people don't know everyone's names. . . . Often, we just know the kids' names!" She asked parents to state their name, their child's name, and their child's class. They started at the back. The first person, a black mother of a girl, stood up, still wearing her down jacket. She said her name and her child's name; she then laughed sheepishly and said, "I don't remember the teacher's name!" Everyone laughed. One by one, parents stood up and followed suit, warming up as someone cracked an icebreaker joke. It turned out many parents did not yet know the names of their children's teacher. At the last table sat a group of parents who seemed to know the names of the others and of their teacher. When the last person in that table recited the teacher's name, it was clear that all were in the same class. "All right!" someone said, "Let's hear it for Ms. Robinson!" More laughter.

There were many additional items on the agenda, which had been arranged by Serena, the president, Hector, the vice president, and Samantha, the center's director. The next item was candy. Many parents, required to raise $200 in candy sales, were already behind target only three months into the year. The secretary of the parents association said she could indicate how much each parent still owed. The next item was a pizza event. Hector, a tall, heavy-set, Bronx-born Latino with straight, salt-and-pepper hair slicked back, led discussion. After introducing himself, he explained that he had spoken with the management of a restaurant, Pizza Party, about organizing a fund-raiser that had previously been mentioned to the parents. The center would receive a portion of the sales made during the time parents and their families attended the parties. "The manager said if we make over $1,000, we get 10% [back]....If we make $2,000 it's 20%...." He continued: "The manager gave us four hours, but normally they give...two hours. They won't give us the weekend or Friday, but they'll give us Monday through Thursday. So, we started looking to see if there was a holiday we could go." He explained that he works for government, so "I have the holiday schedule right in front of me for the whole year. They give us the whole year in advance." As he said this, he waved his palm up and down in front of an imaginary wall calendar, for impact. He then ran through the numbers. "So, the way I figure, if we have 75 children, plus one parent, that's 150. Then you add cousins, other family who wants to come.... He said, "They gave us four hours because I had said 'That's not enough time for people. They work, so they're going to be coming for several hours.' So, I thought we could do it in shifts." He concluded: "If we get up to $2,000 that's . . . $400 we can use for the center."

The next item was the Christmas party, where "Santa," said Samantha, "will be there with gifts" for all the children. Samantha, the director, was a slight, soft-spoken African-American in her sixties whose large eyeglasses often dangled near the tip of her nose. One mother asked where the gifts were coming from, and Samantha explained that at some point over the previous weeks, children had written their wish lists on a card and posted these on the center's main bulletin board. A large nonprofit foundation had received these lists and would bring gifts the children had requested. At this point, another mother worried aloud about her child: "I didn't know we were supposed to do this." A third interjected: "All gifts they get are appropriate for the child's age, and they also give books and things like that. And all children will receive a gift, even if they didn't put in a request." The party would take place in the middle of the day at an off-site location. Serena stood up and asked for volunteers to walk the children over.

The meeting proceeded at a fast clip. The next item was a request for special emergency volunteers, whom Samantha referred to as "classroom representatives." The center would generate a list of parents, two per class, whom the director would call in an emergency. Each person in the list would be responsible for contacting half the people in the class or, if the other representative were not available, all parents in the class. After several parents offered themselves, Serena took over, encouraging parents to bring any skills to the group. One mother stood and said, "I know we all have a math phobia. Well, I'm a math teacher and I was thinking we could have a math day, where parents come with their children and we help them all do their math." She smiled as she said this, and a few people nodded their head.

By this point, the meeting was winding down. Samantha requested donations for the two school custodians who had stayed late to keep the school open for the parents. "If everyone could donate a dollar or two dollars for them, that would help." The treasurer, a Latina in her thirties wearing a camel-colored sweater, picked up a tin square can and started collecting dollar bills, in a ritual reminiscent of collection during mass.[7] They netted more than thirty dollars. After a prayer led by Samantha, the group disbanded, as parents paired off, continuing small conversations on the Christmas list, the logistical details of upcoming events, and the dry, cold weather.

A PARTIAL TEST

We can partly test the idea that the opportunities we have discussed substantially contribute to friendship formation, by using the national survey data on mothers of young children employed in chapter 2. Since that survey was designed by a separate team to examine family formation and dissolution, it does not contain extensive data on whether the mothers' centers ran field trips, parties, fund-raisers, or other activities likely to lead to tie formation. However, it does contain data on whether the centers had a parents association, and we know that parents associations are instituted to run these activities. In fact, centers in New York City with parents associations are significantly more likely ($p < 0.004$ or lower) to have held any of the field trips shown in table 3.1 and to have conducted a fund-raising activity than centers without parents associations. Thus, we can use the presence of a parents association as a proxy, albeit an imperfect one, for the opportunities and inducements a center is likely to present. If the theory is correct, mothers in centers with a parents association should be more likely to have made new friends at the center than those in centers with no association, net of the mothers' own characteristics.

To conduct this test, I limited the sample to mothers in childcare centers and estimated the probability that the mothers made any friends in the center as a function of whether the center had a parents association, after controlling for demographic variables. To help account for selection bias—for the possibility that friendlier mothers chose centers with parents associations—I adjusted for the total number of close friends the mother has (see appendix B for details). Figure 3.1 exhibits the results.

If the center has a parents association, a mother's probability of making a friend there is about 12 percentage points greater, net of her personal characteristics, including how many friends she has in general. (This difference is statistically significant.) Thus, the opportunities presented by the

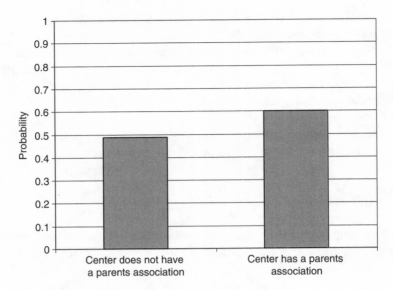

Figure 3.1. Predicted probability of making a friend in a center, for statistically average urban mother of 5-year-old enrolled in a childcare center.
Source: Families First survey. Logistic regression model; including controls for no close friends, income, race, age, education, no. children, no. adults in household, employment, and marital and cohabiting status. Robust standard errors account for city clust ering.

center and the activities it requires of parents appear to exert an influence on the mothers' ability to make friends.

CONCLUSION: MORE TO DO, MORE TO GAIN

Mothers formed friendships in childcare centers so often because centers, purposely and otherwise, provided opportunities and inducements for them to spend time with others, often by insisting that mothers participate in the center's routine activities. Thus, many centers in New York City do not free mothers' time but instead constrain it, requiring more, not less of them. How could this possibly contribute to well-being?

The never-ending demands on working parents' time has probably been the predominant theme in recent research on working parents.[8] In a culture that increasingly expects mothers and fathers to devote serious time and attention to both their work and their children, the suffocating need for more hours in the day stands out as the overriding predicament of this generation of parents. The additional responsibilities introduced by many childcare centers may be difficult at best, daunting at worst.

Nevertheless, these responsibilities serve multiple purposes: for example, parents must chaperone children while simultaneously taking one-day vacations in the countryside, prepare for and attend a potluck dinner while also sampling foods from other countries, or organize a fund-raiser while also preparing for a holiday party or attending a comedy event. Therefore, as described throughout this book, the additional requirements are not so much an extra burden—though they certainly are partly this—as a rearrangement of how vacations, trips, quality time with children, cooking, and, ultimately, socialization are practiced. They constitute a reconfiguration of the mothers' time to the parameters set by this new organizational membership, one that may require extra hours but also reward them with more interaction with the child, a Kodak moment, or a chance to meet other adults. These routine events serve multiple purposes.

Two books help place this reconfiguration in perspective. In *The Time Bind*, a study of how, for many parents, the office has become a greater safe haven than the home, Arlie Hochschild argues that work transforms how parents use their time: "The social world that draws a person's allegiance also imparts a pattern to time."[9] The same may be said of the childcare center, a social world that draws the allegiance of parents and shapes, in smaller and more haphazard but equally persistent periods, how they use their time. The office forces the worker to clock in daily, for eight or more hours, with the threat of the pink slip; the center forces the parent to clock in daily for a few minutes, and only weekly or monthly for several hours, but with the equally daunting threat of the lost slot. This threat earns the center the right to make demands, but with the gentle admonition that the stakes are the good of the child, such that the parent's allegiance is usually secured and her patterns of time subsequently altered.

In *Changing Rhythms of American Life*, Suzanne Bianchi, John Robinson, and Melissa Milkie describe their study of how American parents have occupied the hours of the day over the past 40 years. They found that even though the amount of time parents spent at work increased over this period, the amount of time they spent with children actually had not decreased.[10] This paradox, more time in the workplace but no less time with children, was resolved in part by the fact that mothers today multitask much more than they used to, combining their child time with their time for other activities. The center, in that light, is the answer to the multitasker's prayers, the reason Denise was among the first in line to volunteer to chaperone the field trip. The center permits and encourages mothers to pursue multiple global purposes. Through the fund-raisers, center parties, field trips, and other activities, mothers can temper the guilt of not devoting enough energy to the child, save some dollars on childcare, spend time with their children, eat or party or sunbathe or breathe cleaner air, and take time away from the pressures of work and the stress of home. All of these activities accomplish more than one task.

The one common task among these "multitask" activities, as described throughout the chapters in part II, is the opportunity to socialize with other adults, to generate, sometimes purposely but often not, the ties that produce social capital. For this reason, childcare centers played a major role in decreasing social isolation.[11] A refrain among first-time parents insists that, after the birth of their children, people make most of their new friends through their children. If true, it might well be so because an increasing number of those children are enrolled in childcare centers.

POSTSCRIPT: WHY CENTERS INVOLVE PARENTS

Before continuing, it is important for the broader understanding of the organizational embeddedness perspective to examine a question: why centers delegate so many activities to parents. This question is, in fact, two: Why do centers arrange so many field trips, spring cleanings, and other events? And when they do, why do they involve parents? The discussion above has offered several hints. Below, I briefly elaborate on and summarize the factors underlying the centers' motivations. I suggest that these are both internal and external, encompassing both economic and institutional motivations: the need to maintain low costs in a difficult industry; the internal pressures of staff members themselves, whose professional orientations encourage activities that require parental participation; and the external pressures of the state.

Internal and External Pressures

Childcare centers involve parents in much of what they do because economic needs in a difficult industry demand it. Centers are precarious organizations. The National Childcare Staffing Study found that of 226 centers sampled in 1988, 30% had closed by 1997.[12] When centers require that parents fund-raise or ask them to sew together costumes, bring foods for holiday parties, request time off work to chaperone children at field trips, and scrub, mop, and paint during spring cleanings, the centers are pooling group resources for the good of the center and its members. Incorporating these processes into the roles of formal parents associations helps ensure their stability and cut yearly startup costs for the activities even further. As Deirdre, director of A Place Upstairs, explained, when asked why she tried to get parents involved, "it takes a lot [of pressure] off you."

Economic imperatives constitute only part of the answer. For example, while it appears economically rational that centers include parents when they conduct field trips, it is unclear why they bother running field trips, especially if trips are costly. In addition, while the cost-cutting benefits of asking parents to participate in beautification campaigns are self-evident, the benefits of having them participate in staff hiring are not so clear. (In fact, it seems like a recipe for conflict.)[13] To understand these practices, I suggest we must rely not merely on the market, but also on at least two additional factors that, in their theoretical work, organizational sociologists Paul DiMaggio and Walter Powell have described as institutional in nature.[14]

A second factor is the set of professional norms among childcare professionals. Many staff members in childcare centers believed that providing proper childcare required the participation of the parent. The professionalization of childcare provision has been associated with the proliferation of certain norms regarding the proper provision of service.[15] Many of these are norms discussed in chapter 7, but several are worth noting now: the beliefs that one cannot care for the child without somehow caring for the household, that children should be exposed to diverse experiences and environments, and that part of the role of the center is to provide resources that might not be available from home. For this reason, staff members conceive the organization of trips to the zoo, museums, and parks to be a natural extension of their services, much the same way high schools organize athletic teams even though their global purpose is to provide an academic education. These norms are so institutionally accepted that centers failing to organize such activities may give the impression of providing subpar services.

A third factor is external—the pressures that the state, as a powerful authority, exerts on certain centers. Many state-funded centers must, by government mandate, involve parents in curricular and other administrative decisions. The most notable are those funded by the Head Start program, which provides the financial backing for centers operated by local community organizations. Head Start regulations require that centers "establish and maintain a formal structure of shared governance through which parents can participate in policy making or in other decisions about the program."[16] These regulations explicitly mandate an annually elected parent committee "comprised exclusively of the parents of children currently enrolled" in the center.[17] The responsibilities of the parents' committee include the following:

1. Advise staff in developing and implementing local program policies, activities, and services;
2. Plan, conduct, and participate in informal as well as formal programs and activities for parents and staff; and
3. Within the guidelines established by the governing body [or other committees] participate in the recruitment and screening of Early Head Start and Head Start employees.[18]

Many centers, that is, form parents committees because they must comply with the pressures of external authorities.

In addition, Head Start centers are mandated to solicit volunteers as much as possible: "Special efforts must be made to have volunteer participation, especially parents, in the classroom and during group socialization activities," which presumably include field trips and holiday events.[19] Thus, these centers must ask parents to participate in curricular policies, activities and events, and staff hiring. In New York City, the Administration for Children's Services (ACS), which administers Head Start centers, also funds its own centers. In recent years, these programs have been consolidated, such that ACS-funded centers must operate by many of the rules that govern Head Start centers, including the operation of a parents association.

Survey Data

Testing the notion that these three factors motivate centers and their staff to institute tie-building activities is difficult. The Childcare Centers survey did not ask center directors to explain why they conducted each activity. However, we can exploit the data in several ways.

First, since centers differ in the extent to which they are subject to state control, we can assess whether this difference is associated with the presence of the aforementioned activities. We saw that the Head Start program required its centers to institute a parents association. The survey asked directors whether the center was a for-profit or nonprofit and whether it was primarily privately funded or publicly funded. Table 3.4 categorizes centers by primary funding source and profit orientation, and exhibits the percentage of centers in each type (private for-profit and nonprofit, and government funded) that has a parents association. While about half of privately funded centers, whether for profit or nonprofit, had such an association, almost 90% of government-funded centers did.

Second, although the survey did not ask directors to provide the motivations behind all of the center's institutional practices, it did ask them why they had instituted a parents association, providing them the opportunity to provide more than one answer. Table 3.4 shows that, among government-funded

Table 3.4. Prevalence for and motivation behind having parents association's, by center sector

Center characteristic	PFP ($n=59$)	PNP ($n=98$)	GNP ($n=134$)
Among all centers			
Center currently has a parents association	49%	53%	89%
Among centers with a parents association			
Required by government agency	12%	20%	86%
Required by private agency as condition for receiving funds	11%	8%	34%
Requested by parents	50%	51%	26%

PFP, privately funded for-profit center; PNP, privately funded nonprofit; GNP, government-funded nonprofit.

Source: Childcare Centers and Families Survey. $n=293$. Centers could report more than one reason.

centers, the primary motivation was the state mandate, even though other factors, including parental requests, played a role, as well. Government mandates played little role in the actions of private-sector centers, which helps account for their having comparatively fewer associations.

The influence of the state also becomes clear when we evaluate the centers' fund-raisers, teacher or staff hiring, and spring cleaning activities. Table 3.5 shows the percentages of centers that held specific activities in the previous 12 months, and the percentage of these in which parents participated, by category. While most centers fund-raised, a substantially larger number of government-funded centers did so. Yet whenever a center fund-raised, parents were involved. This pattern suggests that while the decision to fund-raise was externally motivated, the inclusion of parents—once the decision was made—was driven largely by operational needs. Regarding personnel, more than 70% of centers in all three categories hired teachers or staff during the previous 12 months. Yet only among government-funded centers were parents often involved, since at least among some of them (Head Start centers), they are required to do so. Among government-funded centers, 46% of centers involved parents; among privately funded centers, less than 14% of them did. Finally, no government mandates involve the institution of spring cleanings. Consequently, there were no major differences across center categories in this practice.[20]

Our ability to observe the role of professional norms depends on how widely shared they are. We saw that center staff often reported believing that children should participate in multiple activities outside of the class-

Table 3.5. Activities held by center at least once in previous 12 months, and parental involvement, by center sector

Activity	PFP (n=59)	PNP (n=98)	GNP (n=134)
Held fund-raising event	66%	65%	80%
If yes, involved parents	97%	95%	100%
Held teacher or staff hiring	71%	73%	70%
If yes, involved parents	10%	13%	46%
Held spring cleaning	34%	22%	24%
If yes, involved parents	30%	73%	31%

PFP, privately funded for-profit center; PNP, privately funded nonprofit; GNP, government-funded nonprofit.

Source: Childcare Centers and Families Survey. n=293 Centers could report more than one reason.

room, such as trips to zoos, parks, museums, and other events. We also saw that, when centers established these field trips, they almost always found it economically rational to request parent involvement. If these norms and beliefs are truly widely held, then field trips should be prevalent across centers, regardless of the level of state control, since the motivation to execute the activities is largely internal.[21]

Table 3.6 shows the percentage of centers in each sector that conducted different types of field trips, along with the percentage in which parents participated the last time the center held the trip. Two patterns are apparent. First, the rates of parent participation are nearly identical across cate-

Table 3.6. Field trips held by center at least once in previous 12 months, and parental involvement, by center sector

Field Trip	PFP (n=59)	PNP (n=98)	GNP (n=134)
Museum or zoo	76%	68%	88%
If yes, parents participated	91%	83%	95%
Library	64%	58%	80%
If yes, parents participated	38%	56%	59%
Farm	67%	52%	78%
If yes, parents participated	97%	92%	93%
Event in large stadium	45%	26%	44%
If yes, parents participated	100%	84%	93%
Children's park outside city	28%	19%	40%
If yes, parents participated	100%	89%	100%

PFP, privately funded for-profit center; PNP, privately funded nonprofit; GNP, government-funded nonprofit.

Source: Childcare Centers and Families Survey. n=293.

gories, suggesting the importance of economic imperatives. Trips to museums, farms, and major events outdoors require parents; thus, whenever events occur, parents are asked to help. Second, the differences across categories in whether the field trip is held at all are smaller than the difference in whether centers had a parents association (though there are exceptions). This pattern is consistent with the idea of widely held beliefs about how centers should operate, beliefs that exerts pressures independent of those of the state.

I suggest, then, that many of the activities through which mothers formed friendships—and thus gained access to a potential source of social capital—must be traced not only to the imperatives of local actors but to institutional pressures as powerful and external as those stemming from state authority. By conceiving of actors as embedded in organizational contexts, it is possible to trace the practices occurring at the most macro levels of society to interactions as micro level as whether a mother can expect the opportunity to chat regularly with other parents at center-run fieldtrips. The implications of these processes for a revised theory of network inequality are discussed in chapter 8.

4

Weak and Strong Ties
Whether Mothers Made Close Friends, Acquaintances, or Something Else

Mothers, we have seen, typically develop friendships in their centers. But how close do these friendships tend to be? Do they tend to be strong bonds of intimacy and camaraderie, or thin acquaintanceships that demand no obligations and yield few social goods? The question is as important as whether mothers made friends at all, since the ties may be so slight as to be meaningless. For example, chapter 3 described how Denise reported that the center parents she met were "very nice"—an informative detail, but far from confirmation that her newly acquired networks improved her well-being.

A standard distinction in the sociology of networks helps refine this question and generate expectations about how the relations may be useful: the difference between "strong" and "weak" ties.[1] The idea of strength was defined well by Mark Granovetter: "[T]he strength of a tie is a (probably linear) combination of the amount of time, the emotional intensity, the intimacy (mutual confiding), and the reciprocal services which characterize the tie."[2] Sociologists of networks expect strong ties, which they also call "intimate ties," to improve well-being because they provide social support: they provide assistance during emergencies, lend cash in times of need, help ward off loneliness, and provide the opportunity to share intimate feelings.[3]

Weak ties, however, may possess their own advantages. In an elegant study, Granovetter showed that only weak ties serve as bridges between separate networks. Bridges matter for a simple reason. People tend to be friends with their friends' friends; that is, strong ties tend to cluster, and information or resources owned by one in a strong cluster tend to be known or shared by all. A bridge, defined as the only tie between two networks of individuals, carries information and other resources from one network (or cluster of friends) to another. Since strong ties tend to cluster, only weak ties are likely to be bridges. Consequently, weak ties are most likely to offer information that a person did not already know or resources from a network to which a person did not already have access.[4]

The difference between weak and strong ties provides alternative accounts of the gains mothers acquired from their center friendships. We saw that enrolled mothers experienced greater well-being on average, due in large part to their new friendships. If these tended to be strong ties, then mothers likely acquired new sources of support; if they tended to be weak ties, then mothers likely gained valuable resources from alien social networks.[5] The former implies that centers represent a community of support; the latter, that they function not as a space for community but as a terminal where mothers make superficial yet useful connections. Given the time constraints that mothers reported, and the general decline in *Gemeinschaft*, or traditional sense of community, that sociologists have documented, we have reason to expect a preponderance of useful weak ties.[6]

AN ANSWER

To determine whether mothers largely made weak or strong ties, we turn to the Fragile Families survey of urban mothers. The survey asked enrolled mothers how many friends they made in centers and how many of those they considered "close friends," which indicates strong ties.[7] Table 4.1 presents the results. As described in chapter 3, among all enrolled mothers, 60% had made at least one friend at the center, and smaller percentages had made larger numbers of friends. The bottom panel shows that, perhaps surprisingly, 68% of these mothers reported that at least one of the center

Table 4.1. Friends and close friends made among urban mothers with children in childcare centers

	Among all mothers in centers, percent who made	Among all mothers *who made friends* in centers, percent who made
Number of friends		
1 or more friends	60%	
3 or more friends	40%	
6 or more friends	15%	
Number of close friends		
1 or more close friends	41%	68%
3 or more close friends	14%	24%
6 or more close friends	2%	3%

Source: Fragile Families national survey. Figures weighted to account for survey design.

friends was a *close* friend. In fact, 41% of *all* mothers in childcare centers made at least one friend whom they now considered close. Close friendships abounded. The survey makes clear that most mothers formed ties in centers, and that most of those who did, perhaps in spite of expectations, formed *strong* ones.[8]

WHAT IS A CLOSE FRIEND?

That most mothers made strong ties represents this chapter's point of departure. The preponderance of strong, rather than weak, ties generates a rather specific set of expectations. Mothers should tend to be friends with their friends' friends. The friendships should yield relatively little new information, but much all-around support, since strong friendships imply strong obligations. To paraphrase Granovetter, the friendships should be characterized by intimacy, mutual confiding, and a measure of emotional intensity. For many mothers, the average center should be a place of community in the traditional sense. Is this the case?

To answer this question, the chapter turns to the in-depth interviews. While the survey provided valuable knowledge on the distribution of close friendships in a national sample, it cannot tell us what mothers mean when they report a "close friend." It does not explain how close these friendships truly are, what obligations they entail, or what resources the parties are willing to exchange. With the interviews, we probe beyond the theory to the everyday experience of friendship.

The findings reveal two surprises. First, some developed precisely what Granovetter and other network theorists expect of strong ties. In an age in which social capital has been said to be in decline and social isolation on the rise, many center mothers developed nothing less than a small, family-like community, an all-around source of support with deep obligations, mutual confidence, and emotional intensity. For these mothers, *Gemeinschaft* was not dead.

Second, however, other mothers who reported "close friendships" developed a rather different kind of strong tie, one that violated many expectations of social network analysts. If theorists expect strong ties to be intimate they often expect weak ties to be domain specific: "[A] common interest in chess, work activities, [or] sports" to quote Edward Laumann, might characterize the relationship among acquaintances.[9] A golf buddy seen only on the course will not be the source of an intimate relationship; he will be the source of conversations on golf. Nevertheless, many mothers formed friendships, both genuinely intimate *and* domain-specific ties, that in many senses were both weak and strong. In these relationships, conversation, activity, and interaction were limited to implicitly understood and strictly delimited domains, while nonetheless attaining remarkable depth within their domain. If the *Gemeinschaft* mothers developed standard "intimates," these mothers formed compartmental intimates.

Compartmentally intimate ties reveal how organizations may contour the closeness and strength of friendships. As we shall see, these theoretically unexpected relations produced an especially advantageous form of social capital, wherein mothers were saved from the more daunting obligations of standard intimate ties. We shall also see that these relations were made possible by something rarely considered in conventional models, that organizations can institutionally perform much of the "work" required to sustain strong friendships. When institutional conditions sustain a friendship, the burden of maintenance inevitably shifts.

We begin, however, with the first unexpected finding, the overwhelming evidence of standard intimate relations among enrolled mothers.

STANDARD INTIMATES

Some mothers developed remarkably intimate friendships in the centers that they patronized. Katherine was a sharply dressed, New England-born, white redhead in her late thirties who worked as a consultant to small businesses. Thoughtful and earnest in conversation, she handled the many cell phone calls that rang during her interview without fluster, apologizing for the interruptions and quickly refocusing her thoughts. Her daughter attended and her son had graduated from the Little Friends Day Care, located in the upper middle-class neighborhood where she lived.

Katherine enjoyed being involved in the activities of her center, but her global purpose in doing so was getting closer to her children:

> I'm trying to be involved, and I don't think I participate that much but I just like to really hear what's happening, what's coming up. . . .
>
> They seem to do weekly field trips now in the preschool class, so I'm going on later this month as a chaperone. Whenever I can I try to. At this age they're young enough that they don't, they can't really tell you that much about their day, or they don't. So any kind of involvement I think is great, just to be able to see what it's like. Although . . . the child's not the same when you're there, when you, the mother, are there. But it's always fun to see how they interact.

Guilt played a role, too, even though Katherine had what many mothers would consider a dream job, a consulting position that allowed her flexibility: "I just want the time with my daughter, too. I think I feel a little bit guilty on the days that I don't work. I work but not in an office; I do consulting work, so I always feel like I should make the time when I can."

Over time, Katherine and her husband developed friendships with Amy and Bob, the parents of two other children in the center. She considered these to be "incredibly close" friends:

> KATHERINE: [When] my son was probably two, there were two other families that each had kids the same age as my children and the three families got to be incredibly close and we're still close today, but one lives down near [another neighborhood] and they ended up taking their kids [to a center there] . . . [and] the other moved to Pennsylvania. . . .
> INTERVIEWER: [Are you] still close to those . . . families?
> KATHERINE: Yeah, yep.

Some friendships, when separated by distance, remain close only in an ideal sense; they are no longer sustained through social interaction. This was not Katherine's experience. Despite the distance, she said, "we get together every month or two months or so." She elaborated on what they did together:

> Playgrounds, we go down to the family in Pennsylvania's house, we went to a state fair and rode the rides and just really anything. They're wonderful, we really think of it as family and feel like this place [*Little Friends Day Care*] is responsible for bringing us together. [Interviewer asks what topics Katherine feels comfortable discussing with them]. Well, now we know each other so well because it's been, I guess, five years that we've known each other. So, it used to always be the kids and now it's sort of everything from relationships, marriages, travel, and of course the kids, too.

A friendship that began with conversations on the children then blossomed into much more, into relations that are essentially "family." After Katherine referred to the couple as "good friends," her interviewer asked, "How would you define a good friend?":

> The ones that you consider family that you know you'd leave your kids with, with no qualms. And you can talk about anything and, as one of the couples described, one of the women described, it's as easy as breathing. You're just together and it's you know, it's like yesterday and you catch right up where you were from the last time you were together. As one of them keeps describing, it's just like our, it's just an extended family.

For Katherine, the center had effectively created a small tight-knit community.

Katherine's experience was not unique. Agatha was a black, vivacious secretary with thick long braids down to her neck who sported casual-chic clothing at her midtown office. Mother of four, she had three years earlier enrolled her youngest daughter (now graduated) at the Tweed Center because she appreciated the religious values she believed the center inculcated. "I was the secretary on the PTA," she recalled. "So, I knew most of the parents. Even if I didn't know them by name I knew them by face." Agatha explained that she had made close friends with whom she still kept in touch. There was a recent dinner event for currently enrolled center parents; nevertheless, the parents at the center insisted she should attend:

> [They] were all, like, "Come to the dinner." I was, like, "I don't know if [the staff] want me to come to the dinner; my child's not in the school anymore!" But, yeah, I [went]. I keep in touch with about five parents on a regular basis and then there are others that they know, like I said, I'm always the one looking for information, so when I find out about things I email them. . . . And they do the same thing. They're, like, "You [are] always sending us good stuff." [M]y [oldest] daughter [is] in a sorority and they're having a youth symposium coming up. So, I just sent out the flier for that today and I sent it to the parents [at the center] so they could take the kids.

Agatha described herself as "close" to several of the center parents. Her interviewer asked Agatha to rank them on a scale of one to ten, with ten being the closest: "Well, I have one that I would say is probably a ten. And then I have about two or three more that I would say maybe seven." Her interviewer pushed Agatha further. Were any topics of conversation off limits with these parents, sensitive issues she would not discuss?

> No, because, see, the difference with parents at [the center] is you, you're growing, you're all growing together, especially with little kids. And a lot of stuff comes out that . . . you know, little kids talk. They talk about their parents. They tell [their friends about] the argument you had last night. . . . So my close friends, yeah, I'll talk to them basically about anything.

Agatha's close friendships in the center erected few walls to delimit topics of conversation. It could have been her, rather than Katherine, who said, "And you can talk about anything."

At times, the centers helped parents sustain and deepen already-existing ties. Nancy, whose daughter was cared for at Little Friends, was a native Upstate New Yorker and also a secretary. Above average in height and stick thin, Nancy dyed her naturally blonde hair even blonder, painted her toenails chrome silver for the summer, and had bleached her teeth to a blinding white. Friendly by nature, she knew several parents in her center. "Yeah, I do now, quite a few. . . . Ten." She explained, when prompted by her interviewer, that one of them, Nadia, whom she knew before, was a close friend, "and I'm getting to be friendly with some." Her interviewer asked what she and Nadia tended to talk about:

> I don't know, we complain about men. Man bashing, exhaustion complaints, getting old and out of shape complaints. Things that are children, I mean we talk about their development, her son is about five or six weeks younger than

Tammy. We do talk about the children and things to do with them, all kinds of things actually. Politics, we're both [*unintelligible*] interested in politics and Nadia is very interested in the arts. She does the talking and I do the listening, she's very into the arts. Books we read, we both ... when we read, it's rare, it's a rare thing.

For Nancy, as for Agatha, conversation with her close friends in the center was unconstrained, the relationships an important source of social support, companionship, and confidants.

We heard something similar from Linda, the black secretary enrolled at Tweed who worked at a local university and who believed parents should be active in their children's education. When asked explicitly about the nature of her friendships, Linda told her interviewer,

It's funny, I was talking about this with somebody today. . . . [W]hen you don't have children your friends have a tendency to be people who don't have children also, but when you become a parent your closer friends tend to be people who have children because of like interests. So, yes, I would consider some of them to be my close friends.

Given Linda's answer, her interviewer asked whether their conversations tended to also center only on the children. They did not:

LINDA: Oh [we talk about] the school, what activities are going on at the school, our own personal lives, I mean I'm talking about just the close ones . . . . Our own personal lives, our career goals, spirituality. . . .
INTERVIEWER: How would you define a close friend?
LINDA: . . . I guess someone who I can share things with and is reciprocal with. . . . Yeah someone I can share things with, who has common interests.

Linda believes they have much to talk about in part because of their common interests (more on this below). Important sources of social support, these friendships were not limited to talk, nor were they constrained to the mornings and afternoons when they ran into each other in the center. Linda explained that she and her friends spent leisure time together outside the school. Her interviewer asked her to elaborate:

[We] go on trips, like last year we went on a, a group of us went on a trip to Virginia Beach and a lot of us belong to the same summer camp group so they all go, all of our children go there. We may get together and go swimming together and then just the parents, like maybe one of the mothers and I, will go to a movie or meet for dinner or something like that. Or like, some of the parents, we email each other all the time that type of thing.

These are unconstrained relations.

The friends of Katherine, Agatha, Naomi, and Linda may be characterized as standard intimates. In this context, intimacy simply refers to willingness of the parties to reveal something private about themselves.[10] These mothers shared a sense of closeness; they were, for each other, predictable sources of everyday support. No topic was inappropriate, and both their knowledge about each other and the activities they shared transcended the confines of the center. It is not surprising that these relationships may help ward off depression and other hardships, not only because they provide support on raising children, marriage, spirituality, career, and the work-life balance, but also because they provide opportunities for leisure together, trips out of state and out of the city, the opportunity to raise children in conjunction with other adults. The experiences reinforce that many of the "close friends" mothers reported in the survey were, indeed, very close.

COMPARTMENTAL INTIMATES

Suppose the strength of a tie between two actors can be determined by the privacy of the topics on which they converse, the informality of the activities in which they participate, and the intimacy of the things each knows about the other. When two actors are strongly tied, they share private feelings, spend time together even if not coerced, interact effortlessly and support each other selflessly. To this point, the contrast between strong and weak ties remains useful.

The contrast misses, however, that the intimacy of conversation or of activity can be domain specific.[11] For example, at work, I share a strong relation with a colleague I will call Cameron. I share with Cameron very personal things, such as rough drafts of papers that I would be too embarrassed to show others. I would collaborate with Cameron on conferences, even though I do not have to, and I would do so with pleasure. I speak to Cameron often, and we never small-talk, and if a survey were to ask me whether Cameron was a close friend, I would probably respond in the affirmative. Nevertheless, if I were to get married, I probably would not invite Cameron to the wedding. In addition, I have never spoken to Cameron about my love life or my family, nor has Cameron been over to my home for dinner. This is for no other reason than it has never occurred to me, or to Cameron. Cameron and I share a strong tie, but one limited to the domain of work, scholarship, intellectual pursuits, and the profession of sociology.

Likewise, mothers (and fathers) in childcare centers developed different types of "close friends." While many of these friends were standard intimates, relations with few restrictions on conversation or activity—strong ties in the traditional sense defined by Granovetter—many others constituted compartmental intimates, domain-specific strong ties, such as my tie to Cameron, except the domain was not work but the center, children, and raising families. I define a compartmental intimate as a relation characterized by openness, trust, and the revelation of privacy, but only within confined domains. In centers, conversation among compartmental intimates was open and highly personal, but only in the domain of children, family, and the center. Activity transcended polite conversation, and even the physical confines of the center, but only with the involvement of children, such as the coordination of play dates (among the middle class) and the celebration of birthday parties at each other's homes. Compartmental intimates knew personal details of each other's lives, but only center- or child-specific ones. Center-based interactions could remain compartmental for long time periods, resulting in increasingly deep and truly intimate relations, even if the parties remained unfamiliar with entire categories of each other's lives.[12]

Conversation, Activity, and Interaction

The nature of mothers' compartmentally intimate relations may be understood through conversation, which was frequent, personal, and always child-related. Tina, a gentle-spirited African-American in her late thirties, wore her long kinky hair in thick pony tails and preferred tie-dyes and denim skirts in the summer. Self-employed, she provided personal assistance services for professionals. Tina had enrolled her son in the highly recommended Tweed Center after his difficult experiences in the public school system. In the public schools, she explained, "he came home every day full of aggression." She and her husband had been highly involved in the school, and by the time of her interview, she knew most of the parents in the center. Still, her closest friends in the center were made when her child was younger, thanks in part to her membership in the parents association. Her interviewer asked if she would "consider any of [these] parents to be [her] good friend." "Yeah," she explained. "Quite a few, quite a few, I'd say at least a dozen, at least a dozen including ones that aren't there anymore but I still keep in contact with them." Like Katherine, the New England-born small business consultant, Tina had made strong ties in the center that had lasted well past her son's graduation, and she met with at least two of them, still, outside the center. Nevertheless, when her interviewer asked explicitly their topics of conversation, she explained that their conversation was limited to the domain of children and family: "The school [*laughter*]. Mainly the school. . . . And we meet and we [*unintelligible*] socially and talk about family issues and the kids growing up and the preadolescent thing, those kinds of things."

Blanche was even more direct about the nature of her conversations with her center friends. Blanche was an East African immigrant in her late twenties with dark brown skin, thin long braids, and a round, welcoming face. A full-time student in a nursing program, Blanche enrolled her daughter at the Sunflower Center, an almost all-black center in a predominantly poor neighborhood in the city. "The only thing we have in common is the children," she explained, "so we used to talk about the children, children, children. Some time we ask about [other things] but most of the time it's about the children."[13]

By contrast, recall Katherine, who explained that "it used to always be the kids and now it's sort of everything from relationships, marriages, travel, and of course the kids too." Or Linda, who explained that she spent adult time with her new relation: "One of the mothers and I will go to a movie or meet for dinner or something like that." Or Nancy, who explained that she and her friend made at the center cover an array of topics: "men . . . the children and things to do with them . . . politics . . . the arts . . . [and] books we read." Whereas these relations were unconstrained in conversation, those of Blanche, Tina, and Denise remained domain specific, they were compartmental.

The idea that conversation among intimates may be compartmental is supported by a recent study by Peter Bearman and Paolo Parigi.[14] The authors assessed the question in the General Social Survey in which people were asked with whom they discussed matters important to them. This question had originally been asked in order to identify respondents' intimate ties. However, when the authors examined what people actually talked about, they found a great deal of what they called "topic-alter dependency": whom people talked to about important matters depended on the topic: "One-third of the conversations about life and health are between spouses, conversations with relatives are more likely to be about relationships than anything else, and so on."[15] Similarly, in relations between compartmental intimates, topics depend almost completely on the alter.

Among compartmental intimates, not merely the *conversation* but also the *activities* between friends were primarily child related. Brittany, a slim white doctor in her late thirties who wore rectangular black glasses and betrayed a peaceful and professional disposition, enrolled her daughter and son in the Rainbow Center. Her close friends in the center were, indeed, close—at least she was beginning to think of them that way—but this closeness was always child specific, or, in her words "kid oriented." Her interviewer asked whether she would consider any of the parents she had met a "close friend":

> BRITTANY: . . . there are several, yeah, that we see several weekends a
>   month . . . three couples . . . three families.
> INTERVIEWER: So what is your definition of a "close friend" . . . ?

BRITTANY: Well I mean, maybe it isn't like a close, well . . . one of them is becoming a close friend. Well these are people that we do—I mean it's all kind of kid oriented now, that we . . . speak on the phone, or email, actually make a plan, have a meal, go play together like you know go to the park together that kind of thing. . . . A lot of shared parenting. My husband picked up the term from another guy, "married to a doctor of zone defense." Which means nothing to me cause I don't play football but I guess it's like two dads on a bunch of kids. So there's a lot of that that goes on. You know, like, "Oh my God I have the kids all day for 24 hours. . . . Can I bring my kids over? Can we order dinner?" That kind of thing.

The relationships Brittany formed helped to release stress, to find some reprieve from balancing children, her husband, and the clinic. It is also not difficult to imagine that, in response to a telephone survey, Brittany might have responded that, yes, she had made close friends in the center, even if, in the context of a longer interview she would have found reason to qualify her statements. The families did come over, and they did share meals—yet the relationship, at least at this juncture, depended on the children. *Without* their presence—"it's all kind of kid oriented"—the parents might not spend much time together. The relations were by no means superficial; they were, instead, rather limited to the process of collective child rearing.

We have been discussing the experiences of women in this book because most of our interviewees were women, given the gender distributions of childcare centers. But the men we interviewed did not differ much on this particular issue. Xavier was a black man in his late forties with short-cropped hair, fine lines around his eyes, and a serious demeanor that nonetheless easily broke into a smile. A bus driver, he almost always wore his uniform. When his interviewer asked how many parents he knew at Tweed, where his daughter was enrolled, he explained: "Quite a few. Wow . . . maybe about 20." Many of these he had met at the parents association meetings. His interviewer followed up the question: "Do you consider any of them to be your close friend?" Xavier counted aloud while considering the question: "One, two . . . three." And how would he define a close friend? "A close friend is somebody that you talk to at pretty much anytime. And a close friend is someone who will give you his or her honest opinion opposed to just saying something to pacify you. That's my definition . . . also somebody who has the same Godly beliefs as you do, that's very important."

Just about all interactions with the three close friends, however, had been limited to the center. When he was asked if he had seen them much elsewhere, he explained, "I haven't so far . . . well one of them, one of them yeah. I just started to. . . . But not too much of them on the outside." There had been some exceptions, but all of these were child-related: "They come to my kid's party, I'll take my kids to their kid's parties, and we've been out a few times to . . . Play Land [in Upstate New York]."

Compartmental Intimates and the Phrase "Close Friends"

Compartmental intimates, even the closest among them, are above all *center* friends. Yet while some compartmental intimates identified their relations as "close friendships," others explicitly did not, which is a reminder that respondents' words should not determine our perception of their underlying practices. Consider Jasmine, a researcher in her early thirties whose freckled cheeks and tucked hair removed years from her appearance. Her 2-year-old daughter was enrolled in the Rainbow Center. Jasmine explicitly told her interviewer she did not have relations in the center she would consider "close friends":

> Not really. There're people there who I would like to go to that kind of relationship, that I haven't done anything outside of the day care center with any parents or any families. . . . I've never called anyone in sort of a social situation. Never confided anything, like, extremely personal. There are definitely a few parents there I feel closer to than others just because our kids are in the same class and we'll talk about certain things and situations. But we've, I've never had an interaction outside the work or day care setting. And that's what I would consider a closer friend.

To this point, Jasmine has explained that she had not developed *standard* intimate ties. Nevertheless, the relationships that Jasmine did develop were far from mere "hi and bye" acquaintances. Since Jasmine insisted she had never confided anything "extremely personal," her interviewer asked what she had confided in or talked about:

> Our kids. We talk about, you know, sometimes the struggles of balancing work and having a child. I mean if there is anything particular happening at the day care center that week, the strategies for general child care. I talk about potty training at this age, what did you do, when there are certain kids ahead of my daughter, getting advice about that. Some logistical stuff like about how to label the bottles on your child's cup. So, a lot of practical things about, what did you do with your children. Sometimes I talk about personal things about moving out of the city and moving to the suburbs, some of them have done that, the adjustment for them. Definitely about what to do when your child gets sick cause that's always an issue.

The confines of the center, and the expected homophily with other center mothers (more on this below) provided a focus whereby certain topics were implied to be acceptable and even encouraged for conversation, such as the balance of work and family. For Jasmine, discussing personal topics *within* the appropriate domain—"personal things about moving out of the city and moving to the suburbs"—were par for the course, and advice defined by the domain was widely given and received. The relationship, which Jasmine defined as "not really" close, still provided a key source of everyday support, much informational support, and some emotional support.[16] Regardless of what Jasmine called the relationship, it provided all of these elements of strong ties, even if only within the domain of children and the family.[17]

NONINTIMATES

Naturally, many relationships lacked any form of intimacy. Ernest, a black male in his thirties with a bald head and a thin beard around his chin, had developed few friendships in the center he would comfortably consider close. When asked on the nature of most of his relationships, he responded, "'Hi and bye,' you know. Speaking to them but not by name but just speaking to them in general: 'how you doing today' and things like that." Or in the words of Winona, a middle-age black stylist who was asked the same question: "Not personally, just in the passing." "How many would you say you know?" "A few of [my son's] classmates' parents, maybe three that I say hello to." "Do you associate with them any other time or do you just say hi?" "Hi and good bye."

Many parents developed what some low-income black and Latina mothers referred to as "associates," something perhaps a notch above the "hi-and-bye" relationship.[18] Irina was a sharp, pugnacious, second-generation Latina in her late twenties who pulled her straight black hair under a baseball cap. As I learned from another mother who grew up with her, Irina was known in high school as a bully, and her own son, at Alegre Daycare, had begun to follow in her mother's footsteps. After I heard her use the term "associate," I asked Irina to explain the difference between an associate and a hi-and-bye relation: "'Hi and bye?' Oh, [in that case] I wouldn't even waste my time with you. It's just, 'Hi, how you doing? Hey, hey, bye.' But the associate I'd be more small talk with you a little bit. . . . And be like, 'How's the family? Good? Oh, sorry, oh, you know, got to go.'" With some humor, Gloria, a black mother who herself works as a teacher in a childcare center, explained the difference between an associate and a friend in terms of the time allowances granted true friends:

> INTERVIEWER: So do you consider [the parent we have been talking about] a
>   friend?
> GLORIA: No, not really. Just an associate. 'Cause the friends I have, I had them
>   over 20 something, 30 years.
> INTERVIEWER: . . . well my next question was going to be what to you makes
>   the difference between a friend and an associate?

GLORIA: An associate knows when to go away and a friend just hangs around [*laughter*]. So you know what time of day it is and a friend just stays around.

An associate was in many ways an acquaintance that required some, but not much, time and emotional involvement.

Table 4.2 outlines the three types of relationships and the differences among them. As we have seen, some relationships, which I have referred to as standard intimates, transcended the domain of the family and the center in talk, activity, and interaction. For this reason, they provided support in all realms, from the family to spirituality, with few constraints. Other relationships were strong as well, but the intimacy was limited to conversations about children and the family, the activity to play dates and collective babysitting, and interaction to those settings appropriate to child-centered activities. These relationships, however, also provided important information, such as how to deal with children's diseases. Other relationships were not intimate in any sense, being relegated to polite greetings and

Table 4.2. Characteristics of social ties among mothers in childcare centers

	Standard intimates	Compartmental intimates	Non-intimates
Type of tie	Strong, domain-transcendent	Strong, domain-specific	Weak
Conversation	Topics transcend domain (children, family, politics, books)	Topics domain-specific (children, family)	Topics domain-specific (children)
	Intimate quality (problems with children, men, career, spirituality)	Intimate quality (problems with children)	Superficial quality (greetings)
Activity	Planned activities	Planned activities	No planned activities
	Activities transcend domain (play dates, baby-sitting, dinner, movies)	Activities domain-specific (play dates, baby-sitting)	—
Interaction	Beyond center (parks, playgrounds restaurants, theaters)	Beyond center, within domain (parks, playgrounds)	Within center

superficial conversation; they involved no revelation of privacy, not even within narrowly defined domains. (There were circumstances, however, when nonintimate relations were characterized by trust and support, as described in chapter 5.) I reiterate that these categories are ideal types, categories that rarely manifest themselves perfectly in practice.

ARE COMPARTMENTAL INTIMATES USEFUL?

The discussion above has described the value of standard intimates. They help mothers deal with children, marriage, spirituality, career, and the work-life balance; they afford the general fulfillment derived from either sustaining close bonds or belonging to a small community. To understand the value of compartmental intimates, we must consider them in the context of the significant constraints on mothers' time.[19]

Center mothers were nothing if not busy, regardless of their class background. Low-income mothers, such as Griselda, experienced severe time constraints when they were employed. When Griselda dropped off the children at the center, she explained, "I would have to run out because I would be late for work. So I didn't even have time." And her manager's flexibility had its limits. Middle- and upper middle-class mothers, such as Lorraine, the white doctor in her thirties we saw in chapter 3, experienced a different version of the same process. Fully engaged in her career at the time of her son's birth, she found herself confronting the decision, faced by many women, whether to temporarily leave work to raise her son.[20] She decided not to, at a cost: "I feel like I've struggled enough with it because the last three years are probably going to be the hardest years of our lives I will have to have gone through in terms of neglecting my family."

To a parent constantly negotiating work, family, and children, part of the advantage of a compartmental intimate is having ready access to practical resources within one of life's domains. Probably the most valuable of such resources was service. Consider Serena's description her relationship with another mother, Daniella:

> [There's a] woman, a single mom. Her daughter is in my class. I met her daughter, the most beautiful kid, and the most mischievous, the worst-behaved kid in the class, but if she wasn't there it would be my daughter so that's fine. . . . When Daniella needs backup, she needs to go to something at night, I take her daughter [to my] home. I feed her dinner. We play. I give her a bath. Daniella comes and picks her up later. She would do the same for me. . . .
>   When I teach a night class or a seminar, she will come. I pick up the girls [at the center] and bring them to my house. I have to leave at six. She arrives at

six, at my house, . . . and then she does homework with them. They eat dinner
and [then] my husband comes home [from work].

Daniella and Serena were by no means best friends or even confidants in the
broad sense of the term, though they could eventually become close in that
way. Theirs was a kind of weak strong tie, one in which the practical
demands of their daily life imposed constraints while the similarity of
their needs allowed for depth. Their relationship was instrumental, to be
sure, but also strong and even affective, since the intimacy of bathing each
other's children was an unselfconscious part of their commitment. Most
important, it yielded a practical advantage.

The particular way Serena and Daniella were useful to each other was
not unique, nor was it specific to them as black women living in low-income
neighborhoods.[21] Consider Naomi, a petite, married, white mother with jet-
black hair who worked as a middle-manager at a cosmetics company and
whose only daughter was enrolled at Little Friends Day Care. An extrovert-
ed, loquacious, and hyperorganized workaholic, Naomi developed one relationship that, while compartmental, was especially close. She sought another
mother, Tessie, much as Serena did, explicitly to exchange babysitting
duty and save some money on sitters:

> I have an informal arrangement with one of the other mommies [Tessie] for
> swapping child care duties so everyone gets a Saturday night date once in
> a while. So she'll take my daughter with her little boy for a few hours on
> Saturday and then I'll take her kid and, at night so the kids get an all-day play
> date. And each set of parents gets some [*unintelligible*] without having to pay a
> sitter. You have to work for it: it's not exactly like you pay the sitter and you
> don't owe anybody anything and you don't have the challenge of chasing
> two kids around. But it's a pretty sweet arrangement and that was informal
> networking.

It is not difficult to see that having a friend like Tessie might help Naomi
deal with everyday support, that it constituted an important component
of the household's support network.

Naomi's relationship also reveals the difference between how standard
and compartmental intimates are useful. Naomi's "informal arrangement"
with Tessie was helpful to her in ways different from, say, Katherine's
relationship with Amy, whom, as described above, Katherine considered
"family." Tessie made Naomi's life simpler, more efficient, in some ways
cheaper, and easier to handle; she did not, as Amy did for Katherine, fulfill
Naomi's deeper sense of community. Naomi's commitments were delimited
and more limited. Katherine had found a confidant; Naomi, only a partner,
yet an especially useful partner to the parent of a young child. Katherine
made a standard intimate; Naomi, a compartmental one.[22]

The child-related resources mothers acquired from compartmental ties were not limited to services. Information and even material goods—all within domain—were routinely exchanged. Naomi explains her use of such relations (in this case, compartmental though not quite close):

> [I] used informal networking to learn a lot about childhood diseases, talk about things the kids come home with and what are the symptoms. I have scored some awesome hand-me-downs from other parents because for a long time my baby was the littlest so she got the choicest cast offs. She got, I mean she got jumpy toy things and snowsuits and some good stuff.

Naomi, it is clear, is a "networker," a purposive mobilizer of her connections.

The fact that compartmental and standard intimates were useful in different ways should not encourage us to forget that ties are fluid, that an instrumental tie may later become affective, and that the boundaries delimiting a relationship may wither with time. Naomi, speaking about Tessie, illustrates: "We, they recently proposed that we hire a sitter one night for both kids and that we go out all four of us. That was nice." Her interviewer asked if this had already occurred:

> Uh . . . we haven't done it yet, they just suggested it a couple of days ago. And in fact this morning [Tessie] and I got into talking about where you like to shop and we both like Loehmann's. And I was thinking, "Oh, I could invite her to go shopping and we could bring the kids. And maybe we could both handle trying on clothes if one of us is up on kid duty while the other one's trying on." So, that's occurred to me too. They'll definitely come over when the football season kicks off because we have a very, very large TV. And in fact we were talking about what we'd done for Father's Day and she just mentioned that her husband, all he wanted for Father's Day was KFC and the park. I was like, "Oh my husband's really into KFC too." Although now, OK we have a plan for when the Bears play the Vikings there will be KFC and the big TV. So, yeah, the plans are sort of, they're loosely but they're coming together.

It would be little surprise if, a year hence, Naomi and Tessie's relationship relaxed the domain-specific boundaries that had so far defined it.

WHY MOTHERS FORMED INTIMATE TIES

Homophily

What accounts for the prevalence of intimate ties? An important factor is "homophily." Coined by Robert Merton, the term refers to the tendency of people to associate with others who resemble them.[23] Thus, we saw, for example, that Tessie and Naomi resembled each other in several ways: they both were white, professionally employed, comfortably middle class, and mothers of young children enrolled in childcare centers; they both shopped Loehmann's, a store selling discounted designer fashion; they both were married to fast-food-loving sports fans. Homophily helps account for the prevalence of both standard and compartmentally intimate ties, since similar people tend to form stronger bonds.

Nevertheless, the prevalence of homophily was not accidental; on the contrary, in many respects it was organizationally induced. The fact that Tessie and Naomi—two people so similar—patronized the same center did not occur by chance. On the contrary, two people who decided to bear children in their late, rather than early, twenties in order to settle their professional life first, who therefore enjoyed the income to live in an upper middle-class New York City neighborhood, and who sought the amenities, lifestyle, and racial composition of this particular neighborhood, were likely to find themselves in the same childcare center, or in another center in the same neighborhood with the same price structure and to meet a group of parents who would also seem a lot like them.

By virtue of their operations, centers tend to attract similar strangers under a single roof. First, centers secure their members through income requirements. These may be, in fact, formal requirements, such as the upper limit set by Head Start centers, or the sliding scales set by New York City's Administration for Children's Services centers; or they may be institutional barriers that occur naturally as a result of prices. Whether by requiring that parents earn less than $28,000 a year or by charging $1,200 a month, centers establish, purposely or not, a rather economically homogeneous population. Second, centers serve the residents surrounding them, since most patrons prefer centers within their own neighborhoods. For example, a survey of Maryland parents revealed that 80% preferred a center in their neighborhood.[24] Thus, in the Childcare Centers survey of New York City centers, 78% reported that either "all or almost all" of their clients lived in the neighborhood. People in the same neighborhoods tend to share not merely incomes but also racial and demographic backgrounds, lifestyles preferences, and geographic predilections, such as proximity to a bus line. Third, centers tend to attract parents with similar extraneous tastes. Strongly atheist parents are unlikely to patronize a center that, like Tweed, advertised a Biblical passage on the proper way to train a child beneath a 15-foot cross at the front entrance. Parents highly uncomfortable with germs, dirt, or mold are unlikely to find comfort in basement centers with exposed pipes and prewar heating systems. Instead, within the constraints imposed by practicality, parents gravitate to the centers that meet their needs, placing them in the presence of others with similar predilections. In fact, in many organizations, actors will encounter homophilous actors—that is, actors who, with respect to the functions of the organization, resemble them more than actors elsewhere. In this particular sense, homophily, and the ensuing forms of intimate relations, must be seen as organizational products.

Homophily helps explain not merely why ties were so often intimate, but also why they proved so useful, since people who share traits often share problems and, as a result, solutions for one another's problems. Consider Brittany, the slim white doctor described earlier in this chapter. Among the three couples with whom Brittany and her husband had formed compartmentally close relationships, she felt comfortable calling only one couple "good friends," a couple who happened to live in the same building. The importance of homophily was made clear:

> [At] this point it's probably like this couple with their two girls who ended up becoming really good friends. One it was that our kids, you know, it's all . . . meeting through the kids now. And [the couple] lived 11 to 12 stories underneath us, [which] became convenient. And then, you know, it's two mothers who are doctors kind of dealing with the same things, two dads who are doctors dealing with two mothers who are doctors. They have it a lot rougher than we do. And just being in the same stage, we're pretty much in the exact same place that they are. You know financially, emotionally, spacewise, how we're crammed into our space. I mean all the issues are the same. "Where the hell are we going to send our kids to kindergarten?" "Are we going to go through this whole insane New York thing?" "Where are we going to live?" "Why are we here?" There's no benefit, essentially. You know the perceived benefits of living in New York are not a [unintelligible]. . . . So, it's the same discussion all the time.

For mothers to explain the strengths of their center-based relations in light of their homophily was not uncommon. In fact, mothers were often surprised by how much they resembled other mothers. But this similarity—of race, age, language, life stage, income, and education—shaped how comfortable they felt sharing vulnerabilities. Katherine, the New England-born small business consultant, was experiencing the anxieties about aging, success, and family that befall many people about to turn 40. She explained:

> Almost 40, September I'll be 40. It's funny to meet—a lot of the parents are the same age. You know, I feel a little bit like an older mother and it's funny how we all went through the same kind of waiting and doing our own thing with our careers before we had children.
>
> And [I have met] a lot of people who've had the same [experiences]. [For example], my husband and I have been married for 12 years and a lot of people [in the center are] celebrating their same like 11th, 12th anniversary too. It's really weird. So, I don't know if it's just a coincidence or if that's an indication of living in New York and working in a career then doing daycare. I don't know, somehow we all ended up in the same—whatever. That's a separate study. [*Interviewer asks if this makes it easier to talk to other parents.*] I think it helps, I think you definitely feel like you're older than . . . some mothers, and you just

feel "I'm so old compared to her." But I don't meet that many that are that much younger than I am, honestly. We're all really about the same age and, yeah, that does [help], you know, all going through the same time, we're just about to hit a pretty big milestone.

Apparently unique anxieties are often common to people in the same organizational settings. This similarity creates the space where sharing particular vulnerabilities is safe and social support is made easier.

Duration

While homophily contributed to the prevalence of strong ties in centers, so did time. Few would dispute the notion that time is necessary to strengthen relationships. Granovetter probably expressed common knowledge when he defined the passage of time as the first indicator of a strong tie.[25] In fact, mothers who reported intimate ties often spoke of the time required to develop them.

However, the experiences of mothers suggested that time mattered in different ways for different kinds of relationships. Developing compartmental intimates required *frequency* (that parents encountered each other often), while forming standard intimates required both *frequency* and *duration* (that their encounters were long lasting). Naturally, mothers' agency and temperament ultimately decided the connections they developed, including how often and for how long they spent time with others. However, organizational practices played a central role. While practices such as constrained pickup and drop-off times and monthly meetings with teachers facilitated frequent interactions, only practices such as parents associations with active agendas and repeated out-of-state field trips encouraged interaction that was both frequent and long-lasting.

Jasmine's account of her failure to form (standard) intimate ties illustrates why frequent interactions alone are insufficient. Jasmine had enjoyed many of the activities her center organized, which included short holiday celebrations, picnics, and even bake sales. However, few parents attended: "A lot of time I've gone and been the only parent or there'll be one other parent." She had few opportunities to engage other parents for extended periods. In addition, while her center organized the extended field trips that both required parental participation and allowed for long-lasting interaction, her own child was too young for Jasmine to participate. "Yeah, they don't really have field trips at this age. I guess the biggest trip that they have is over to the hospital garden, which is like five blocks away. But they, at this age, they don't go on buses or those kind of field trips." Similarly, the center had a parents association, but it met infrequently and at inconvenient times.

It is especially notable that Jasmine *wished* to form strong bonds. The structural conditions of the center, however, undermined her interests in purposive networking. For example, when asked what she would improve about the center, she explained the problem with the parents association meetings:

> JASMINE: [The] meetings are usually like 5:00 on Friday which I just think is extremely inconvenient. I mean most people by the end of the week you want to go home, but that's one minor thing. Change it to a different day, [and] maybe think about making it once a month during the week, you know, at lunch time. I don't know how flexible that would be but also publicizing that more. I don't think that there's a big emphasis on like getting the parents together. . . .
>
> I don't even know when [the meetings] are: once every month, once every two months, once every six months. But the few times when I saw like a small sign, "Parents Association," it was a Friday when we were going away for the weekend. That it would be great to have like a master email and to have the Parents Association email us all that this is when we want to have it and see if it's convenient.
>
> INTERVIEWER: Well so what would be different be then, what would the benefits of that be?
>
> JASMINE: . . . I think I would like to have strong relationships with other parents. I think we could all benefit from that.

Comments from other parents reinforce her observations. David, who was an officer at this same center's parents association, had also reported making compartmentally close, but not "best friend" close, relations. Reinforcing Jasmine's statements (in a separate interview), he described a PTO not oriented toward extended social interaction. "I looked at some other places and other day cares and sometimes the Parents Association is like kind of a social thing like they try to organize social activities; we don't try to do that at all. We don't really."

Other strongly social mothers, such as Naomi, found it difficult to break through the boundaries of domain-specific friendships because of the absence of opportunities for long-lasting interaction. "I'm not able to because of my work schedule. I mean the [center] is 8:00 to 6:00 every day. My business hours are 8:30 to 5:30 so that gives me just barely enough time to [get to the center]." And later: "I haven't gone to any of the parents meetings; I haven't gone to any of their little parties. . . . I wish I could go." It might seem surprising that she even found the time to develop the compartmentally strong relationship with Tessie discussed above. However, when she explains how, it becomes clear that even if her interactions lacked *duration*, they did not lack *frequency*, because of the similarity of her and Tessie's schedules: "We're on similar schedules with our kids so I'd walked in and out with her a couple of times and then we bumped into them once on the weekend sort of outside of school.... And when I felt like I knew her well enough I suggested, 'Hey, do you want to try a baby swap?' and they were open to it."

WHY MOTHERS FORMED TIES COMPARTMENTAL YET INTIMATE

Standard network models predict that people will form ties either domain specific or intimate, but not both. The reason is simple: strong ties, for all their benefits, demand work. As Pierre Bourdieu argued, maintaining the ties that generate social capital "presupposes an unceasing effort of sociability, a continuous series of exchanges in which recognition is endlessly affirmed and reaffirmed. This work... implies expenditure of time and energy."[26] Close friends, like close lovers, require maintenance to be long-lasting, which theorists have thought of as a "cost" of social capital. If two people make no effort to interact—a natural tendency for people, like new mothers, with limited leisure time—the relationship will likely weaken. In this respect, Bourdieu would argue, maintaining a friendship remains a purposive endeavor.

But for enrolled mothers, the center itself either guaranteed or encouraged repeated encounters, not merely through the many tasks that required their participation but also through mundane rules such as required times for drop-off. This helps explain why relations could be compartmental yet strong: organizations can institutionally perform much of the maintenance work. A "center friend" resembles a "sports friend" in that both relations are compartmental, defined around a focus. But a busy person who fails to call a sports friend will weaken the relation; a busy mother who fails to call a center friend today will still see her tomorrow, and the next day, and the following day, at the center, because that is how centers organize participation by their members.

The contrast between two of Naomi's ties is instructive. The compartmentally strong relationship between Naomi and Tessie was sustained *by* the center, rather than merely in it. The center unintentionally helped ensure that the mothers would continue to run into each other, since their children shared a classroom. Without the center's de facto guarantee that they interact (aided, of course, by their own similar schedules), the relationship was likely to wither. By contrast, consider another relationship that Naomi had hoped to cultivate: "There's another mommy that I'm very friendly with who I've seen outside of day care, too." The relationship had potential, but it did not flourish. Why? "[H]er little boy graduated to the toddler room so we've grown apart a little bit." A structural change in the opportunities for interaction cut short that budding friendship—while the tie to Tessie blossomed.

Centers create a focus in the purest sense, a separate point of attention that orients the actions of the parties. And therein lies the advantage and disadvantage of this type of relation: a place to interact and institutionally set times for the parties to do so sustains the relationship without requiring much effort from the parties to maintain it. Thanks to the organization, the relationship both deepens week by week and remains within its bounds; without it, the relationship will likely wither.

STRONG TIES IN ORGANIZATIONAL CONTEXTS

Almost every mother we interviewed cited time as the biggest constraint on her activities, on the possibility of making relations that provide social, emotional, or instrumental support. In these circumstances, it is not surprising that the types of attachments mothers developed were so often compartmental and selective, limited by what they could offer and the time they could devote to sustaining a new tie. That the parties faced similar circumstances helped strengthen the relations. That the centers instituted policies guaranteeing their encounters helped maintain them. Like standard intimates, compartmental intimates became a source of social support, and one would expect parents who made either type of friendship to experience less hardship and depression than one who made none at all. But the compartmental intimate offered a kind of support especially useful to a mother of young children, a relationship understood by both parties to be limited in scope and, therefore, expectations. The organizations, whether purposely or not, mediated the operation of these intimate relations.

5

Trust and Obligations

Why Some Mothers' Support Networks Were Larger Than Their Friendship Networks

Social support neither begins nor ends with friendship. A shoulder to cry on after the death of a loved one can be, instead of a friend's, a priest's. A listener's ear can be a therapist's; an offer to help, a lawyer's.

Consider two facets of these three relations. The priest, the therapist, and the lawyer assist their patrons because formal obligations, whether written or implicit, compel them to do so. Even if the lawyer and the therapist are more likely than the priest to expect financial remuneration, the three of them are driven by the obligations of fulfilling a professional mandate. The support of these professionals depends, ultimately, on their mandate. It also depends, in spite of its formality, on trust. The relationship assumes a patron willing to confess personal intimacies—an adulterous affair, a suicidal thought, an undisclosed theft—that she might not even share with her closest friends. The receiver must trust; the provider must feel obligated. In the absence of trust or obligations, the support that clients derive from these relationships would vanish.

These elements of professional support, as we shall see, bear relevance to relations among mothers. Chapter 4 examined support among friends; the present chapter probes support among acquaintances or nonintimates, among people so weakly tied that they would have no reason to expect social support. The chapter asks how an acquaintance becomes a source of support.

On its face, the question seems to violate the elegant rule of thumb by which the strength of a tie determines the goods to be gained from it—that is, strong ties, such as friendships, provide social support, while weak ties, which are acquaintanceships, yield references and information.[1] An acquaintance is not generally expected to provide social support, and professional relations are the exceptions that "prove" the rule. Such principles, however, often prove more useful to the theorist preparing a formal model than to the observer struggling to understand what happened on the ground. The student curious about whom a mother turned to when asking for a favor, or why she felt compelled to help another parent, may learn less by adopting a formal rule of thumb than by asking the mother, free from preconceptions, to explain whom she turned to and why. Adopting this perspective, we explore two of the mechanisms by which centers can engender social support among acquaintances, among mothers who hardly know one another.

The present chapter does not provide a novel theory of either social support or its etiology. Instead, it suggests that centers can condition relations among weakly tied mothers—among complete nonintimates—in ways conducive to social support. It finds that centers, either intentionally or unintentionally, (a) facilitated *trust* among parents and (b) established *obligations* that mothers felt compelled to follow, thereby creating a network of support—of certain kinds of support—even among otherwise weakly connected actors. The chapter discusses the willingness of mothers to trust others they did not know well, in ways contrary to rational expectations, and the mothers' willingness to make themselves available to others when requested to do so by the center. These circumstances mattered for only some mothers. While they had little consequence for the many mothers who had developed strong friendships in centers, they dramatically affected those who were truly socially isolated.[2]

SOCIAL SUPPORT AND TRUST

One of the most important preconditions of social support is trust. People rarely support others they distrust, and, just as critically, few are willing to *accept* support from a provider deemed untrustworthy. A mother must be willing to trust the intentions, the competence, and the expectations of another to take advantage of an offer to help. What determines a mother's willingness to trust another?[3]

Coleman's Model

Perhaps the most elegant answer in social capital theory was produced by James Coleman. Coleman would argue that the critical prerequisite of trust is *information*, because without it people cannot assess risk. In one of his simple yet perceptive models, Coleman proposed that an actor would trust another when the ratio of the probability of being right about trustworthiness over the probability of being wrong was greater than the ratio of the losses from being wrong over the gains of being right. That is, people will trust others when they have sufficient information to determine that the risk of being disappointed is low.[4]

Coleman illustrated his point by explaining why a banker did something that seemed risky: lending a very large sum to a ship owner. The banker explained:

> Actually, the risk isn't as terrible as it seems to you. I know the company, I know the ship, I even know the cargo. It's my job to know all these things. Admittedly, one has to be careful. Other banks have burned their fingers in this business. One has to keep a lot of useful information in one's head.
>
> A merchant banker lives on his information and I try to get all the available information in my territory.[5]

The banker's information made trusting the ship owner a rational thing to do.

The key, from Coleman's perspective, is the actor's certainty about being right, and this certainty requires information. And perhaps most important, as the costs of making the wrong decision increase, the importance of having sufficient information rises.[6]

Did the Mothers Follow Coleman's Model?

But the attitudes of mothers in centers seemed to belie the expectation that actors require abundant information about a potential trustee if the risk of being wrong is high. Consider a hypothetical question. Would a rational mother trust her child with a person whose name, address, and occupation she did not know? Coleman (and most of us) would probably respond that she would not, since not knowing such basic information is a good proxy for not knowing enough to assess trustworthiness, an especially damaging condition considering the potential costs. It is, after all, her child.[7] Nevertheless, our interviews revealed that mothers' willingness to trust other mothers with their children rarely required much information about the potential trustee. More than once I interviewed mothers who told me they would have no problem trusting another mother—the parents association vice president, their son's friend's mother—only to confess later in the interview that they did not know this person's name, or where she lived, or what she did for a living. It was as if the center had preapproved the others, confirmed by proxy their trustworthiness.[8]

Consider the attitudes of Griselda. As described in chapter 3, she had met other parents in the center, which had given her the opportunities for "adult conversations" she had craved since losing her job months earlier. By contrast, she explained, at "home ... it's *Dora* all day or *Blues Clues*, or everything baby, baby, baby, baby. And I have no one to talk to." These parents, whom she encountered during holiday events and their preparations, were a relief to an otherwise isolated mother. Despite this, Griselda had not become close enough with any parent to consider her or him a good friend. Two of them might eventually become friends: one was a former coworker; another had begun to be a partner in conversation. She explained to me: "I would say there's one [parent] who [is] pretty good, not bad. Not outta here [in terms of our relationship] but when she comes we... talk a little. Or when I see her out on the street: 'Hi. How are you, how's [your son]?'"

I asked Griselda whether, if she had an emergency and needed someone to watch her children, she would trust this mother to do so: "Trusting her?...I mean I would [first] ask my ex-coworker. But if [my coworker] wasn't [available], I think I would." I assumed this mother might be what I was then beginning to think of as a compartmental intimate of Griselda's. As we concluded our interview, I asked for references for other mothers I could speak to; she agreed. I suggested the mother she was willing trust with her child; she thought it was a good idea. I asked for the mother's name, and Griselda's response surprised me: "I don't know her name. Maybe the teacher can get you her name. I know she has light green eyes and her daughter's name is Erin or [unintelligible]." Clearly, neither friendship nor much formal information seemed preconditions of trust for Griselda.

Ula, a Puerto Rican who had migrated to New York City as a toddler and whose son attended Bright Colors, saw things similarly. Ula was married, in her thirties, and always pressed for time, commuting more than an hour each way and running errands perpetually in the green scrubs of a physical therapist in training. Her primary worries when finding childcare were safety and convenience. She found the center "through work.... [T]he only thing that I felt safe with was the childcare center here," which had been recommended by other parents whose children had attended it. In addition, the center was easy to access given her commute. "Oh, we commute on the train about an hour, fifteen minutes.... But the only reason [my son] goes here is because it's right close to" work. From work it was a four-minute walk, in fact, she had timed it. "And I went to visit... and I just felt good about being able to go and visit whenever I felt like it."

By her own admission a finicky yet shy parent, Ula had opened up out of necessity after the birth of her son and daughter, becoming acquainted with some of the parents, but not actually making any friends. While once she had asked another parent, a doctor, for advice on dealing with her son's rash, this had happened almost by chance, when she ran into the parent and her husband. "I wasn't planning on approaching them. We were just sort of there and we started talking and [I said] my son is experiencing this and that." Her interviewer asked why she would not just approach them. "For one, we're... we see each other casually. It's not like we have a strong core or we're friends outside of the daycare." In fact, she explained, "I've only really had a chance to know one of the parents. . . . And . . . it's just [a] hi/bye [relationship]."

For this reason, it was not surprising that, when asked whom she would trust to care for her son in a short-term emergency, Ula explained that she would first turn to her family. Since her mother still lived in Puerto Rico, "I would call . . . my brother or sister. . . . I'm very . . . I'm a little too, I think . . . too cautious," to trust her children with just anyone. In some respects, Ula would seem to be Coleman's classic rational actor, who required abundant information about the person being trusted, especially given the considerable costs of being wrong. As she explained, it has to be "somebody I could really trust." Nevertheless, when asked if she would "ever consider asking other parents at the center" Ula replied without hesitation: "Yes, yes." While not her first choice, what were technically strangers at the center were nevertheless trustworthy if she felt she needed to turn to them: "Yeah, I would definitely [turn to them as a] last resort."

Words and actions are different things, and though these mothers did not seem insincere—after all, parents of young children have an incentive, if any, to represent themselves as especially careful, rather than especially trusting, people—their statements do not guarantee that they will turn to others whom they do not know well when they are actually faced with an emergency. In these circumstances, they might, in spite of their statements, hesitate.

In this respect, the circumstances of Blanca and Helena are instructive. When I interviewed Blanca, a divorced mother of two who worked in the support staff of a local hospital, she had recently ended her year as officer of the parents association of Alegre Daycare. Petite, pale, and intense, Blanca tied her thick black hair with a scrunchy and wore practical T-shirts and jeans that made her seem ten years younger than her actual thirty-two. Born in Puerto Rico but raised in New York, she betrayed a nervous energy in conversation, repeatedly shaking her hands at the wrist and clasping them together for emphasis. Blanca had difficulty developing new friendships after her divorce (in Spanish):

> [It is] incredible that these days I almost don't have a *friend* friend, because when my ex-husband and I got together—he was my first boyfriend—we were in "high school" and then . . . I paid more attention to him, and I set everyone else aside, which was very bad.
> . . . Well, by the time we separated, well . . . things were different. Now [*unintelligible*] the children, my world [revolves around] them. . . . I don't really have time for myself, to have friends as much, just work.

Nevertheless, she had made many acquaintances in the center, because she sometimes told stories to the children when she went to the center to pick up her daughter. "So then the children [when they saw me] would tell their mothers, 'Hey look, that's Bella's mommy.'" She also met other mothers at the parents association.

Like other mothers, Blanca told me she would trust at least one of the mothers she had met, the vice-president, with her children, even though when she first felt comfortable doing this, she knew little to nothing about her. Blanca had not only reported this to me; she and the mother had previously agreed to do this for each other: "She used to say, 'If you can't or if I can't [take care of our children] if by any chance [the center] is closed, we'll see if one of us can take care of them.' We did all of this."

As if to confirm they did not know each other well at the time, Blanca had difficulty, less than 6 months later, recalling much information about this mother during our interview. "What's her name?" I had asked. "The vice president?" Blanca asked rhetorically, and she paused to think, flushing. After a few seconds, she opened her purse and began to sift quickly through its contents. "You know, I have her card here—wait, I feel bad about this."[9]

Helena (whose name Blanca eventually recalled, after finding a card in her purse) saw their relationship in similar terms. A Dominican-born mother of two, Helena (whom we revisit below) was, by her own account, not a trusting person: "How do I say this?" explained Helena, in a separate interview (also in Spanish). "I don't trust many people. I need time to develop trust in others. I am maybe a little timid with respect to this." Helena's conservatism when it came to trust was very reminiscent of Ula's. And yet not only was she willing to trust her children with Blanca, but she had, in fact, done so. One time soon after their agreement, when Helena was confronting an emergency at work and could not get to the center before closing, she left a message for Blanca to retrieve her young son from the center—which Blanca did, backing up by action a fleeting promise made in conversation. When it comes to trusting other mothers in centers, something more than information is probably at play.

It is worth noting that while more than a few mothers were willing to trust others they did not know well with their children, almost *all* mothers we interviewed were willing to take care of the child of another they scarcely knew. As Griselda explained, when asked if she would do the same for the hair dresser: "Oh, yeah. Definitely. If she was in a situation like that and she asked me. Or left a message [with the center] and said, you know, 'Ask Griselda to pick up the kids for me,' I would."

Not Only Strong Ties Are Trustworthy

The experiences of Griselda, Ula, and Blanca, and other parents tell us something small about Coleman and something larger about friendship and support. Whether one believes that these women's experiences disconfirm Coleman's theory partly depends on one's definition of the term "information." A strict reading would conclude that Coleman was wrong about these mothers, since the risk they would assume was certainly high and the information they knew, certainly limited. Coleman's banker may have known the company, the ship, and the cargo, but the center mothers sometimes did not even know the *name* of the potential trustee—and still, despite the risk, they were willing to trust. A generous reading of Coleman would argue that "information" is a general term, and mothers may have acquired implicit knowledge about the trustworthiness of others even if they did not know them as a friend would (more on this below).

Either way, these experiences make clear a larger fact: whether a mother turns to another for support is not merely a function of what is normally understood as the strength of the tie. Recall the rule of thumb that "strong ties" provide social support while "weak ties" provide information. My critique that two people with little information on each other may still trust each other in risky situations reflects the broader point that two people who are not strongly tied may still serve as reliable sources of support, because support is shaped by other factors as well.

One of the most important of these factors—and the most directly affected by center participation—is repeated interaction. The more two actors interact, even if they do not become friends or intimates, or acquire formal information about each other, the more they trust each other.[10] This hypothesis has been confirmed by a large body of empirical research in social psychology.[11] Researchers in the exchange theory tradition have probably done more than any in sociology to demonstrate this relationship, by focusing on interactions in which goods are exchanged and studying how people react to varying conditions in experimental settings. For example, Peter Kollock divided participants in his experiment into "sellers" and "buyers" and asked them to trade multiple times hypothetical goods of varying quality. To add uncertainty, buyers in the experimental condition could not verify first-hand the quality of the good until after the (binding) trade was made. At the end of the experiment, Kollock asked participants to evaluate the trustworthiness of their trading partners: participants ranked their most frequent partner as more trustworthy than their least frequent partner, regardless of the quality of goods bought and sold.[12] Probably hundreds of similar studies, with seemingly innumerable variations, have demonstrated a positive relationship between frequency of exchange and trust.[13] Frequent exchange builds trust in the way that jewelers who have traded gems for years do not need a receipt when dropping off a load for a bid, regardless of its value.[14]

The relevance of this point for the relationship among trust, availability of support, and strong ties among center mothers becomes clear when reconsidering the case of Ula. Figure 5.1 exhibits four of Ula's relations: her mother, her sister, a childcare center parent with whom she has a "hi and bye" relationship, and her interviewer for this book. For clarity, figure 5.1 represents the strength of the tie as the *closeness* Ula would express feeling toward the actor. The standard theory that strong rather than weak ties serve as sources of support operates mainly on the vertical axis. It suggests, for example, that Ula's mother was more likely to be a source of support than her interviewer for this book, because the tie to the mother was a stronger tie.

But the so-called weak ties, or acquaintanceships, also differ among themselves as a result of how frequently the parties come into contact. While Ula and her interviewer seldom interacted, she encountered the other center parent, to whom she did not talk about personal matters, almost every day. In so doing, Ula developed enough familiarity to break down the discomfort of asking a stranger for a favor. A strong defender of Coleman may refer to this as accumulating a type of information. The term "intuition" seems more appropriate (more on this below).[15] Either way, the important issue is that similarly weak (or nonclose) ties may be greater or lesser sources of support depending on the frequency with which the parties interact. And in routine organizational settings, it is not uncommon for actors who have not become friends to nonetheless encounter each other repeatedly.

The importance of repeated contact, and the fact that it may encourage social support independently of how strongly participants are tied, becomes

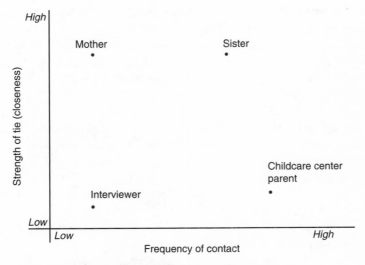

Figure 5.1. Two axes along which Ula's relations vary.

clear when we consider ties that are *strong* but *infrequently encountered*. Since Ula's mother still lived in Puerto Rico, the mother was less a source of support for this particular crisis than the childcare center parent, even though Ula felt much closer to her mother. That is, weak ties may be better sources of emergency support than strong ones depending on the circumstances of interaction.[16]

By extension, a study of social support that focuses on *strong connections* and ignores the *context of interaction* will miss much of what matters about how mothers, day to day, deal with crises.[17]

Trust in Centers

Childcare centers exhibit several characteristics generally understood to support trusting relations. They are noncompetitive contexts, removing the threats to trust that naturally arises from competition. They are nonhierarchical, such that mothers' willingness to trust one another is not complicated by differences in power. They are homophilous contexts, giving rise to the trustworthiness that arises from one's ability to identify with the concerns of others.[18] Yet centers are also spaces for interaction, buildings with halls, stairs, and lobbies where mothers certainly have an opportunity not only to make friends but also, when friends do not emerge, to see each other and each other's children repeatedly, becoming part of the daily marches from home to center to work to center to home that organize the habits of many working mothers. If mothers' explanations for their willingness to trust others pointed to one factor, it was to the consequences of repeated encounter.

Repeated encounter worked through at least two different processes, one largely informational (perhaps consistent with Coleman's model), and one largely not. For some mothers, repeated encounters were the source of fleeting clues about behavior that informed (in the strict sense) a gut decision. The clues were captured, perhaps unintentionally, in brief but telling encounters: the way another mother addressed others at a meeting, the way she disciplined her child, the way she spoke to teachers, the way her child was dressed. When asked why she was willing to trust a mother whose name she did not know, Griselda explained that previous encounters with the child made the difference: "She has her daughter going here as well. And her daughter seems very well taken care of so I don't think I would have a problem with [trusting the mother]." Griselda, indeed, acquired a kind of knowledge that informed, in the strict sense, her decision. Griselda would belie Coleman's model in the sense that she did not require abundant information to take a risk with major consequences. And yet she would, as Coleman might expect, explain her trust by describing an informational process. With Griselda, Coleman's model was half right: information mattered, just not a lot of it.

For other mothers, centers provided something rather different, a familiarity engendered by mere force of repetition. This familiarity generated confidence, the way the sight of the same vendors, stores, families, parks, and street corners may make a resident's neighborhood feel like a safe haven. Habitual practices produced trust by increasing comfort.[19]

Consider Donna's impression of her center. A thin, bespectacled white professor in her thirties, Donna worked at a college in the city about an hour from her home. Thoughtful in demeanor and straightforward in attitude, she and her husband had enrolled her first son in a center near their neighborhood because it seemed the most practical solution to their predicament: "I brought him downtown to the financial district near where we live. Because I thought it would be easier for us in terms of drop off and pick up. My husband could do the drop off and I could do the pick up and [my son] wouldn't have to leave so early in the morning with me." By the time her daughter was born, their schedules had changed enough that she could enroll her in the center administered by her college.

Donna was struck by the differences between the centers. The first reflected the financial-center environment in orientation and clientele. First, the parents spent little time exchanging pleasantries with each other. The parents were "really not interested in what the other kids are doing. Nobody's playing with the kids.... No parents sitting down and chatting or anything like that. Very few parents did that." Second, the center afforded few opportunities for parents to interact. As she explains, the differences with her daughter's current center were "twofold. I think it's the profession, number one.... The majority of the people that have dropped their kids off here [at the campus center] have chosen a [different] profession, [where] there's this humanistic, caring quality that comes along with them.... I think the other part of it is the childcare center, because they really encourage that participation." Unlike her old center, the current center had a parents association, regular meetings, and frequent field trips.

Donna was busy. Though she appreciated the monthly meetings, she had not attended any of them. "There's a parent organization that's at this day care which is very nice. I have not attended the—they usually happen right after, like at 5:00. And that's too, that's difficult for me 'cause I have another child that I have to manage to pick up and [do] stuff for after school. So I've not gone to any of the meetings." As a result, she did not yet know anyone well in the center.

However, because of her frequent encounters throughout the center and campus, she "sort of" knew everyone well enough:

You sort of, because the center is affiliated with . . . the [college], even though people from the community can enroll their children, most of the kids are from, their parents are affiliated somehow with the university. . . . And it's just . . . if you don't see them in the hallway and know them personally you just, you just know everybody. Everybody sort of knows everybody. You kind of know all the kids in your class. . . .

There's forty of them or so, whatever.

Donna had a wide network of recognized-by-face acquaintances.

The familiarity that Donna had acquired, added to the warmer environment of the center, was sufficient to inspire a particular kind of trust, and in a sense knowing formal information such as names and addresses would be beside the point. If she needed someone to take care of her son in an emergency, her frequent encounters had provided what she needed: "You know that hasn't arisen but in the event that that would arise, heaven forbid, like an emergency situation I would feel comfortable knowing that with *any* of the parents that [my child] would be fine."

For both mothers, frequent interactions gave way to trust. For Griselda, it provided subtle informational clues about the behavior of a particular mother that rendered her, in Griselda's mind, as trustworthy. For Donna, it provided something different, a general familiarity and recognition that supported the inclination to trust—that is, it provided a basis for what some organizational scholars call "noncalculational trust."[20] In short, the conditions that social psychologists have found to foster trust are reproduced in centers, where interaction is frequent and often predictable, creating both opportunities to observe the behavior of others and increased familiarity with an institution. For this reason, mothers did not need to make strong ties to gain access to social support.

SOCIAL SUPPORT, OBLIGATIONS, AND INSTITUTIONALIZED CONTACTS

If social support among nonintimates in centers owed something to the operation of trust, it also owed something to the formal norms institutionalized by centers. Social capital theorists refer to the stock of social capital available in a network as a type of emergent property created and sustained by a natural feeling of solidarity or the enforcement of purely social norms. A network or group is a source of support for an individual because the group feels solidarity or because informal norms encourage everyone to give to others, such as the pressures among gang members to share goods in difficult times. Through either mechanism, the social capital to which an actor has access is said to result from informal dynamics.[21]

Support Lists

But if centers created access to social support by increasing trust, they also did so by *formally* institutionalizing obligations. I illustrate this point by discussing one instance of this process, centers' creation of emergency contact networks.

For many of the operations required to run a center effectively, including organizing field trips, maintaining emergency procedures, and coordinating fund-raisers, centers needed to establish effective communication among parents. Often, this meant assembling a list of all parents' contact information and making it available to all others—that is, creating a formal social network of acquaintances that were thereby allowed and encouraged to call each other for certain forms of support. In fact, such a list was a way for Head Start centers to meet federal requirements. Head Start centers are expected to institute procedures to contact parents quickly in the event of an emergency.[22] A center with one or two telephone lines will find it difficult to contact 100 parents quickly. Thus, centers often established parent representatives whose job it was to contact a given set of parents in case of an emergency. In creating such lists, centers of all types exerted their institutional pressure even on those parents not naturally inclined to "network," or even to share their personal information.

The Little Friends Day Care provides an illustration. A 10-year-old center founded by a church, Little Friends cared for about 40 children, most of whom were white, in an upper middle-class neighborhood in the city. Most parents lived within a few blocks of the center, and many parents knew other parents in the center. The center had instituted a parents association to plan its many activities. During one of its early fall meetings, attended by a handful of mothers and fathers, a fieldworker observed that, "In the first order of business, [the president] said that she wanted to have a parent representative for each classroom who would make a class list. The list would be distributed to each of the parents and would contain contact information for all of the parents of children in the class." Everyone provided and everyone had access. To make the process easier, the representative produced a form to slip in children's boxes, requesting names and phone numbers.

Little Friends merely institutionalized what may well have happened anyway. A parent with a bit of initiative—a purposive networker such as Naomi or Serena—might have put together a contact list to distribute at parent meetings for all mothers and fathers to enter names and phone numbers. But by instituting the process into its formal procedures, the center implicitly vouched for the reliability of other actors and made them available during times of crisis. These parents did not need to be friends in any real sense, compartmental or otherwise: by formalizing their membership they were effectively available for each other, at least for some types of emergencies (more on this below).

The Tweed Center instituted a somewhat different policy. The center posted a bulletin board in front of each classroom, a board containing notices pertinent to parents. After several weeks of daily drop-offs and pickups, most parents checked the board habitually. At Tweed, the director designated a "parent representative" for each classroom, a person whose job included keeping classroom parents abreast of issues related to the particular class and answering questions regarding events or activities. The director used the board to get parents used to the idea of a representative. Agatha, a black mother of four in the center who worked as a secretary, explained: "At the beginning of the year . . . , to get you to know the parent reps they put their names up on the board so [a parent] and her daughter . . . would know who to go to if you had questions."

The board also helped the parent representatives perform their duties. One of their duties was collecting contact information for every parent in every classroom. In Agatha's classroom, the process was effective. The parent representatives obtained, for "the entire class, address, phone number, email address, everything. And they gave it out to the entire class. So everyone has everyone's email address."

Agatha explained that, in her opinion, for the center to have instituted this practice made a difference, since the center first asked for the information and then shared it with all parents: "Because some places you go and people don't want to share their information. . . . So, by [the center] doing it—they actually went around and had each parent put their information down so . . . you gave them what number you wanted them to have, and then they let you know that everyone in the class would receive it." As in the case of the Little Friends Day Care, Tweed had created access to a potential form of social capital, by instituting a parents association, publicizing a contact list, and thereby making parents available for one another.

Compartmental Utility

Whether this remains only a *potential* source of social capital depends on whether mothers actually turned to the list when they needed something. In fact, one might expect this type of social capital to be weaker than informally generated capital, that mothers would be less likely to turn to those in the list than those with whom they have shared information personally. And, indeed, for many types of social support, this must be true. In the end, it is only a list. Nevertheless, the most pertinent concern is less the *depth* of available support than the *type* of need for which it is mobilized.

That is, parents may access this form of social capital, but largely to meet domain-specific needs.

For example, Agatha explained how the contact list at Tweed provided a source of support during a small crisis:

> [One] day, one parent was supposed to go on a trip with [the children, staff, and other volunteers]. And unfortunately she had to work. She couldn't get off. So, she sent out an email and said, "Help! I'm supposed to go on the trip tomorrow and I can't make it. Is there anyone out there who can go on the trip tomorrow in my place?" And the parents answered her. So, it's really good.

The crisis here was the parent's inability to make a center-related commitment. The parent may well have hesitated under circumstances unrelated to the domain of the center, such as borrowing money or requesting help with a medical emergency. On the other hand, she may have had no one to contact had the center not provided a list. In so doing, the center had implicitly made each parent in the class available to the other for at least certain types of crises—those contained to the domain of center activities.

Negative Social Capital

Despite these gains, social capital from formal, rather than informal, sources leads to a potential conflict between the actor and the organization. A center's pressure may supersede a particular person's reluctance to participate, substituting for the group pressure that manifests itself in informal settings. In this setting, a parent may fear losing a coveted center slot or retaliation by the teachers toward her children for not cooperating, fears that, rational or irrational as they may be, would effectively result in a type of coerced action.

This is not merely a theoretical possibility. Agatha's interviewer asked her whether some parents felt uncomfortable revealing their information. Agatha explained:

> Every parent gave. I think in the beginning a couple parents didn't really feel comfortable doing it, because they kept saying "I'll fill it out tomorrow, I'll fill it out tomorrow." And then the first time when [the director] sent [the list] out it was missing probably about five parents. They needed their information. And then I guess when [these missing parents] realized that everyone else had done [it] then they finally gave in.

Agatha's language—that the parents "finally gave in"—makes clear that the center induced effective social pressures.

Under the rubric of *negative* social capital, theorists have discussed the pressures that actors may feel to conform to informal norms.[23] The case of Tweed suggests that these pressures may be exacerbated in organizational settings, since mothers may pay financial or membership costs for noncompliance. Thus, the institutionalization of "social support lists" illustrates that organizational settings may exacerbate the paradox of social capital—they may heighten the negative and positive dynamics of social capital among individuals. By formalizing a process that actors in other settings perform informally, centers expand the support sources available to mothers, but the more effectively centers perform this task, the more they pressure mothers to participate in the group process. And while we did not witness any cases where mothers who did not yield their numbers and email addresses suffered serious consequences, it may be the case that at least some mothers feared such consequences, informal and formal, from not participating. In centers, as outside of them, few social gains are unaccompanied by costs.

CONSEQUENCES

Access to an Extended Support Network

Our larger question prompts us to examine how these institutional dynamics affect mothers' access to social support. The result of these circumstances—multiple opportunities for frequent interaction and organizationally derived support contacts—was that mothers in childcare centers acquired an extended support network that was not limited to their standard or compartmental intimates. That is, some mothers who made no friends nonetheless acquired support ties. This turned out to be a significant advantage, but only under certain circumstances.

We can see why by returning to the case of Ula's relations in figure 5.1. Suppose we populated the figure with all persons in Ula's social network and assumed a threshold on the vertical axis such that those above this point are Ula's friends and those below it are not.[24] Regardless of the point of the threshold, as long as Ula interacts frequently enough with someone below it to request and receive from that person social support, her support network (the set of people she would turn to successfully for social support) extends beyond her friendship network (the set of people she considers her friends). The same is true if, instead of considering the frequency of interaction, we considered the presence of people, friends or not, in an emergency contact list created by the center.

This extended support network becomes a predictable advantage when considered as a type of last resort. If each of two actors, A and B, have three friends or family members while only B has additional extended-support "nonfriends," we still would expect both of them to turn to their friends or family when faced with a short-term emergency.[25] But if these friends were unavailable—because they lived in Puerto Rico or were stuck in traffic an hour away or did not have cash on hand—we would expect B to turn to her nonfriends and thereby have an easier time resolving her crisis. As Griselda explained, if she needed emergency care, she would *first* turn to her coworker (friend), but then she would comfortably turn to the mother whose name she did not know.

This advantage, however, depends on three conditions. First, the advantage of B over A depends in some measure on the type of emergency. Feeling comfortable asking someone to watch a child for a few hours differs from asking someone to take the child to the hospital or to lend a hundred dollars. The more serious the emergency, the smaller the difference between B's friendship network and her support network—because B will be less willing to ask and the nonfriends less willing to offer—and the less of an advantage B will have over A.

Second, the advantage also depends on the type of social support available, since not all types of support are solutions to emergencies. Some forms of support are domain specific, while others are not, and some are more personally demanding than others. Asking a person to watch one's child differs from asking someone to listen to one's story of domestic abuse—in the latter, a request that is at once less directly tied to the domain and more personal, how strong the tie is will become important. In their review of network models of social support, Michael Walker, Stanley Wasserman, and Barry Wellman, identified four types of social support: emotional support, informational support, material support (in the form of goods, money, or services), and companionship.[26] Mothers in childcare centers acquired support of all four kinds. However, it is likely that, within each category, the more personal or the less compartmental the form of support, the less either frequency of interaction or trust by proxy alone will do to engender access to social support.

Third, and perhaps most important, the advantage of B over A depends on their having very few friends. If A had not three but six friends, then one of them would surely come through, so why care about the extended support network? The significance of the extended support network comes about primarily for those who are socially isolated.

The term "socially isolated" here does not refer merely to the urban poor, as in William J. Wilson's classic conception.[27] Social isolates may also be those who have experienced a social transition, such as moving to a new country or becoming divorced, as in Blanca's case. These individuals sometimes find that their friendship network has narrowed dramatically, as the friends they had in their home country have failed to maintain the bond, or those they had while married have remained friends only with the other spouse. People who have no close friends have everything to gain from having a support network of nonfriends to turn to in an emergency. And this category of people is not rare. Among respondents in the Fragile Families survey, 11% of urban mothers reported having only one close friend, and 8% reported having no close friends whatsoever. In these cases, having an extended support network may mean the difference between getting by and experiencing significant hardship. This would help explain why, as we saw in chapter 2, poor mothers with children in centers experienced less hardship than those not in centers even when they did not develop relationships they would consider to be friendships.

For Whom an Extended Support Network Mattered

Our interviews confirmed that the consequences of an extended support network depended on the circumstances of the mother. For resource-rich mothers, the presence of an extended support network was, effectively, inconsequential. Consider the case of Tammy, a successful white photographer in her forties who wore her brown hair long. She worked in a downtown office and enrolled her son at Little Friends Day Care. Tammy had assembled an effective support network around her to deal with childcare issues. Her interviewer asked what she would do if an emergency arose and neither she nor her husband could pick up her son:

> It has happened, and actually it happened last week when we were moving offices.... [W]e have a babysitter who's in college right now who's in for the summer and we called her and she was able to help us out. We also have another babysitter who lives right near our house who most of the time is available. And I could also call my parents who live in the West Village. So those three resources are tremendous.

For this reason, "I would do that [turn to these resources] before I would ask any parent at the school."

In fact, the use of available resources to establish preset emergency mechanisms was not uncommon. Mary, a married, brunette white mother in her thirties, worked full time in a corporate office while pursuing, nights and weekends, a career as a comedian. Witty and high strung, she referred to herself as an often "neurotic" mother to her only daughter, Jennifer. Mary's home and her work were located in different boroughs, which gave her an incentive to cover her bases for emergency situations. Her interviewer asked what she would do if she had a short-term emergency and could not pick up her child. The comedian replied without hesitation:

> I'll show you just because you can see just exactly how neurotic I am, and then it will just answer everything for you. I have a bag of tricks, a laminated "Jennifer Emergency Contact List" of people who are able to pick up my

child with ID and phone numbers and a call tree if there's drama in Manhattan and I can't get to her. 'Cause her being so far away from me is an issue. I'm lucky to have my husband available to pick her up. There's a . . . tree of people who can get her. . . .

[On this list are] friends and relatives . . . it's a neurotic breakdown people in the vicinity who could get to her in case—it's really an emergency card for another disaster if one should happen.[28] And it's people in the neighborhood that could walk to her, [first]; and if they're not available [my instructions are] "You call the person ahead of you to see if they got her until someone gets her." There's so many people on the list it's hysterical. My brother-in-law wants to put it on Saturday Night Live or something like that, "Neurotic Parents in Manhattan" [laughter]. But it's clear after the blackout no one [I normally relied on] had printed out where her school was, so no one knew if I could get to her. But no one knew how to get to her because it was all on their computers! So I was pissed off [laughter] and I said, "Well, I'm leaving you in care of my child and none of you know where to go? Here's a little card. Don't do it again." And now everyone carries their card. . . . There's a lot [of people] with cars, a lot without cars; a lot with scooters, I mean, everyone's got a way to get to Jenny. The golden child [laughter]. Poor thing.

Mary's laminated emergency contact list was only a peculiar instance of the rather common practices by which mothers already rich in social resources created protection for themselves in emergencies. For these mothers, having people in the center, other than their friends, to call on for support was of little consequence.

Consider, however, the case of Helena, described above. A soft-spoken, entrepreneurial, Dominican-born immigrant on Medicaid, Helena had opened a small grocery store on a quiet street about one hour away from her home and the Alegre Daycare, where her son was cared for. He had asthma, which made him more demanding of her time and more susceptible to emergencies. Before entering the center, Helena was almost completely socially isolated. As she explained to me (in Spanish): "I don't have that many friends. I'm not the type to have many friends. . . . It's not something that I have done on purpose. But . . . how do I say this? I don't trust many people. I need time to develop trust in others. I am maybe a little timid with respect to this. I am not very open to know people when I know people. I need time." She was especially sensitive about the needs of her son, who had recently also been diagnosed as suffering from ADHD. I asked her what would happen if an emergency came up and she could not pick up her children. Before I could finish, she explained her aforementioned relationship with Blanca:

Well, I ended up doing this with Blanca. She one time picked up my son. I called her, I have her cell phone and she has mine. . . . I used to get out of [work] at five . . . and I didn't have anyone to pick them up, and I was always on the highway running or on the train, and I was late a few times. So I [have] had my [children stay] with Blanca, Blanca and another woman who was the mother of a friend of my son.

Helena had met Blanca when they both served on the board of the parents association. Helena did not have at her disposal two babysitters, or a mother nearby, or friends with cars or scooters. A near isolate, she certainly needed support and therefore, as an emergency presented itself, soon took the risk of trusting Blanca, whom she had not yet gotten to know. The experience of having trusted Blanca with her children without incident helped Helena out of her shell. Over time, as they worked together to coordinate Alegre's holiday celebrations and field trips, Helena and Blanca even became compartmental intimates.

CONCLUSION: HOW TO ACQUIRE AN EMERGENCY SUPPORT NETWORK

"I can tell you a story!" said Katrina, mother of an infant girl at the Little Friends Day Care. Animated, social, and taking nothing for granted, Katrina carried close to a dozen Tupperware containers with foods and items for her daughter in a large canvas bag wherever the two went. "I recently had an emergency with daycare. My daughter got sick, but I couldn't stay home with her because I am involved in the 9/11 investigating commission, and I had to be at work. I could have lost my job! But the teacher here knew someone that could babysit. She came in for a week, and I had never even met her before."

Carol Stack's *All Our Kin* and Kathryn Edin and Laura Lein's *Making Ends Meet* succeeded in alerting researchers to the fact that single and low-income mothers in urban areas relied on others facing the same circumstances to make ends meet, avoid hardship, and deal with everyday emergencies. However, as Margaret Nelson notes, this finding has been taken to mean that being a mother provides instant access to a support network. Referring to her own research among rural mothers, she explains, "[I]t is important to note here that the relationships I have described are *not* automatic, and that becoming a single mother does not ensure entry into a network of like-minded or similarly situated friends. Some single mothers, in fact, know no others in their same situation."[29] Making the social ties helpful to a mother is a task in its own right, a task easily and wrongly assumed to occur naturally among parents of young children. Chapters 2-4 have shown that, for mothers in childcare centers, these ties are formed and sustained in large measure by the organizational conditions in the centers themselves, a situational context that provides a considerable advantage to the formation of these supportive ties.

The present chapter has shown—by articulating one way centers shape trust and one way they impose formal obligations—why acquaintance ties can matter more to everyday social support than common rules of thumb might suggest. Though many mothers developed strong ties, they did not need to do so to gain access to social support, because the latter stemmed from conditions that transcended the closeness of the bond, conditions created by an organizational context in which interaction was institutionally moderated. Through membership in the organization, mothers entered sets of relationships that, like Katrina's, transcended how close they felt to anyone.

Similar sets of relationships in different social contexts have been referred to by anthropologists as generalized exchange systems, in which each person gives to or receives from any other without expecting direct reciprocity, provided there is sufficient solidarity in the whole.[30] In centers, as in generalized exchange systems, two people need not be close to be supportive. In centers, however, the system does not depend on the solidarity or cohesiveness of the group. Every mother's formal relationship to the center, and the obligations it entails—from the simple mandate to retrieve a child from a classroom, rather than the curb, to the complicated task of organizing a fund-raiser—provides, either intentionally or not, the access to other people that cohesive groups ensure through strongly enforced informal norms. Mothers are tied formally to the organization, and thereby informally to a support network. For these reasons, much of the support mothers experience is ultimately an organizational product.

Part III

ORGANIZATIONAL TIES

6

Ties to Other Organizations
Why Mothers' Most Useful Ties Were Not Always Social

Destino, a short, black-haired, brown-skinned, plain-spoken Puerto Rican in her early thirties, had developed no friendships, compartmental or otherwise, in her center, a predominantly black organization in a high-poverty neighborhood in the city.[1] She had never arranged play dates or swapped babysitting responsibilities; she would not, she insisted, trust *any* other parents in the center with her children. And although she volunteered in her center's parents association, she rarely spoke with even those parents about any topic other than association business. Destino had no interest in purposive networking; she seemed reluctant to express even an occasional interest in making a friend or two. She had chatted a few times with one mother and even attended her son's birthday party. But she ranked their relationship as a "4 or 5" on a 1-to-10 scale, and when I asked why it was not higher, she explained that something not too strong was "good": "Because I don't know her. . . . You know, we've had talks but, I think five is nice and good in the middle. . . . I know her enough, but I don't know her that well." As for other parents, "I don't really know any other parents or [when I do] it's not that close."

The fleeting relations Destino developed in the center played, at best, minor role in her social life and they certainly played no role in her ambitions. Born poor, in the Bronx, but driven and hard working, she had slowly climbed the income ladder, now making a living as a certified public accountant for the state in a messy cubicle in a vast, cramped public office in her old borough. Destino and her husband hoped their son, who was now ready for kindergarten, would receive the very best education the city could offer. In this ambition, the other low-income parents in the center played no part. Nevertheless, through her center Destino formed a kind of tie that dramatically improved her chances of attaining her ambition.

Her wish was for her son to enroll in one of the city's top private elementary schools, all of which she knew she could not afford. Destino, resourceful and self-efficacious, had begun to pursue her options. Shortly thereafter, she realized that identifying, applying to, and getting funds for these schools would be more difficult than she imagined. "It's a whole process," she explained to me. "It's more stressful than your college applications.... Probably more stressful than you trying to get into a Ph.D. program.... [Y]ou have to be interviewed, you have to fill out applications, you have to give [a reason] why [your] child should [be there]."

Despite her good intentions, Destino, herself a product of the New York City public schools, did not possess the cultural capital to know the many facets of the process, such as contents of the entrance tests, the subtle signals of a successful application, and the availability of full scholarships.[2] She explained how she discovered that testing, which parents were expected to pay for, was part of the process:

> Well, last year the PTA did ... an informational meeting. At the PTA meeting, they provided information about the process, the testing, you know, just the nuts and bolts of how the testing is done. [The center] arranged so that the students can be tested at [the center] because ... the students have to go in and get tested [to be eligible for admission]. So either, if you are in the thousand-dollar preschools, the testers will come to the [center] and you don't have to pay extra for it. The teacher comes to the [center], they test the kids ... where it's a familiar environment. Or, you have to go down to the testing facility.

By providing crucial information and even free entrance exams, her center had begun to be useful in ways she had not anticipated.

Standardized testing was only part of it. Just as important was finding both the right school to apply to and the funds with which to pay for it. In this process, the critical tie Destino made was not to an employee of the center, but to an outside expert on the private school admission process, who gave a presentation at the meeting:

> There's a woman that's associated with [the center] who's very knowledgeable about the whole private school process, and then there was a parent that approached my husband [who was on the PTA at the time] about it, saying she wanted to try to do this, 'cause she had already gone through it, and ... she felt it was better for the kids to be able to be tested in a familiar environment. She thought they would do better. So, between her and the other lady, and my husband, they put up a presentation together for the PTA ... that was the first PTA meeting last year. And they provided information about all the schools, the kinds of things [included in the] test ... other ... things about the schools ..., how much the test costs, and programs available to help you with the test or getting into the schools....

The expert had been to the center several times throughout the year.

She was helpful when I asked her: "Since you've seen [my son], and you know the private schools, where do you think would be a good fit?"...And she gave me some recommendations, some suggestions. I told her which schools I was thinking of and, you know, she gave me her opinion on those schools, so that was helpful.

Destino trusted the expert instinctively. In fact, this stranger's opinion superseded her own:

One of the schools that she recommended that I wasn't even looking into is now one of our...number one schools that we hope he gets into....It's an all-boys' school. And I really didn't think about doing an all-boys' school, but you know, she...thought it was a really good program. She thought it was a really good school. So we went to the school and my husband fell in love with it.

And cost? "Twenty-five thousand dollars a year, something like that. I don't know. They're all between eighteen and twenty-five thousand dollars a year....We hope to get, we hope to get scholarships, because [the school provides] scholarships 'cause [the school wants]...economic diversity, ethnic diversity."

Although Destino did not form the intimate or otherwise supportive ties that other mothers did, she certainly acquired a valuable, even priceless, resource: information. This expert provided Destino information about the testing process, advice on the city's best schools, and the critical bit of knowledge that the schools often granted their own scholarships. The $25,000 yearly price tag, enough to scare off all but those at the very top of New York's income distribution, became less daunting to a parent who knew to expect a scholarship that was not a precondition for applying but a guarantee from the school itself upon acceptance. The information that other mothers lacked, or accessed through informal social capital, or instinctively possessed through cultural capital, Destino obtained through a formal tie, the tie between the center and the expert.[3]

While this book has been examining how mothers gain social support and other resources through their newly acquired *social* ties, the present chapter argues that center mothers often acquired valuable resources, as Destino did, through *organizational* ties. By organizational ties I refer to the connections, brokered by the childcare center, that mothers made to other organizations or to their formal representatives[4] (see figure 6.1).

Understanding the nature and value of organizational ties occupies chapters 6 and 7. They make clear why students of network inequality would be remiss in ignoring this type of tie, and articulate how organizational ties differ from the social ties we have hitherto examined. In so doing, chapters 6 and 7 unravel the basic character of what some have called this "institutional" form of social capital.[5] The present chapter begins by answering

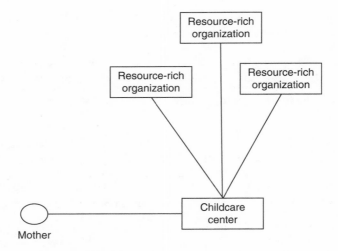

Figure 6.1. Childcare center as broker between mother and resource-rich organizations.

three questions that probe the basic nature of these ties: To *what organizations* did the mothers form ties? What *resources* could they acquire through these ties? And exactly *how* did mothers acquire these resources? (Chapter 7 explains *why* centers brokered organizational ties.)

The chapter proceeds in three sections. The first identifies the organizations from which mothers in the 23 centers we observed acquired resources. The second specifies what these resources were, revealing that they generally fell into one of three types: information, services, and material goods. The final section identifies the mechanisms by which mothers acquired each of them—information, services, and material goods—arranging the discussion by type of resource. It introduces four mechanisms, described as forms of brokerage: storage, validation, referral, and collaboration. The section suggests that organizational ties provided access to goods often difficult to acquire through social ties, and through mechanisms different from any this book has examined so far.

ORGANIZATIONAL TIES OF CENTERS

Connections to Multiple Organizations

Childcare centers, like most organizations, were not organizationally isolated. More often than not, they were connected, through relationships of either greater or lesser stability, commitment, parity, and formality, to organizations as diverse as the centers themselves—businesses, nonprofit agencies, and government bureaucracies, large and small organizations, and neighborhood and citywide entities.[6] An effective tool to understand this heterogeneity is the concept of "organizational field." Sociologists have defined "organizational fields" as systems of interconnected organizations constituting a recognized area of institutional life.[7] A somewhat elusive metaphor employed in several branches of sociology, the idea of a field nonetheless helps capture the tendency of organizations to orient their activities toward some organizations and not others, to purposely form relationships with organizations with which they have attributes in common.[8] These relationships may serve different purposes, and chapter 7 explores what purposes they served for childcare centers and their directors. First, however, this chapter identifies the fields in which centers tended to operate. We shall see that the concept helps delimit the universe of organizations with which centers formed relationships.

Childcare centers cooperated, competed, and exchanged resources with organizations in several different fields, reflecting the multiple purposes to which the centers, and their members, were oriented. Centers operated at the intersection of multiple fields: the *childcare field*, which included for-profit and nonprofit daycare providers, daycare teachers unions, New York City's Administration for Children's Services, child development organizations, and the federal Head Start office; the *education field*, which included private and public elementary schools, teacher's unions, elementary-school testing organizations, afterschool programs, adult-education centers, and the city's Department of Education; the *healthcare field*, which included pharmacies, hospitals, mental health clinics, domestic abuse centers, the WIC (Women, Infants, and Children) Program offices, the U.S. Department of Health and Human Services, HIV/AIDS testing centers, and nutritional supplement businesses; the *community development field*, which included local and national community development organizations, youth-leadership programs, neighborhood churches, schools, ethnic organizations, immigrant-focused organizations, the city's Human Resources Administration, and sponsoring businesses; and the *cultural field*, which included theaters, museums, zoos, philanthropic agencies, corporate sponsors, and schools. In the fields of childcare, education, and health care, childcare centers were major actors; in community development and culture, less so.

Childcare centers both provided to and received from the organizations in these fields various resources—information, staff, funds, legitimacy, clients, services, political capital—to meet their institutional needs.[9] For example, in the summer of 2004 many childcare center workers in New York collaborated with other centers and with childcare workers unions to organize a strike for higher wages.[10] The political capital acquired through the collaboration was an instrumental resource in the pursuit of higher wages. While many resources such as these benefitted the centers as institutions, many others—and these are the focus of our chapter—primarily represented a benefit to the parent. For example, certain university hospitals sent health professionals in training to some childcare centers to perform free oral or general health exams on children. These patron-specific resources derived from organizations in all fields. Table 6.1 lists those organizations that, among the 23 centers we visited, provided, sent, or distributed resources acquired by parents of the center.

Table 6.1 demonstrates the remarkable range of organizations in the fields of childcare, health care, education, community development, and culture to which centers were connected. They were businesses selling a product (at a discount) or agencies providing a service; they were nonprofit organizations disseminating information or firms providing charitable contributions. They included New York City's Administration for Children's

Table 6.1. Some organizations to which centers were formally tied

Federal childcare agencies
New York city Administration for children's Services
Other childcare centers
Nonprofit child well-being organizations
New York City Department of Education
Public schools
Youth organizations
Hospitals
Mental health centers
Dental vans
HIV/AIDS clinics
Substance abuse centers
Domestic abuse centers
Domestic violence centers/hotlines
New York City Human Resources Administration/Department of Social Services
Fire department
Community organizations
Ethnic organizations
Soup kitchens/food pantries
Movie theaters
Circuses
Museums and other cultural institutions
Zoos
Department stores

Source: Twenty-three centers in four neighborhoods in New York City visited by author and research assistants.

services, social service agencies, other childcare centers, public schools, several local university hospitals, small community clinics, HIV/AIDS testing centers, domestic abuse centers, and community building organizations. Many centers were tied to the city's Human Resources Administration, a large, highly networked agency that provides a host of resources, such as work training, essential services for individuals with AIDS, adult protective services to the mentally disabled, and public health insurance.[11] Many centers were also connected to large or otherwise powerful nonprofit organizations that turned to childcare centers in poor neighborhoods as a means to target low-income parents—hospitals were in this category, but also churches, community or ethnic organizations, child well-being organizations, museums, soup kitchens, and youth organizations. In fact, centers often were a subunit of a much larger nonprofit organization located elsewhere. Several centers were tied to cultural organizations, such as museums and zoos, which provided reduced admissions at cultural events, and others to businesses that sponsored scholarships for center children, provided reduced admissions to their services, or produced "Dear Santa" gifts at Christmas time.

Three Types of Resources

These organizations provided many types of resources, which fell under one of three categories: (a) information provided or available to the parent, (b) services provided for free or at discounts to mothers, fathers, or children enrolled in the center, and (c) material goods offered at no or reduced cost to center patrons. The information, services, and material goods that parents acquired tended to reflect domains within the five organizational fields of which centers formed part: child rearing, nutrition, and development (childcare); child and adult mental and physical health (health care); adult education, elementary schooling, and testing (education); housing, immigration, and employment (community development); and the arts and entertainment (culture).

Table 6.2 lists all the resources brokered by the 23 centers we observed. Resources were large in number, often important, and remarkably varied. Accordingly, the mechanisms through which centers brokered access to these resources varied by type of good. Nonetheless, the mechanisms exhibited clear patterns. Whereas childcare centers brokered *social* ties both purposely (e.g., when they assembled networking lists) and nonpurposely (e.g., when they required mothers to participate in fund-raisers), they generally brokered *organizational* ties on purpose. The remainder of this chapter describes in detail each major type of resource and identifies the mechanisms by which parents acquired it.

Table 6.2. Resources from other organizations acquired by parents through childcare centers

Information

        Nutritional information (free)

        Safety education (free)

        Domestic abuse education (free)

        Child health information (free)

        Housing needs information (free)

        School system information/education (free)

Services

        Health exams for child (free)

        Dental exams and instruction for child (free)

        Speech therapy for child (free)

        Domestic violence counseling (free)

        Developmental disability screening (low cost)

        Health exam for parents (free/low cost)

        Substance abuse counseling for parents (low cost/free)

        Vision screening (free/low cost)

        HIV/AIDS testing and treatment (free/low cost)

        Legal aid (low cost/free)

        Adult literacy training (free)

        Adult English language instruction (free)

        Work training (through NYC BEGIN program) (free)

        Housing support (temporary housing) (low cost/free)

        Assistance in dealing with government bureaucracy (free)

        School entrance exam testing (free)

Material goods

        Health insurance (low cost/free)

        Meals (free)

        Tickets to cultural and entertainment events (free/low cost)

        Free admission year-round to cultural institutions

        Employment (through NYC BEGIN)

        Toys (free)

        Scholarships (free)

Source: Twenty-three centers in four neighborhoods in New York City visited by author and research assistants. Refers to resources which were transferred on an ongoing basis or at least once a year. *Excludes* services provided independently by the centers.

HOW MOTHERS ACQUIRED INFORMATION

Just as Destino learned how to get her child into and pay for a top elementary school, parents, poor and nonpoor, obtained important information that ranged from educational to nutritional, to housing, to safety issues. By "information obtained" I refer to any knowledge on any of these topics that the mother acquired, from an external source, through her participation in the center. How to prevent eviction, stress, lead poisoning, or divorce; how to obtain health insurance, a good lawyer, a mortgage, or the child support payments to which one is entitled; or how to cut children's hair, to make sellable arts and crafts, or to get one's child into a good school—all of these were forms of information that parents acquired from external organizations through their centers.

Centers were nothing if not information banks for parents of young children. Information on child-rearing issues, not surprisingly, predominated. For example, in many centers, parents received a version of the flier with nutrition tips from Fun Times Center reproduced in figure 6.2, from an outside expert on nutrition. The nation's concern with food and nutrition, fueled in recent years by reports in the media of rising obesity in adults and children, has contributed to a proliferation of information from marketers, researchers, journalists, and politicians on everything from portion control to the appropriate types of oils. The flier shown in figure 6.2 was produced by a businesswoman hoping to convince parents to consider some of the products and supplements her company offered.

The flier was not anomalous, and some centers routinely disseminated information from other organizations. For example, the staff of the Open Arms center assembled a bimonthly "Parent Newsletter," a glossy, eight-page, color-printed pamphlet with photos of parents and children attending recent center activities, that listed resources available through other organizations and information for parents of young children. A recent issue of the newsletter discussed the causes and consequences of sibling rivalry, which may be caused in part by parents' tendency to treat different children

---

USDA Food Guide Pyramid Recommendations

Check to see if your children meet the USDA Minimum Daily Dietary Guidelines

* Toddlers: 6 servings of whole grains; 2 servings fruit; 3 servings of veggies;
            2 servings of protein; 2 servings of dairy

* Children: 9 servings of whole grains; 3 servings fruit; 4 servings of veggies;
            2 servings of protein; 2 servings of dairy

* Teens: 11 servings of whole grains; 4 servings fruit; 5 servings of veggies;
            2-3 servings of protein; 2-3 servings of dairy

* Use Fats, Oils, Sweets Sparingly For All Ages

Figure 6.2. Flier on recommended daily servings distributed at Fun Times Center.

differently.[12] The newsletter instructed parents to prepare children for the arrival of a new baby ("As arrangements are made for the arrival of a new baby, make sure these arrangements recognize the needs of the older sibling") and to refrain from comparing children to each other ("Parents can intensify feelings of jealousy by holding one child up to the other"). The newsletter also included an article, written by a doctor who worked in one of the satellite agencies of the large nonprofit organization that operates the center, on childhood obesity. The article cited the association between obesity and several illnesses:

> Obesity is an underlying cause of a number of serious medical conditions including Type II diabetes, essential hypertension, respiratory disease, gallbladder disease, stroke and osteoarthritis. These conditions are beginning to show up at increasingly high rates among children who are overweight. According Dr. [*name, university affiliation*], children are "actually developing Type II diabetes earlier, in some cases in their teenage years."

The article recommended strategies for developing "lifestyle changes" for parents and children.

In centers such as Open Arms, a mother could expect to receive similar clusters of information on health care, education, dealing with government bureaucracies, housing, and legal issues. How she acquired this information—that is, how the center brokered the information from the organization to the patron—was largely through two processes. The discussion has already hinted at what they are: storage and the establishment of collaborative informational sessions.[13]

Acquiring Information through Storage

Childcare centers warehoused copious information both stably and accessibly, a practice I define as storage. A distinctly organizational form of brokerage, storage was, from the parent's perspective, often a distinctly institutional mechanism. To see how, consider a contrast. When a *person* is the broker between two actors, the broker must introduce one actor to the other for the information to be exchanged among them.[14] When a *center* is the broker between two parties, it may operate as a passive communicator, because centers are physical spaces with desks, tables, walls, libraries, and bulletin boards, all of which function in part to disseminate information collected in brochures, books, newsletters, pamphlets, and posters. A center can post information on a bulletin board for parents to come across or look over in the daily routine of dropping off and retrieving her child. Organizational sociologists have referred to a similar process as "stockpiling," the accumulation of resources for later use or release to the market; storage differs from stockpiling in that the latter is performed to manage an organizational environment, while the former is in place to attract the attention of the patron.[15]

Consider the Corona Childcare Center. The center occupied a small, cramped space in the basement of a nineteenth-century church building. Visitors were buzzed in at a rear door recessed deeply into a thick wall; they took three steps down into a poorly lit hallway with a damp scent. The main office, which also functioned as a reception room, consisted of two cubicles and several dozen file cabinets, bookcases, and boxes crammed into a space about 10 by 20 feet. The narrow hallway leading to the office, where parents enrolled their children and met with the director, served as a waiting area. On one of the hall's walls hung a bulletin board containing various fliers from external organizations that parents read while they waited. One flier, from a household-oriented human service agency, listed a telephone number for persons to call if they had a nonresponsive landlord or an unfair rent adjustment or a need for information on specific services, such as rent reduction for the elderly. Another flier contained information on how to acquire health insurance; another, on obtaining help from the federal WIC Program, whose mission is "to safeguard the health of low-income women, infants, and children up to age 5 who are at nutritional risk by providing nutritious foods to supplement diets, information on healthy eating, and referrals to health care."[16]

Information-filled bulletin boards such as these were ubiquitous throughout our centers. Among those in our survey of New York City childcare centers, 96% posted bulletin boards in their front lobby or office with information for parents. In fact, among centers that reported helping their patrons with information on the school enrollment process, 75% displayed school enrollment information in a front bulletin board or office. (Most centers did other things, as well, such as hosting speakers or informational sessions, which 63% of centers did.)

Physical repositories such as bulletin boards and newsletters allowed information to be brokered even when it had not been requested, such that part of their value, from the mother's perspective, was access to a resource she would not have thought to ask for. That is, the center mobilized the connection for the parent, effectively procuring the resource in a way advantageous to the least purposive parents. Such repositories contained not only the information that parents were looking for, but often the information they did not know they should be looking for—or information that, in the never-ending hustle of balancing work and family, they simply had not made a priority. Missy, for example, white and a first-time mother, while waiting before her center's bulletin board, happened upon something she had been wanting to know: "the storage of baby food. I didn't know how long to store it, to be honest with you; after I opened it I didn't know how long it was safe to store."[17]

In this light, it is worth recalling how centers helped generate homophily. By mere virtue of their function, centers, like other organizations, attracted individuals with similar interests, problems, inquiries, circumstances, and socioeconomic conditions. They were predictable sites for parents of young children. As such, they became targets for organizations possessing information relevant to this group—such as how to enroll children in private elementary schools, where to obtain health insurance, how to screen for developmental disability, and where to get a mammogram. Fliers and brochures that, if handed out in busy sidewalks and subway stations, might be quickly dropped into a trashcan could be posted on a board, as at Corona, at least temporarily. When assessed against other information dissemination strategies, storage became a viable option.

Acquiring Information through Collaborative Sessions

On other occasions, centers collaborated with external organizations by scheduling and preparing rooms for meetings during which representatives from government agencies or nonprofit organizations presented information about a service, law, or social problem, or businesses pitched a product. Regardless of the source of the information or the objectives of the supplier, most of these meetings were run as interactive sessions during which parents requested and obtained information specifically important to them from a captive speaker. These sessions were decidedly active affairs.

Consider a recent informational meeting on health and nutrition at the Fun Times Center, a daycare in a residential upper middle-class block in New York City. The center was located in one of four large, connected row houses, an elegant three-story brownstone with high front stoops and bay windows. The center occupied the entire basement and first floor, a spacious arrangement in prime New York City real estate. (The basement two doors down was a yoga center.) A for-profit, independent center still run by its founder after 13 years, Fun Times was one of the few centers caring for infants in addition to the standard toddlers; its funds derived strictly from tuition and fund-raising. The circumstances of the meeting suggest how, by brokering such sessions, the center mobilized its ties to provide access to valuable information.

The meeting, attended by one of my research assistants, took place in a basement classroom, 15 by 25 feet, with pale yellow walls, royal blue trim, and two large rugs covering the gray linoleum flooring. Fifteen child-sized seats, miniature versions of standard-issue metal and plastic school chairs, were roughly arranged in a semicircle. The plastic seats on the chairs were coated in different primary colors. On the front of each chair back was still affixed a paper with a different child's name. Attending the meeting were eight parents, half of them men, who constituted a racial cross section of New York's middle class: a black male, two white males, an Asian female and her white husband, another Asian female, and two Latinas.

The session was led by a woman, Susana, who ran meetings in centers throughout the city on child nutrition and health to promote the health products of her company. She began by asking parents, "I want to know . . . whether there is anything specific about your child's health that you are concerned about, or something you have been wondering, whatever it is." Fitzgerald, the black father, answered: "One problem that we have been having with [my child] lately is constipation. The other night at dinner he was very fidgety, he wouldn't settle down, and then we discovered that he just had to go to the bathroom. We try to feed him power food, lots of veggies." He reported this as casually as one talks about the weather, then laughed a bit, and continued, at once discussing and venting:

> But I am concerned that he is not getting enough fiber in his diet, and that it's what's making him constipated. My son is also predisposed to asthma, so we are concerned about that. And before he was always getting sick. He would always have a cold or something, it seemed, all the time, but now he is sick much less, and when he gets sick, he just has a short cold. I think that's because we've been concentrating a lot more on making sure that he gets enough sleep. He is even a more personable, happier child now that he is sleeping more. I think he's been behaving better here too. I think that rest is very important.

Another parent, Helena, shared her concerns: "We have a daughter who's three and a half. We have a lot of trouble convincing her to go to sleep. We've been trying to keep her on a regular sleep schedule but we haven't been having much luck." Fitzgerald suddenly remembered the dark circles forming under his son's eyes: "I know that that is supposed to mean something, but I can't remember what." Another mother added a concern, leg aches. "Yeah," said a third, "my child has aches too." Susana scribbled everything on sheet after sheet of a white paper board.

Upon this backdrop, Susana explained that inactivity, toxicity in the food and environment, and stress tend to make children ill. She distributed literature with detailed information on everything she presented. For a little under an hour, she presented both trivial tidbits and useful information on everything from lifestyle to nutrition. Television, she reminded everyone, was a major source of inactivity. Children needed lots of antioxidants to fight pollutants in the air, water, and food. Table sugar, found in greater quantity than many people realized, was especially unhealthy, particularly if it was inorganic. Motioning to the literature, she presented a chart showing how sugar depleted the immune system: "You need to make sure that your kids have a high fiber, high protein breakfast. Children also need to eat every three hours to keep up their blood sugar. If they don't eat, it really hits them in the brainstem. So you want to make sure that you always pack food and the children get a snack every three hours." Encouraging natural and alternative sources of reducing stress and toxins, she began to discuss oils. "Everyone knows about lavender oil? . . . Well, it is very relaxing. Here, pass this around and so everyone can smell it." She handed a small, open glass bottle with lavender oil in it to the first parent in the room, who took a whiff before passing it on to her left, as everyone else did. She proceeded, then, to discuss the immune system, providing a small lecture on the benefits of small choices in foods purchased, such as brown versus white rice.

The environment was casual: every other one of Susana's statements was interrupted by questions and comments from parents, often punctuated with jokes and laughter. Nothing was taken for granted. After she recommended peanut butter and jelly as an easy snack, one parent asked, "Doesn't jelly have a lot of sugar in it, though?" "You can get organic jelly that doesn't. You need to look for just fruit."

She turned to vitamins. "Not all vitamin supplements are very good. There are three types of vitamin supplements, synthetic, crystallized, and lyophilized." While she said this, she displayed a white cardboard chart listing the three types of supplements and their basic characteristics. Only lyophilized vitamins, she submitted, are good for the body. She provided a handout containing information on what type of vitamins are available in what type of foods. After someone asked where lyophilized vitamins are available, she explained—consistent with the global purpose of her presentation—that she markets such vitamins for her company.

By the end, Susana turned to answer the specific issues participants had addressed, reiterating what she had already said during the talk. "Better nutrition," she said,

> should help deal with the problem of constipation. Finicky, that goes along with general health. Asthma is affected by the immune system and air quality, so better nutrition and air filters for your home will help with that. . . . Dark circles under the eyes have to do with anemia, an iron deficiency. So you have to make sure your child is getting iron.

A mother interrupted her, "But you have to be careful with iron. Iron is very toxic for children." "That's right," said Susana, "children should not get too much iron, because it is very toxic for them. But you can give your children the basic child's vitamin with some iron in it, and they will be fine." She continued: "Leg aches are caused by calcium deficiency. You have to make sure you child is getting enough calcium through supplements."

A father interrupted: "What about having your child drink milk?" "Yes, milk can be a good source of calcium." Another mother: "But my child refuses to drink milk." Susana replied:

> Yes, not all children will drink milk, but calcium supplements are a good option. My son knows to take calcium supplements when he has a leg ache. He'll come to me and say, "Mommy, I need a calcium, my leg hurts." Last time I gave it to him, he told me that the pill had only filled up one leg with calcium and that he needed another to fill up the other leg. [*Laughter*]

A father continued the end-of-session questions: "What about drinking the tap water? Is it safe to drink?" "Well, the EPA says it's fine, but the city simply cannot afford a water filter that can take out all of the impurities. I would recommend an NSF-certified water filter." One of the earlier mothers got specific: "What about [*Brand A*]?" "Well, [*Brand A*] only gets the large particles out, but does not get the really small stuff, so I would recommend [*Brand B*], which is much better at filtering the small stuff." There were more specific questions, on issues such as air filters. Susana described a particular type of filter and informed the group that she markets one for her company. A few questions were very specific, so she asked respondents to provide their contact information for an appointment. By the end, about four of them had done so.

It is not difficult to understand the benefit of acquiring information through such sessions. By assembling parents with collective and targeted problems, they provided external entities an opportunity to reach an audience—or, as in Susana's case, a potential clientele—while providing parents concrete information on problems affecting their or their household's well-being. By mobilizing these organizational ties, centers provided access to a type of social capital.

Informational Sessions Not Uncommon

Holding pointed informational sessions was not unique to the Fun Times Center. In our survey of centers in the city, 84% of centers had held either informational sessions or workshops (more on these below) at least once during the previous 12 months. As shown in table 6.3, the sessions covered many topics.

Table 6.3 both confirms ordinary expectations and introduces some surprises. Child health and nutrition were, as would be expected, the most covered topics. And nearly one-third of centers addressed, as Destino's had, how to enroll children in elementary school. But almost half of all centers covered drugs or drug abuse (among parents), and more than 40% covered health issues directly related to parents. More surprising, more

Table 6.3. Topics covered, among centers that held meetings or workshops in previous 12 months (84% of total)

Topic	Percentage of centers covering topic
Child health issues	79%
Child nutrition	74%
Drugs or drug abuse	48%
Parent health issues	44%
Domestic or spousal abuse	39%
Employment opportunities for parents	35%
Housing issues	31%
Getting children into elementary school	31%
Government programs, such as Temporary Assistance for Needy Families	29%
Legal aid	25%
Any other topic not asked about	83%

Source: Childcare Centers and Families Survey. $n=293$ centers.

than one-third of centers discussed employment opportunities for parents, an issue hardly ever thought of as part of the domain of childcare centers. Nearly one-third covered housing and dealing with governmental programs such as Temporary Assistance for Needy Families, and a full one-quarter of all centers covered legal aid issues at informational centers or workshops. The variety of topics covered reflects the fact that centers interact with organizations in multiple fields, not just childcare, such as the fields of education, health, and community development.

Not all parents attended such meetings, and the high percentages in table 6.3 may mean little for the average mother if only a small fraction of mothers in any given center attend regularly. To examine the percentage that did, I turn to the national Fragile Families survey, which asked mothers whether they had attended such meetings. Table 6.4 presents the results. A high percentage of urban mothers with children in childcare centers have attended meetings in centers on several topics. Nutrition and health, child rearing and discipline, and educational issues were the most covered topics, with more than 50% of urban mothers attending an informational session on each of these topics. Almost a quarter of all mothers in childcare centers attended informational meetings on job finding and job training. Eleven percent attended meetings on legal issues. In all, more than 50% of all mothers formally acquired information from other sources through their centers. As an institution at the intersection of multiple organizational fields, the childcare

Table 6.4. Percentages of urban mothers with children in childcare centers who attended informational meetings

Topic	Percentage who ever attended
Nutrition and health	55%
Educational issues	54%
Child rearing, including discipline	52%
Finding jobs or job training	24%
Legal issues, including legal aid	11%
A topic not specifically asked about	18%

Source: Fragile Families survey. Figures weighted.

center was an informational crossroads for issues related and unrelated to childcare but always pertinent to the mothers and fathers of young children.

Assessing how much such clusters of information affected the lives of mothers, their families, or their children is a difficult task. If Destino's child was accepted at the best school because of a strategy that had not occurred to her, such as writing an especially provocative application letter or prepping her son strategically on the admissions exams, then the value of having acquired information on this strategy is immeasurable. But not all information mothers acquired would have such a dramatic impact, nor would all of it be categorized so easily as immensely valuable. As I discuss later, the value of a given cluster of information is best considered as a function of both its content and the circumstances of the mother. For example, centers brokered information on the best types of sugar to feed a toddler; on the fact that New York eviction laws protect tenants from abusive landlords; and on the illegality of common types of physical punishment. For some mothers, such information will be obvious or irrelevant. For the mother who had been feeding her child too much soda, or the one two months behind on rent, or the one unwilling to "spare the rod," acquiring these clusters of information may well help avoid major catastrophe or hardship, or significantly improve their well-being.

HOW MOTHERS ACQUIRED SERVICES

Many of the resources parents acquired were free or discounted services for which they would normally have to pay. As shown in table 6.2, several of the services involved child-related issues, such a free health examinations, dental exams, and speech therapy or other cognitive development screening. Many were oriented to adults, such as such as free or low-cost health exams and vision screening, domestic abuse counseling, assistance in dealing with landlords, temporary relocation apartments for women leaving abusive spouses, HIV/AIDS testing and treatment, adult literacy and English-as-second-language training, work training, and assistance in dealing with the school system and other government bureaucracies.[18] Centers brokered these resources in two ways, by formally *referring* parents to external organizations and by *collaborating* with the organizations to provide access to them.

Acquiring Services through Referrals

Formal referrals—to clinics, specialists, therapists, and experts of various kinds—were ubiquitous. The Childcare Centers survey asked directors whether, at least once during the previous 12 months, they had referred parents to another organization for one of six different reasons.[19] Table 6.5 displays the results. Almost 80% of centers had referred parents to another organization at least once to address a child's learning disability, which is high but not surprising, given the heightened awareness to learning disabilities and early prevention in the profession and the media. More than a quarter of all centers had referred parents in the previous year to another organization to receive mental health services, and 18% had referred parents, mostly mothers, to another organization for domestic abuse issues. About one in six had referred parents for legal advice, and a similar number for immigration-related services. A smaller number had referred parents for drug abuse or addiction services.

Table 6.5. Percentage of centers referring parents to another organization at least once in previous 12 months, by type of referral

Reason for referral	Percentage of centers
Children's learning disabilities	79.0%
Mental health services for parents	26.8%
Spousal abuse	17.9%
Legal advice	16.2%
Immigration services	15.6%
Drug abuse/addiction for parents	7.8%

Source: Childcare Centers and Families Survey. $n=293$ centers.

Acquiring Services through Collaborative Workshops

Centers also collaborated with organizations by arranging for workshops to be held at the center. These workshops provided direct services such as stress reduction, soft-skills training, and yoga. A workshop held at the Painted Masks Daycare elucidates the mixture of formal and informal elements that constituted the workshops, and the type of impact they were likely to have on well-being.

The Painted Masks Daycare was a government-funded center operated by nonprofit organization and located in a high-poverty, predominantly black neighborhood in the city. The center was on a street of nineteenth-century three-story brownstones and brick townhouses, some deteriorating, some well-kept, that had not yet seen the wave of gentrification that in the early 2000s swept many New York City neighborhoods with prewar architecture. The brick house directly across from the center was abandoned, boarded-up, and fire-burnt black. The townhouse where Painted Masks was located had been stuccoed over and painted off-white, and had a sheet-metal door, with buzzer, installed at the front entrance. In the front lobby, the main bulletin-board posted photos and descriptions of "Famous African Americans," along with children's art and photos of center staff, directors, teachers, and parents. The workshop was held in one of the children's rooms, and it was billed as an exercise in managing stress. The speaker, Bertha, was an African-American, thirty-year-old social worker who worked for the city and was assigned to the center. Bertha arranged the 13 parents, almost all of them black and four of them men, into a semicircle in one of the children's classrooms. Before beginning, she said, "But before we start I want to ask all of you dads to move up! "I don't know why all the dads are at the back." Without skipping a beat, one of the men responded, "Because the food is back here!" Everyone laughed. My research assistant took notes.

Bertha began with a brainstorm. She had taped onto the wall a large white poster with three terms at the top, "Definition of Stress," "Signs of Stress," and "Causes of Stress." She began by asking attendees how they would define stress, particularly, what they see as signs of stress. The answers poured in quickly: "aggravation," "anxiety," "weight loss"—someone quickly added, "or weight *gain*," which prompted another round of laughter—"fatigue," "sleep-lessness." Someone added, "you look nervous." Satisfied, Bertha moved on to ask the group about the causes of stress: "financial," "job," "your children," "family," "illness," "your spouse," "if someone passes away in your family," "planning a wedding." Bertha put the two together: "Even though we might not think that getting married and someone passing away have a lot in common, those are both life changes, right?" She then wrote "life changes" on the poster. She added, "I know someone said 'financial causes of stress'— what about poverty?" Several parents nodded.

Bertha then asked parents to turn to the first information packet she had prepared. It was titled "Self Monitoring," and the second page listed an "Activity Schedule," containing one-hour slots from 8:00 A.M. to 10:00 P.M. on which she asked parents to report what they had done for the current day. She gave them a several minutes, then asked if anyone would like to read what they had written. One mother volunteered to share her daily routine: From 6:30 A.M. to 8:00 A.M. she prepared her two children for the day. By 8:30 A.M., the children were at Painted Masks; by 10:00 A.M., she was at work; at 5:00 P.M. she left work. After that, she retrieved her children from the center, returned home, ironed clothes, and got them into bed, so she could study, from 10 P.M. until midnight, for a class she was taking. Other parents related their stories.

Bertha began connecting the dots. Most parents who had spoken, she confirmed, were sleeping between five and six hours a night. She then asked if things had been different before they had children, at which point the room erupted, such that Bertha had a difficult time writing all of it down. One mother said, "Before you have kids, maybe you have to clean the house once a week. Now I have to clean it once a day." Another mother explained: "You have to cook dinner even if you don't feel like it—you can't order out." Another mother complained that she did not have as much time with her partner. One of the fathers reported that he was always "losing sleep: I like to sleep until noon every day, and I can't do that anymore." (More laughter.) Another mother, agreeing, reported she could no longer sleep if her children were not home. Several parents nodded, and small conversations spread throughout the room.

Bertha then turned to the question of emotions. She asked participants to examine the portion of the packet called an "Emotions Thermometer," which contained a picture of a thermometer with lines to its right, and numbers from coldest ("Feeling Bad") to hottest ("Feeling Good"). She asked them to write what made them feel the worst. She provided an example: "If someone shoved you on the train this morning on your way to work and that made you feel really angry, then put that down next to the number one." After people were finished, she asked them to write what made them feel best, and then to report to the group. One mother reported, "I got to work early today," smiling. A father: "This is my first time at the meeting today and that made me happy." Others approved. Another father: "Hearing my girlfriend say 'I love you' this morning." (This was greeted with the expected "awws" throughout the room.) Bertha then asked what made them feel worst. Another father, who wore a red and blue basketball jersey and sported several tattoos, said: "Being woken up early this morning so I could drive my wife to work." (Laughter.)

By now the group was visibly relaxed. It was clear that this was as much an instructional workshop as a type of group therapy. Bertha provided a take-home package that included a "Mood Monitor," which parents could use to figure out how events that had taken place during the day tend to make people feel. She explained that it helps "take the stress off—help you realize the peaks and the lows." She then pointed to the section of the packet titled "What things or situations make you feel tense?" and asked parents to write a few things from the day that made them feel stressed. She provided an example of one parent running late and her daughter crying while she was being dropped off. "Do you recall feeling anxiety, aggravated, or experiencing the sign of any health problems?" Several parents nodded. "It takes a lot of concentration to go back and remember how you felt, right? What does someone look like when they're tense?" She then pointed to the list that people had made earlier, identifying the effects on weight gain and high blood pressure. Then she asked attendees to identify immediate signs of tensions. Answers poured in: "they bite their nails," "they sweat," "they frown," "they pace," "their face flushes."

Bertha began to end the session by providing a packet of activities that she believed were fun, inexpensive, good at reducing stress, and positive. She pointed to the "Increasing Pleasant Activities" list, but then asked everyone to turn to the next chart, called "Reward Menu," which was a type of reward system to ensure that parents kept up with the program. The idea was to list things they liked to do which they could do if they stuck to the plan. Bertha concluded with a simple relaxation exercise. She instructed the group to focus on a spot on the ceiling, get comfortable, close their eyes, and place one hand on their stomachs and another on their forehead. "Listen to your breathing, feel your stomach expand with each breath." She clicked off the lights, and quieted the room until it was dead silent; she waited. Several minutes later, Bertha asked everyone if they had noticed the slowing of their pulse. A few responded that this was exactly what they noticed. She turned on the lights and thanked everyone for participating, and parents slowly started off, peeling themselves off the chairs one after the other.

Services by Centers and by Other Organizations

Services such as the stress workshop described above were provided by the centers from two different sources: sometimes, the center collaborated with an *outside organization*, brokering the resource for the parent; other times, the center itself was part of a resource-rich organization with qualified staff to perform the service in house. While the former represents the consequence of a direct network process, a connection, the latter does not. The former is brokerage; the latter, participation in a rich organization. The survey of New York City centers sheds light on the difference. Table 6.6 identifies five services that centers offered parents and lists the

Table 6.6. Source of service, among centers providing service at least once in previous 12 months

	Center provided the service	Among these, service provided	
		By center	By external organization
Children's learning disability services	43.0%	44.4%	55.6%
Dental services for children	32.5%	8.6%	91.3%
Counseling for spousal abuse	22.2%	64.2%	35.8%
Services for child neglect/ abuse	22.0%	67.7%	32.3%
Physical health exams for children	8.5%	36.0%	64.0%
Other services not asked about	25.9%	57.1%	42.9%

Source: Childcare Centers and Families Survey. $n=293$ centers.

percentage of centers that provided each service at least once in the previous 12 months, and whether it was provided by the center itself or by an external organization. Centers were asked about services that, in our fieldwork, had been most prevalent; they were also asked if they provided any service the survey had not asked about.

As shown in table 6.6, the provision of services was by no means rare. More than a third of all centers provided learning disability and dental services for children, a fifth provided child neglect/abuse services and counseling for mothers experiencing domestic abuse, a little less than a tenth provided health exams for children, and more than a quarter provided another service not asked about. One of these services, dental exams for children, was almost always provided by an external organization. Among the rest of the services, either most centers or a large minority of them brokered a service provided by an external organization.

HOW MOTHERS ACQUIRED MATERIAL GOODS

Childcare centers also provided access to material goods, including cash substitutes, from other organizations. On occasion, this process operated as an institutionalized type of membership benefit that accrued to all childcare center patrons, in the same way that being a student in an accredited college can provide a person discounts for certain events. The process worked as a type of *validation* by which the center established its members as deserving of the resource. For example, one center, a predominantly black and Latino center in a high-poverty neighborhood in the city, was tied to the citywide "Cool Culture" organization, funded by large businesses throughout the city, that provided center patrons a pass that served as a cash substitute, granting admission (without charge or contribution) at more than 30 museums, botanical gardens, and zoos in New York City, including the Children's Museum, the Museo del Barrio, the Whitney Museum of American Art, and the Guggenheim Museum.[20] The Cool Culture program, targeting low-income families throughout the city, used this and other centers as access points.

On other occasions, relationships between the center and outside organizations were not institutionalized, but rather informal or ad hoc. For example, the director of Standing in Faith, a privately funded nonprofit center in a poor, predominantly black neighborhood, explained how such a relationship developed with a major New York department store: "[One of the company executives] would see our sign [as] he rode past here on the bus. And so he followed up on it and got his company to start helping us with our wish list.... Things that we would like to have." The center's "wish list," common among cash-strapped centers and schools throughout the city, was a listing of items, such as crayons and coloring books, which the center needed. The interviewer asked what resources they had received: "crayons and pencils, rugs for the rooms, valences . . . for the windows. Scholarships!" The department store had donated $9,000 from the proceeds of a sample sale to center parents, a welcome receipt among parents in this black high-poverty neighborhood. Finally, she explained, "they gave us computers, too, for some of the classes."

By and large, material goods from other organizations took the form of in-kind substitutes, such as admission discounts. In one of the most expensive cities in the world, such resources quickly added up. Consider how much a family of four could save through the Cool Culture program. Among the participating organizations were the Museum of Modern Art, the Guggenheim, the New York Botanical Garden, and the Children's Museum of Manhattan. At the time of this writing, their standard admission prices were, respectively, $20 per adult or child 16 and older (younger children free), $18 per adult or child 12 and older (younger children free), $18 per adult or child 5 and over (toddlers and infants free), and $9 per adult or child.

FOUR BROKERAGE MECHANISMS

As described throughout the present chapter, centers helped mothers acquire the information, services, and material goods of other organizations through four mechanisms: validation, storage, referral, and collaboration.

Validation was the process by which a center confirmed to an organization that a patron was deserving of a resource. When a household can enter a cultural event for free or take an elementary school's admission exam without fee, the center has, in fact, validated the household before an external organization. Once done, the benefits of membership were acquired instantly. Notice that while several brokerage processes were driven by directors, staff, or other actors in the center, the validation of the patron before other organizations was largely produced institutionally. *Storage* was the form of brokerage whereby the center stockpiled a resource for access by patrons as sought or needed. When a mother, while waiting to retrieve a child, read a notice on the lobby's bulletin board on pro bono legal representation for tenants facing landlord disputes, she was taking advantage of the fact that centers, as formal organizations, can disseminate information passively and conspicuously, that they can serve as information warehouses. Storage is made possible by the fact that centers are physical spaces with tables, walls, posters, newsletters, lobbies, common rooms, bathrooms, and waiting areas on which to display resources. *Referral* was the process by which the center formally referred its patron to another organization. Childcare centers held semipermanent arrangements with multiple resource providers through which the providers received clients and center parents received a discount or free services (see chapter 7). Such exchange of resources, as resource-dependence theory has argued, is an important way for organizations such as centers to manage their environments.[21] *Collaboration* was the process by which centers cooperate with others to provide access to goods. When a center scheduled a meeting and arranged a room for a stress expert to present a workshop before the parents, it did more than mere referring; it collaborated in the provision of the resource, providing logistical support for the externally provided good. This was clearly the costliest of all mechanisms for brokering resources; it was also the most likely to be seen in the nonprofit sector (see chapter 7).

An important observation is in order. Through the commonly employed distinction between "access to" and "mobilization of" social capital, researchers have identified two different questions: whether people are connected to others who possess valuable resources, and whether people *use* their connections to acquire such goods. The distinction proves its worth to the extent that it forces us to ask when and how people are willing or able to employ their connections for their benefit. But the mechanisms we have identified introduce a different set of circumstances. In organizational contexts, connections may be mobilized by *others*, and predictably so, for one's benefit. The parents did not personally mobilize a connection to Bertha to request her stress-related resources; in fact, they did not know her. The connection was mobilized by the center.

These mechanisms identify *how* centers brokered access to resources; chapter 7 explains *why*. The remainder of the present chapter focuses on mothers, examining the conditions under which a mother's ability to acquire resources through these organizational ties represented a concrete benefit.

FOR WHOM THIS FORM OF BROKERAGE MATTERED

Preexisting Resources

A mother enrolling her child in a center today is not simply acquiring a babysitter, or even just a new place to make friends; more often than not, she is enrolling in a complex broker of information, services, and material goods from organizations in the fields of childcare, health care, education, community development, and culture. Not all childcare centers we observed were equally well connected, but the best-connected among them represented a rich resource base for the acquisition of large and small resources likely to have powerful consequences for well-being. Whether the center's capabilities did help a mother depended on her circumstances; in fact, what improved the well-being of some was little more than a convenience for others.

Among our interviewees, much depended on their preexisting *resource wealth*—not necessarily their wealth or income but, more important, the repertoire of resources they already possessed from friends, family, or other sources. This is clear when we compare how Frances and Katherine, described in chapter 3 and 4, considered the resources available at their center, Little Friends Day Care. Both mothers were financially successful, self-described networkers who used all social ties at their disposal to solve everyday problems. Katherine was a New Englander who made a successful living as an independent consultant for small businesses. While she had benefited greatly from the social ties available at her center, the organizational ties, or any resources acquired through formal channels, were of little consequence. Katherine needed neither the free services (she could afford her own) nor the information (she could easily mobilize her information-rich networks): "I don't really consider [the center] a resource for services. I found my pediatrician through friends, I found . . . other doctors through the pediatrician. There are other resources, really."

Frances, however, found a particularly important piece of information through her center. A white American lawyer with a Russian husband, Frances was raising her son in a bilingual household. As we saw in chapter 3, Frances, in part because of the hours during which she dropped off her son, had not met many of the center's parents. Frances had a problem with her son:

He was approaching two years old and he still wasn't talking.... [At] that time we were living in [another neighborhood] and there were a lot of playgrounds there. And my husband was good friends with a lot of the other people in there. He's Russian and there were a lot of Russians in that community, and they were out there with their children and they were talking and apparently a lot of the children—I don't know if it was because they're [in] bilingual household[s]—have speech delays.

As a result, she soon discovered she needed to locate a speech therapist who could see her son several times a week, beginning immediately, and in the childcare center, since he was there most of the time. The center was connected to a slew of organizations providing multiple types of developmental and early intervention services. As Toni, the director, explained, "We refer [parents] for speech therapy, physical therapy, sometimes it's a hearing issue, or an emotional disorder. Basically, we refer for the whole panoply of early intervention services. [In fact], there is also occupational therapy." To make her point, Toni then named five private and public organizations to which the center had referred parents. Consequently, when Frances approached Toni, as Frances explained, "she... had the name of a speech therapist who was located in the... area so it would be very convenient for her to see him at the school. So, the... speech therapist [my son] has is actually the one that we got the recommendation from Toni for."

Frances's situation highlights the importance of distinguishing wealth in finances from wealth in resources, especially given that the latter is conditional on the circumstances of the mother. Resources, in a sense, are compartmentally relevant and problem specific; information on the kindergarten admission process is irrelevant to an aging grandfather, but critical to a low-income mother. The domain specificity of centers works as much to shape the resources available through organizational ties as it did the support available through social ties. The gains Frances acquired from her center derived from the fact that centers, as brokers of resources related to children (and to health, education, community development, and culture), are small bundles of solutions searching for child-related problems to solve. Because of the intersection of organizational networks at which it lies, the center is, under many circumstances, a combination of concierge, telephone operator, and emergency service line—always with a specialty toward the problems the parent of a young child is expected to experience.

Nevertheless, the difference between finance wealth and resource wealth can be pushed too far. The former, in the end, is often exchangeable for the latter, and richer mothers can be expected, all factors held constant, to need such organizational brokerage less. While the life of a mother such as Frances is certainly more convenient due to the newfound availability of formal organizational networks, it is questionable whether, in the long run, she experiences significantly less hardship. Most likely, the finance rich, also likely to be resource rich, will gain comparatively less from this type of brokerage. In fact, this would help explain why, as described in chapter 2, while all mothers benefited from making informal social ties in centers, only low-income mothers experienced less material hardship even when they did not make informal social ties. For low-income mothers, organizational ties could yield much, just as they did for Destino, described above.

Agency

The discussion in this chapter assumes that mothers have the agency and self-efficacy to pursue a resource if they need it—that their actions, in large measure, are purposive. Frances needed a therapist and therefore approached her director to request a referral; Destino needed information and therefore asked the expert to recommend a school. But actors differ in their ability and willingness to exercise agency to solve their problems, and some mothers with large and small problems fail, for whatever reason, to do something about them. An important characteristic of organizational brokerage is that some of the mechanisms by which centers broker resources—specifically, the operation of referrals and collaborative exchanges—do not require that parents purposely pursue the resource.

Nan Lin has referred to something related as the problem of *access* versus *mobilization*.[22] Having access to resources embedded in social networks, he argues, is not the same as mobilizing them. To mobilize social ties is to actively turn to them to improve one's conditions. Organizational brokerage introduces the possibility of acquiring resources while exercising little agency in the process.

Several conditions could produce this result. One follows from adopting the critique of rational choice theory that individuals are not always single-actor decision makers. Mothers, for example, often act in light of themselves and their children, such that what is rational to the mother depends, in part, on her assessment of what is rational for her child. In fact, her assessment of what is rational may extend beyond the mother—child pair to the household. One household problem is acquiring preventive services for a child with learning disabilities. From one perspective, a mother would have to know, as Frances did, that her child has a problem and to actively seek a solution. Many centers, however, had independent specialists screen children yearly at the site for potential learning disabilities. This process was institutionalized into center operations, such that parents acquired the screening services without having to ask for them. In Lin's language, they acquired the resource *without* mobilizing the tie, a process made possible because the center mobilized the tie for them.

A different version of this process took place among centers that instituted monthly or bimonthly parent meetings, each organized to provide access to a different resource. Centers commonly provided schooling information in this fashion. Lorraine, a white doctor in her thirties whose older child was enrolled in a center different from that of her younger one, explained that the former center did much more for parents:

> Yeah and they do a lot more. They have, I've already been to informational sessions about preschool...preschools. They...have testers come in [because] all the private schools need...IQ-type tests...and it's all done there. And they basically—it's kind of sick, but they—hold your hand through the application process as though you were a high school junior applying to college.... That director is very well connected and they have meetings and he knows about all these schools and which ones might fit your child's particular needs the best.

Whereas Destino and her husband organized the activity as she pursued an education for her child, Lorraine simply attended the regular parent meeting, where, as she explained, the center did much of the work for her.[23]

A DIFFERENT TYPE OF CONNECTION

Through their centers, mothers acquired an array of information, services, and material goods so broad that it helps explain why, as we saw in chapter 2, poor mothers in centers experienced greater well-being even if they did not develop social ties in centers. An actor's "connections" are often thought to be social, the type of informal relationship captured colloquially in phrases such as "personal support network" and "old boy network," the standard concern of social capital theory. We live, however, in a bureaucratic society, one in which everyday goods and information travel across formal ties often instituted to supersede the influence of any one individual, an important component of the organizational embeddedness of ties that has been ignored by social capital theory. And while these ties are no substitute for informal social ties, they nonetheless often provide resources that informal social ties do not; they prove especially beneficial to resource-poor mothers, to socially isolated mothers, and to those mothers who only have connections to others deprived of resources. Mothers so deprived have much to gain through organizational ties, provided they are connected to the right center, the one that is itself well connected. And which centers are well connected? Chapter 7 is devoted to this question.

7

Organizational Ties and Neighborhood Effects

How Mothers' Nonsocial Ties Were Affected by Location

Organizational connections confer distinct advantages.[1] For a mother with either few social ties or few ties to well-connected people, participating in the right center may mean acquiring tickets to cultural events, free health and dental exams, tips on successful school applications, pro bono tax advice, job information, domestic abuse support and counseling, and many other resources that might have been unavailable through her informal social networks. But which centers are likely to be well connected, to maintain ties to those organizations rich in valuable information, goods, and services? The present chapter briefly considers this question, shifting attention from the mother to the broader social and organizational milieu in which childcare centers operate.

Our inquiry will pay careful attention to the role of location, that is, of the neighborhood in which the center is situated. Neighborhoods seem to matter. In recent years, theorists of urban conditions have proposed that living in a high-poverty neighborhood lessens life chances and decreases well-being.[2] Poor neighborhoods are expected to exhibit a host of characteristics—including a scarcity of local resources—detrimental to a person's well-being. Neighborhood poverty may complicate a center's ability or inclination to broker organizational connections.

By considering the role of neighborhood poverty in the connectedness of centers, we address a larger question regarding this "neighborhood effects" proposition. Testing the proposition that neighborhood poverty lowers life chances has attracted the attention of urban researchers over the past 20 years, leading to numerous assessments based on surveys and field experiments. These tests have yielded mixed results.[3] Unfortunately, the tests have largely ignored whether participating in organizations such as childcare centers makes a difference. Yet consider the implications

of chapter 6, which described how organizational ties might produce substantial benefits for urban mothers. Depending on how organizational
ties are affected by neighborhood conditions, childcare centers may either
contribute to or buffer against the negative consequences of neighborhood
poverty. If centers, for whatever reason, tend to have *fewer* ties when
they are located in poor neighborhoods, then they would exacerbate the
inequality associated with neighborhood poverty. If centers tend to
have *more* ties in such neighborhoods, they would buffer against the expected negative consequences of neighborhood poverty. In the latter case,
that the negative effects of living in a poor area are offset by the goods
accessible through its local organizations would help explain the inconsistent
findings of the "neighborhood effect" tests, since some people in poor
neighborhoods would be tied to organizations such as childcare centers
and others would not. This chapter asks, then, whether childcare centers
in poor neighborhoods are likely to be better or worse connected than those
in non poor neighborhoods.

Neither answer represents a foregone conclusion. Many research traditions, informed by the Chicago School of urban sociology—a perspective
associated with Robert Park, Ernest Burgess, and others—conceive of cities
as ecological entities in which the distribution of resources across neighborhoods results from competition among groups.[4] Richer, more educated
groups can more effectively secure goods for themselves, resulting in neighborhoods with more and better connected organizations such as banks,
childcare centers, and churches. This perspective expects high-poverty
neighborhoods to be socially disorganized, which would mean that
social and organizational ties are weak and unable to consolidate or secure
resources effectively.[5] An alternative tradition, informed by a belief in the
importance of the political economy, argues that conditions in urban neighborhoods are shaped not merely by the groups living in them but also by
the state and the political actors, both local and external, that influence
all neighborhoods.[6] From this perspective, whether childcare centers or
other organizations in poor neighborhoods are likely to be worse connected
cannot be known without first knowing the role of the state and other
institutional actors.

An appropriate way to answer the question is to first ask why centers
provide access to these resources. In what follows, I rely on the qualitative
interviews with center directors and with key informants in a half dozen
state and nonprofit organizations to examine why centers formed and
sustained those organizational ties useful to mothers of young children.
Then, to assess whether these interviews are idiosyncratic or otherwise
unrepresentative, I test, based on Childcare Centers survey of centers in

New York City, whether these explanations accurately predict which centers—and centers in which neighborhoods—tend to have more organizational ties. The tests uncovered that centers in poor neighborhoods tend to be *better* connected than those in nonpoor neighborhoods, even after accounting for need. As a result, one would expect different conclusions about the consequences of living in a poor neighborhood when participation in a center is taken into account than when, as is often the case, participation in organizations such as centers is ignored. I begin by addressing the motivations behind the actions of directors.

WHY CENTERS BROKER RESOURCES

On first impressions, it is difficult to understand why centers would broker resources. Providing access to some of the resources discussed in chapter 6 requires time, effort, and other expenses on the part of the center. For example, in order to collaborate with a specialist to provide one workshop on stress relief, a director must contact the instructor, arrange a time, inform the parents, rearrange a classroom for use, retrieve adult-sized chairs from storage or offices and temporarily replace the classroom's toddler chairs, pay teachers and janitors overtime, cover the costs of electricity and heating for several extra hours, purchase snacks and drinks, and return everything to its proper location after the workshop is finished. Furthermore, it seems unlikely that parents would seriously complain if they were unable to access many of these resources through their childcare center, especially considering the limited supply of affordable center-based childcare in New York City. Most people, as we saw in chapter 2, enroll their children in childcare centers for the purpose of securing childcare (or preschooling), not because they are searching for information on nutrition, vouchers for elementary school exams, or free toys at Christmas, even if these things turn out to be useful. In short, it does not appear economically rational for centers to broker resources.

No single factor accounted for the motivations of directors to form and sustain organizational ties to resource-rich entities. Instead, directors and other local actors were motivated by multiple purposes, responding to both internal and external concerns. The pressures to follow the mandates of the state or other powerful actors and to follow professionally agreed-upon practices were paramount. The principal factors shaping the formation of these ties were (a) the state, (b) large nonprofit organizations, (c) professional norms, and, in fact, (d) neighborhood location.

The Role of Parents

Before proceeding, a qualification is in order. The four factors discussed below do not include the role of parents. This may present an inaccurate picture of mothers and fathers as passive recipients of the fruits of others—as targets rather than agents. Certainly, much of the drive behind center's brokerage of resources seemed to stem from external actors, but parents, once in centers, sometimes either directly or indirectly requested centers to mobilize their ties for the acquisition of resources. We saw in chapter 6, for example, that, when Frances needed a speech therapist for her son, it was not Toñi, the director, who first offered it, but Frances who approached Toñi requesting a referral.

Other times, a type of collaboration between centers' and parents' interests drove the acquisition of external resources. In these circumstances, even when the use of center networks to acquire information or services was institutionalized into the yearly operation of the center, it stemmed

---

Parent Workshops and Training

Please fill out the following questionnarie so we can better serve your needs.

Name _____   Telephone # _____
Child's name _____

Arts Classes   **Monthly Parenting Workshops**
     Beginners ___ Advanced ___   By [*Name of expert*] _____
Oil Painting Classes   **Sewing**
     Beginners ___ Advanced ___   **Six session course** ___
CPR Classes   Beginners ___ Advanced ___
     Six session course _____   **Flower Arrangement**
Haircutting Course   One session course ____
     Six session course _____
Computer Course
     Six session course _____   **Fruit and Vegetable Decorating**
Baking and Decorating   Three session course ____
     Three session course _____

Comments and suggestions _____
_____
_____

Figure 7.1. Handout at Family Focus Head Start.

from requests of parents. For example, every fall, new parents at the Family Focus Head Start center, in a predominantly white high-poverty neighborhood, received the form reproduced in figure 7.1 requesting information on the courses they would like to take. The list of "training workshops" had been institutionalized over the years, based on what parents frequently requested. As figure 7.1 shows, some of them involved the arts and crafts; others, basic skills training; and others, effective parenting. The discussion here of the role of external factors examines the wider conditions that not only made possible the resolution of such parent requests but also shaped centers' orientation toward brokerage even in the absence of these requests.

The Role of the State

One of the most important reasons centers brokered resources was state pressures to do so. The role of the state in the brokerage process should be understood in light of several factors. First, "the state" here is not a single, perfectly coupled entity; it is, rather, a shorthand for the federal, state, and city agencies playing some role in the regulation and operation of childcare centers. Previous chapters have already hinted at several of the agencies pertinent to the operation of childcare centers as brokers: New York City's Human Resources Administration (including its Department of Social Services and its Office of Employment Services), New York City's Administration for Children's Services (ACS), the New York State Department of Health, the federal Head Start Bureau, and the federal Department of Health and Human Services. Second, childcare centers exhibited many types of relationships to the state, responding to many types of state pressures. These included complying with licensing regulations; cooperating with non-childcare-related state agencies and programs, such as the Temporary Assistance for Needy Families Program; and following protocols to receive state funding. Third, consequently, not all relations to the state were equally important to understanding center's inclinations to connect parents to the resources of other organizations. Rather than attempt to unravel the endlessly complex knot of state–center relations, I focus on those relations central to centers' brokerage.

The most central form of relationship was one in which the center received operational funds from the state, particularly from the Head Start program. In New York City, most Head Start centers are not directly operated by the government. Instead, the federal government, through the administration of the local ACS, provides renewable grants to local community nonprofit organizations to establish Head Start centers. Among all the centers in our quantitative survey, 46% were government funded, and

20% were specifically Head Start. Many government-funded centers were required by the state to establish referral or collaborative ties.

The federal government specifically imposes many such requirements on Head Start centers. Head Start was formed as part of a model through which childcare was combined with education and services to the family, under the idea that it was difficult to educate a child if the household was facing hardship or disarray.[7] Consequently, Head Start centers were expected to do much more than provide childcare, a philosophy that, despite the transformations the Head Start program has experienced over four decades, continues to this day.[8] For example, Head Start centers are explicitly required to determine whether "each child has an ongoing source of continuous, accessible health care."[9] If not, the center must help the parent find care. In addition, the center, working with the parent, is required to screen children to assess "developmental, sensory (visual and auditory), behavioral, motor, language, social, cognitive, perceptual, and emotional skills."[10] Despite these requirements, the government does not provide extensive funds for these resources; instead, it expects that, to provide these resources, centers "take affirmative steps to establish ongoing collaborative relationships with community organizations," such as the following:

- Health care providers, such as clinics, physicians, dentists, and other health professionals
- Mental health providers
- Nutritional service providers
- Individuals and agencies that provide services to children with disabilities and their families
- Local elementary schools and other educational and cultural institutions, such as libraries and museums, for both children and families
- Any other organizations and businesses that may provide support and resources to families[11]

Accordingly, several directors in our Head Start centers reported that they formed ties to schools, health providers, and community organizations because they were mandated to do so.

Centers funded not by federal but by city funds followed the lead of Head Start. In New York City, the ACS oversees the Head Start program but also funds its own childcare centers from the city treasury. In recent years, the ACS has experienced a consolidation, by which Head Start ACS grantees are increasingly subject to the same bureaucratic structure and rules. In our observations, ACS centers, like Head Start centers, seemed to be especially likely to form these organizational ties.

The Role of Powerful Nonprofit Organizations

Pressures to form organizational ties derived not only from state authority but also from organizations in the city's large and powerful nonprofit sector. Several authors have argued that many of the roles and functions once performed by the state have, in recent decades, been increasingly adopted by not-for-profit organizations, either of their own accord or under state-funded contracting arrangements.[12] This trend reflects, among other things, a decline in the availability of federal funds for social services.[13] Our interviews with heads of large nonprofit organizations suggested that this retrenchment had contributed to the formation of ties between these organizations and centers.[14]

One way large nonprofit organizations affected the ties of centers was as citywide, higher order brokers of resources in the face of declining funds. One of our informants, Robert, was a tall, politically savvy Jewish organizer who had spent decades as the director of Kids Are the Future, one of the largest nonprofit organizations in the city.[15] He explained the current predicament: "[Today] there is no money in day care centers for health or mental health.... Head Start eliminated years ago from the federal level any substantial amount of money for [these services], and greatly cut back on three categories of staff—social worker, family assistant, and family worker—that were once part of the Head Start machinery." He explained to me that nonprofit organizations such as his "have compensated for those limitations" by collaborating with businesses and other organizations that provide or sell resources. For large organizations intending to distribute various resources, forming organizational ties was a way to cut costs. As Alexander, a high-level officer currently at the same organization, explained to me, his organization collaborates with others,

> because in our communities we have an adult service, we have day care, we have public school, and we [often] have them in isolation one from the other. So, an effort that really created enough financial capital to improve the interconnectedness of the social system ... would make much more efficient use of existing dollars. It still requires some new dollars, but it would make much more efficient use of existing dollars.

Kids Are the Future had an annual operating budget of more than $60 million, which allowed it to yield great influence over the activities of child-care centers.

Another mechanism through which large nonprofit organizations played a role in brokerage was by running their own centers, which would form part of a network of sister organizations providing different resources, all ultimately governed by a main office. La Familia was a large Latino organization in New York City with a staff of 400 whose main office was located in a high-poverty predominantly Latino neighborhood. In addition to running its own childcare center several blocks south of the main office, it administered the Clínica Popular, a mental health center, also in the neighborhood, staffed by psychiatrists and therapists; the Fuerza Family Center, which organized popular workshops on stitching, sewing, cooking, and other crafts; the Futuro Youth Leadership Group, housed in the basement of local school, which established an afterschool program; the Back on Track Center for women with drug problems and under rehabilitation (it was also skills based: women were taught crafts focused on sellable Latino folk art); and the Positive Health Program, which provided free HIV/AIDS 30-minute tests, free condoms, and HIV/AIDS counseling and education. Because all of these organizations were funded through La Familia, they were part of the same network, and parents in the childcare center gained information about and access to the resources of the sister organizations. The director of the center estimated that 30% of the parents in the center had some connection to another organization in the agency at large.

The Role of Professional Norms

Childcare centers do not run themselves; they are run by directors, teachers, and other staff whose actions are guided by personal beliefs and professional norms. Many of the directors and other professionals we interviewed, whether in centers or in larger organizations, subscribed to certain norms relevant to our question. These norms were, specifically, (a) a "holistic" approach to childcare, expressed in the idea that one cannot care for a child without caring for the family (as Alexander explained, "we're always aware of the family, and we're always conscious of what we need to do for the family as the unit of service, even though most of our direction may be toward children"), and (b) a firm belief in expertise and specialization, expressed in the idea that a staff member should not perform a role for which she or he is not qualified.

The dual mantra of holistic provision and specialization was ubiquitous. In fact, it was so pervasive that it seemed obvious to our informants. During one of her visits to the Kids' Place Preschool in a low-income neighborhood, a research assistant wrote: "[According to the director,] the center also refers [parents] for domestic violence issues. They work with 'Victim's Services,' which has a domestic violence program. I asked why the center does this. [The director] made a face that told me he thought it was an obvious question. 'Because there's domestic violence,' he said." Another director at a privately funded center expressed a version of the same sentiment when asked why the center held informational meetings for parents: "For information purposes. To help parents decide . . . what's best for their children." And later: "You know, it's just something we do. All the private schools do this at some time or another . . . either in the form of parent meetings or workshops or seminars." (As described below, public ones do, as well.)

Directors of centers often met with other organizations in the childcare field, to address common problems and exchange ideas about providing childcare. These meetings seemed to cement a collective orientation toward collaboration. A director at a private nonprofit center in a predominantly black low-income neighborhood explained how she found out about the free auditory, visual, and dental screenings available for children from the Board of Education:

> I used to be the director of the YMCA, [and] these are things that came throughout my office then so [I asked myself], Why not [have them] come to the office here? Also the other schools I worked at up at Westchester County—these were also services that were provided in the Westchester County area, . . . and they're free, so why should that not be provided here in [this] district.

This sentiment was consistent with the professional social service literature, which in recent years has called for greater interorganizational collaboration among service providers.[16]

The ethos extended from center directors to the directors of large organizations. Kaitlin, a white officer in her fifties at the city homeless agency, explained a pilot project by which a small nonprofit organization would "bring multiple agencies together at the local level in the event there are at least three government agencies involved in a household's life." I asked her to elaborate:

> [S]o, if there's a . . . brother getting out of jail, a child who's at risk of dropping out of school . . . and the mom is just getting referred to child welfare . . . the brother's about to come back, that's gonna screw up the household. The kid's already acting out and the mother is having all this stress and then suddenly she has to defend herself to child welfare. The goal is that . . . the public agencies [will] come together to see the family holistically and then develop plans that are gonna support the family in the best way. So the probation officer, the child welfare specialist, the education guidance counselor, all [are] working together about how to bring resources that solve the problem.

She explained that an international nonprofit funder "buys into this argument [and] gives us money to fund a program, as [have] a number of other foundations."[17] There were versions of this belief—in a holistic approach and in professional specialization—in centers of all types, regardless of sector or profit status.

The prevalence of such norms suggests that, along with loose coupling at the center level, there was strong coupling at the field level. The idea of coupling refers generally to the extent to which the interests or orientations of actors are independent or oriented toward the same end.[18] Childcare centers were loosely coupled entities to the extent that multiple actors within them—directors, teachers, staff, parents, and boards—pursued multiple interests, not merely childcare. But among the organizations in the health, education, community development, and childcare fields in which centers operated, there was a common orientation toward holistic and collaborative exchange of resources.

The Role of the Neighborhood

In an environment in which practitioners in and outside centers believed in the provision of resources through ties, and in which external actors such as the state, large businesses, and large nonprofit organizations had vested interests in redistributing resources toward the poor, the perceived poverty of the neighborhood seemed to play an important symbolic role. Businesses, large nonprofit organizations, and the state all used the neighborhood as a signal for the characteristics of the populations to which they sought to sell or distribute resources.

Kyle, a restrained black male in his early forties, was an officer in the part of city's education bureaucracy that addressed community affairs. Among other tasks, his office coordinated the relationship between schools and either businesses or nonprofit entities, to match the needs of the former to the offerings of the latter. That is, his office was a type of higher order broker that coordinated relationships among organizations themselves. As part of the process, he explained to me, the city instituted in many schools a "parent coordinator," a person whose job was, among other things, to identify what parents needed and to broker relations to organizations that could provide needed services. He provided an example:

> Around tax time, for example . . . you have a number of our parents who are eligible for earned income credit, but a number of them don't apply for it . . . [because they don't know about it]. So, we have a number of nonprofits who fill it out, who help on a pro bono basis filling out income taxes. And they work with [the] parent coordinators [in our schools] to inform parents that (a) you may be eligible for earned income credit, depending on your income; and [(b)] if you need a tax preparer, we can provide you that service free of charge. So, you have cases where parent coordinators have nights where parents come into the schools and you have these tax preparers in the school helping parents fill out their tax returns.

Kyle, through his position, turns schools into brokers for parents and families.

The city and the nonprofit organizations, however, must decide where to send their volunteers. Not surprisingly, they seek to provide the service where it is most needed. Nevertheless, this need was not determined by the income level of the parents in the schools—it was determined by conditions of the neighborhood.

To understand the implications of this difference, consider the two options at Kyle's disposal. He could obtain a list, from another colleague on his floor in the education department, of all schools in the city sorted by some indicator of need, such as the percentage of students eligible for a free lunch. Then, around tax time, he could send the tax preparers to the poorest school on the list. Or he could assess which was the poorest neighborhood in the city and send the preparer to any school located there.

Kyle did the latter, except he did not figure out which were the poorest neighborhoods; he just sent the preparer to a school in a neighborhood "known" to be "in need." Kyle explained that most actors in his networks agreed that interorganizational coordination of this sort should focus on poor neighborhoods. As he explained to me:

> And, again, we know where the areas . . . are [in which this is] happening. If you had to ask me what are the five areas where this is happening, where there's the greatest need: Harlem, Washington Heights . . . South Bronx, central Brooklyn, southeast Queens. . . . [T]hose are the five areas where . . . we have the most problematic schools, most challenging schools, where our kids are generally under-performing and also. . . . Seventy to 75%, I believe, of the prison rate of the State of New York [comes from] those five Zip codes.

That is to say, when he came across businesses or large nonprofit organizations seeking to provide a good, service, or other resource, his office directed them to schools located in the poorest neighborhoods.

Kaitlin made a similar observation when I asked her to elaborate on a new homelessness prevention program being piloted: "They've been in place for a year and they're in six of the [city's] 59 community districts. But the six districts that they're in are among the fifteen highest need districts in terms of homeless demand for shelter among families."

Why does this matter? The two strategies Kyle could have pursued appear to have the same result, but this is not the case; in fact, his adopted strategy reveals an important aspect of how resources travel across organizational ties. In the strategy based on the need in the neighborhood, rather than in the organization, those centers with great need but unfortunate enough to be located in a low-need neighborhood are likely to be missed. A childcare center serving the immigrant children of service workers in an affluent neighborhood would be unlikely to be targeted. Conversely, a low-need center in a high-need area, such as one caring for the children of gentrifiers in a historically poor neighborhood, may reap unnecessary gains. The neighborhood-based strategy reveals that, for access to certain resources, a poor actor may find it easier to be targeted if he or she is connected to an organization in a poor neighborhood, given the place-based orientations of high-level brokers of organizational ties.

A TEST

Our review of the factors playing a role in the organizational ties that would matter to center mothers has been schematic—an attempt not to understand the entire constellation of actors, organizations, and conditions shaping how centers in New York City function but to pinpoint the factors likely to affect which centers are well connected. Our interviews suggested that much depends on the state, the nonprofit sector, the norms of both internal and external actors, and the poverty level of the neighborhood in which it is located. To test whether these factors do matter, I turn to the quantitative survey of centers in New York City.

To obtain useful data on the outcome variable, I had to impose some constraints on the survey questions. A telephone survey would not produce reliable answers by asking a director, "How many organizational ties do you have that carry resources conducive to the well-being of your patrons?" There would be several problems with this question, including that the word "resources" means too many different things to different people, and that directors may not understand the meaning of "organizational tie." Instead, my research assistants and I pursued two strategies. From pilot work, we knew that centers connected parents to other organizations through several processes, two of which were concrete tasks a director could recall—explicitly referring parents to the organizations and collaborating with the organizations to provide the resource in house. It was also clear that directors had a better idea of what interviewers were talking about when they had examples.

Therefore, we focused on referrals ties and collaborative ties. For referrals, the survey asked directors whether over the previous twelve months they had formally referred any parents to other organizations for six specific resources we had observed in the fieldwork, making sure to include resources targeted at parents. For collaborative ties, the survey asked directors whether over the previous 12 months they had provided one of five resources. As a validity check, the survey also asked if the center had provided any other resource not asked about. (All analyses and figures presented in this chapter refer to services provided by external organizations, not those provided by the center.) The result was two outcome variables, indicating the number of referral ties (0 to 6) and the number of collaborative ties (0 to 6).[19]

Table 7.1 presents the number of referrals and services from other organizations transferred by centers. This section examines how state, non-profit, and neighborhood factors are associated with the number of resource-providing organizations to which the center is connected.

First, the qualitative work suggested that centers dependent on state funds would exhibit more connections, because the state often required funded centers to broker resources. While researchers have uncovered that organizations often ignore or distort state mandates to serve their needs, we witnessed a clear tendency among centers to conform to state pressures.[20] The qualitative work also suggested that privately funded nonprofit centers might be subject to similar external pressures from large or powerful nonprofit organizations, such as Kids Are the Future. In addition, if these institutional pressures are important, we expect them to be greatest where market-derived demands such as the need for profits are weakest, which suggests that state-funded and privately funded nonprofit centers should have more active organizational ties than do for-profit centers.[21] Second, professional norms seemed to be important. Center staff members found ways of locating outside resources even when, as in the case of "Victim Services," it was neither required nor profitable, because it appeared to be a need among center patrons. Therefore, not merely the sector but also

Table 7.1. Percentage of centers with active ties, by type

Formal referral ties	%	Collaborative ties	%
Children's learning disabilities	79.0%	Dental services for children	29.8%
Mental health services for parents	26.8%	Children's learning disability services	24.6%
Spousal abuse	17.9%	Counseling for spousal abuse	8.1%
Legal advice	16.2%	Services for child neglect/abuse	6.8%
Immigration services	15.6%	Physical health exams for children	5.2%
Drug abuse/addiction for parents	7.8%	Other services not asked about	10.9%
Average number of referral ties	1.6	*Average number of service ties*	0.8

Source: Childcare Centers and Families Survey. $n=293$. Active ties are those activiated at least once over the previous 12 months.

the level of need among patrons should make a difference. Finally, the interviews suggested that location mattered. If many resource providers are using the neighborhood, not the center, to assess need, then, after accounting for center need, those centers in high-poverty neighborhoods should still exhibit more referral and collaborative ties. In this respect, our expectations would differ from both a simple demand model (which would expect more resources in high-demand centers, regardless of location) and the deinstitutionalization model (which would expect fewer resources in high-poverty neighborhoods).

To determine the impact of these factors, I estimated the number of active ties, separately for referral ties and collaborative ties, as a function of several predictors. Two of them were especially notable: whether the center was located in a poor neighborhood, and whether it served children likely to be in need. The measure of high-poverty neighborhood as an indicator variable was coded 1 if the center was located in a neighborhood at least 40% poor, the standard yardstick for high-poverty status in studies of urban poverty.[22] This indicator matched the many of the tracts in the poor neighborhoods (e.g., upper Manhattan and central Brooklyn) that actors such as Kyle perceived to be those with the "greatest need." The proxy for need in the center as an indicator variable was coded 1 if at least 30% of the children in the center were on government vouchers or some type of government subsidy (regardless of the center's location).[23] Thirty-nine percent of centers fell in this category. The models controlled for a number of other neighborhood characteristics.[24] Additional details behind the survey are given in appendix B.

Table 7.2 presents the percent increase in number of expected ties associated with each variable, after adjustment. (For Poisson regression coefficients and standard errors see appendix B, table B.8.) Government-

Table 7.2. Percent increase in number of active ties associated with sector, need, and location

Variables	Referral ties	Collaborative ties
Center		
Government non-profit	49%**	220%**
Private non-profit	50%**	55%
Center has high proportion of poor children	53%**	24%
Center located in a high-poverty neighborhood	28%**	44%**

Exponentiated Poisson regression coefficients. Models control for neighborhood percent black, percent white, and percent Latino; residential instability, population density, and borough. Full models are given in appendix B.
*p <.05   **p <.01

funded centers had 49% more referral ties and 220% more collaborative ties than did for-profit centers, consistent with expectations. Private non-profit centers had 50% more referral ties of than did for-profit centers. They also had more collaborative ties, but this association was not statistically significant.

Although the centers' primary funding sources and sectors mattered, so did their expected amount of need. Centers in which at least 30% of the children were poor had 53% more referral ties, as is expected, since their needs for organizational ties are likely greater. Surprisingly, however, the effect of center need on collaborative ties was not statistically indistin-guishable from zero. It seems likely that the costlier, collaborative ties require strong influence or mandates and support from the state.

Table 7.2 also indicates the impact of location. Net of the poverty level of the center, centers located in high-poverty neighborhoods had 28% more referral ties and 44% more collaborative ties than did centers located elsewhere. These findings suggest that the sentiments of Kaitlin and Kyle, by which resource providers look for centers in poor areas, are prevalent across the system.

To properly understand, and be confident in, the finding that centers in poor neighborhoods have more connections, several issues should be con-sidered. First, it is possible that the standard measure of neighborhood poverty, 40%, may be too high.[25] I estimated versions of both the models with the threshold set at 30% and then 20%. For referrals, the threshold did not affect the significance of the coefficient; the size of the effect was roughly the same. For collaborative ties, the same was true except when the threshold was set at 20%. At that point there was no effect, suggesting that those powerful organizational actors deciding what consti-tutes "needs," and therefore where they should send resources, tend to focus on the very poorest neighborhoods. Second, it is possible that results might differ if, rather than asking whether a neighborhood is poor, we asked what its particular poverty rate is. When I estimated versions of the models in which I specified neighborhood poverty as a continuous variable, the effect was not significant. This is consistent with the idea that powerful actors such as Kyle and Kaitlin observe need in neighborhoods imperfectly. To be sure, they can ascertain the socioeconomic differences between upper Manhattan and, say, the Upper East Side. But finer, continuous distinctions—such as that between parts of Hell's Kitchen and the poorest areas of the Upper West Side—do not fall within their purview. As described above, these higher order brokers do not base their decisions on careful analyses of the demo-graphic characteristics of every neighborhood in the city; instead, they focus on those key, discrete neighborhoods that are commonly believed or known to be in need, such as the South Bronx. This would lead one to expect the number of ties to increase only after poverty rises past a certain threshold, which is what we see.

Third, it is possible that neighborhood poverty affected the number of ties positively only as a result of the particular resources directors were asked about, some of which may be disproportionately needed by residents of poor neighborhoods. The survey included a question asking whether the center provided any service not specifically mentioned. Many responded affirmatively, and their answers included "insurance policies," "first aid and CPR training," and "aerobics." If the specific issues we asked about are a source of bias, there should be no effect of neighborhood poverty when the outcome stems from this open-ended question. I estimated the odds that a center provided a resource not asked about, based on the model in table 7.2.

The results, shown in table 7.3, are largely consistent with those in table 7.2. A center located in a high-poverty neighborhood has odds of having a not-asked-about collaborative tie 5.37 times as great as one located in a nonpoor neighborhood.

A PARADOX OF PLACE

Centers differ in their connectedness, and this difference is patterned. The actions of directors depend strongly on external factors such as actors in powerful state and private nonprofit bureaucracies. As a result of these factors, centers benefit, with respect to their organizational connectedness, from being located in a high-poverty neighborhood. For example, Destino would have been less likely to find an outside expert providing knowledge on getting into private school and access to subsidized entrance exams, as described in chapter 6, had her center not been located in a high-poverty

Table 7.3. Effect of sector, need, and location on the odds of having an active collaborative tie providing a resource not asked about

Variable	Logit coefficients
Center is a	
Government non-profit	3.15+
Private non-profit	2.59
Center has high proportion of poor children	0.45
Center located in a high poverty neighborhood	5.37**

Models control for neighborhood percent black, percent white, and percent Latino; residential instability, population density, and borough. Full models are given in appendix B.
$^{*}p < .05$ $^{**}p < .01$

neighborhood—even if the center itself had had as many low-income parents.

This finding seems to fly in the face of much of the research by Chicago School sociologists and others that poor neighborhoods lack not only organizational density but also the effective interorganizational ties that ensure the well-being of their residents.[26] That research, however, too often neglected the differences across cities in the level of penetration by the state and private nonprofit sectors in conditions in low-income areas. What our findings suggest, instead, is that Chicago and New York are radically different cities, the former with a well-known history of institutional and state neglect in many of its poorest South Side neighborhoods, and the latter with a strongly institutionalized nonprofit infrastructure dating back more than 150 years. When poor neighborhoods are situated in organizationally connected cities with strong nonprofit sectors, the residents of these neighborhoods will do better than they would in other cities. To the extent that a person's social capital relies on formal, not merely informal, ties or organizational, not just social, ties, the conditions of the city in which the person is located may matter.

Therefore, the findings ultimately tell us something about the connections that carry valuable resources for individuals in today's cities and something about the conditions in poor neighborhoods. Regarding connections in today's cities, it is clear that the organizational ties to which a mother has access are shaped by conditions much larger than not only her but also the center to which she is connected. The sources of these ties, and the motivations of the many actors and organizations involved in transferring resources across them, cannot be understood by resorting to the traditional concepts of social capital theory, such as the ideas of solidarity, interpersonal trust, or informal obligations. These ties exist in the realm of institutionalized arrangements, formal agreements, reciprocal exchanges, and cross-sector partnerships that our discussion has only briefly addressed.

These findings also tell us that conditions in poor neighborhoods are shaped not merely by group competition for resources but also by the state and other powerful actors.[27] That centers in high-poverty neighborhoods in New York City are better connected calls into question an all-too-common and rather narrow interpretation of the neighborhood effect hypothesis: that moving an actor from a poor to a non poor neighborhood will make it easier for her to acquire the resources conducive to well-being. Our discussion suggests this expectation is simplistic, because it ignores not only the role of organizations in the practice of accessing resources but also the institutional factors shaping how connected neighborhood organizations are.[28] The result is a paradox, by which New York City low-income mothers, were they to move to non poor neighborhoods, might enjoy the greater safety and improved schools associated with middle-class neighborhoods but lose contact with the resources available through organizations such as childcare centers. These and other implications of our discussion are explored in chapter 8.

Part IV

BEYOND CHILDCARE CENTERS

8

Extensions and Implications

When a mother enrolls her child in a center she simultaneously enlists herself in a set of obligations, expectations, and norms that, more often than not, transforms the nature of her networks. In the course of their day-to-day operations, centers create opportunities for strangers to meet, for acquaintances to become friends, and for friends and acquaintances to exchange favors. Centers develop and maintain complex arrangements with other organizations to mobilize the goods, information, and services of these entities for their own patrons. Not all centers broker social and organizational ties in equal measure. And within a given center, not all mothers develop these ties. But if mothers, in fact, do better when their children are in centers, then much of the explanation must lie in the resources acquired through these ties.

This study of childcare centers has illustrated a perspective on personal networks and the resources available through them. The organizational embeddedness perspective suggests, above all, that what researchers have called a person's social capital depends substantially on the institutional practices of the organizations in which the person routinely participates. If embedded in the right organizations, a person can acquire significant advantages, through the workings of these networks, which yield palpable effects on their well-being.

The organizational embeddedness perspective builds on social capital theory while also directing attention to a different set of questions (see table 8.1). When Nan Lin wrote on the investment in social relations, James Coleman on the purposive theory of action, and Pierre Bourdieu on the unceasing effort needed to sustain ties, they prioritized individuals' actions over the organizational contexts that either guide or give meaning to those actions. The organizational embeddedness perspective reverses the orientation, probing the nature of the context and investigating actions, purposive or nonpurposive, in light of their context. This difference carries on to the most recent trends in social capital research. Over the last decade or two, many researchers have continued Coleman's effort to formalize social capital theory based on the elegant models of social network analysis, an approach in which relations are conceived as nodes and the ties between

Table 8.1. Two perspectives on personal ties

Element	Social capital	Organizational embeddedness
Basic assumption	Actors invest in ties to eventually secure resources from them	Actors encounter others in organizational contexts that shape the ties they form, their use of those ties, and the resources available through the ties
Orientation	Structure Network composition	Context Everyday interaction
Ties	Social	Social, organizational
Formation of ties	Secondary importance	Primary importance
Consequences of ties	Primary importance	Related to the formation of ties
Mobilization of ties	By actor	By actor, by organization

them. Some, such as Ronald Burt, have studied the structure of total networks; others, such as Lin, the composition of personal ties. The organizational embeddedness perspective directs attention less to structure than to context—to the everyday settings in which people interact with others. It assumes that while many contexts matter, few matter more than organizational contexts, given the power and persistence of institutional practices. In this light, the perspective insists that ties among organizations, which have been largely neglected in social capital research, constitute an important component of a person's repertoire of connections, given the vast array of resources—information, material goods, and services of various kinds—potentially available through them. Two additional differences in orientation stand out. While social capital theory has focused on the consequences of personal ties, the organizational embeddedness perspective assigns primacy to their roots, suggesting that the process of tie formation, to the extent it is organizationally embedded, conditions other aspects of personal relations. To know what good a tie does an actor, one should know how the actor formed the tie. And while both perspectives insist that mobilization matters, the embeddedness perspective suggests that not only people but also organizations may mobilize connections for an actor.

The present study of childcare centers has not only illustrated the perspective; by identifying the mechanisms through which centers brokered social and organizational ties, it has also proposed concrete hypotheses about how other organizations might do so. Childcare centers brokered social ties effectively to the extent they presented multiple opportunities to interact (a) frequently, (b) durably, or (c) in a focused manner; instituted (d) formal obligations that encouraged pro-social behavior; and (e) induced cooperation on collective or shared tasks. They brokered organizational ties effectively to the extent they (f) maintained relationships to (g) resource-rich organizations in (h) diverse fields and, specifically, engaged in (i) validation, (j) storage, (k) referral, or (l) collaboration. These processes, I suggest, are not unique to centers.

Childcare centers are unique in their ability, due to their remarkable variety, to broker both social and organizational ties through many different mechanisms. They are also unique in other senses. They are primarily female institutions, which may help explain the prevalence of strong ties.[1] They are especially noncompetitive settings. They come alive daily with the heart-warming innocence of babies and toddlers; they exhibit, by institutional orientation, an explicit ethos of caring. This uniqueness demands some clarity in exposition, an explication of how much the mechanisms observed in childcare centers might, at least in theory, be evident in radically different settings. In fact, I argue that studies of networks in other urban organizations—such as beauty salons, diners, schools, bathhouses, churches, and community colleges—confirm several of my propositions about how organizations condition personal networks.

EXTENSIONS

Social Ties

The key to how organizations broker social ties is how they affect social interaction. To comprehend how interaction conditions social ties, one must first abandon the tendency, common in the study of urban processes and social inequality, to examine organizations in light of their global purposes: the childcare center as a place for childcare, the recreation area as a place for recreation, the grocery store as a place for groceries.[2] Changing orientations helps unearth the possibility that organizations not normally conceived as brokers may perform such roles.

Consider why a car repair shop might generate more friendships than a neighborhood restaurant. In chapter 3, I argued that opportunities and inducements, which differed from center to center, facilitated friendship formation. A small study of friendships between clients and employees at various neighborhood establishments supports the hypothesis that ordinary instances of repeated interaction matter more than the basic functions of the organization. Harvey Farberman and Eugene Weinstein surveyed 461 residents of St. Paul, Minnesota on the establishments they patronized and the relationships they formed there.[3] For each establishment, the authors asked respondents if they knew the name of any employee, whether that employee knew the respondent's name, and whether the respondent and employee would consider each other friends. If all three questions were answered affirmatively, the researchers considered the respondent to have formed a friendship. To understand differences among types of establishments, the authors also recorded the "frequency" with which the establishment was used, and what they called the "intensity" of usage, which referred to whether the transaction involved the purchase of a service or the purchase of a material good. Since the former implied more interpersonal interaction, they considered it more intense. To be sure, the authors ignored several issues that the present book has shown to be important, such as the fact that establishments with the same global purposes (e.g., hair dressing) may vary in their institutional characteristics and that people vary in how frequently they patronize establishments. Nevertheless, the average trends they uncovered, exhibited in table 8.2, remain instructive.

The first column exhibits the percentage of clients, among those patronizing each type of business, reporting friendships formed in the establishment. It shows, for example, that 34% of people who patronized haircutting establishments developed friendships there. The second and third columns report how intense and frequent interaction was. When both were low, as

Table 8.2. Friendship formation in commercial establishments in St. Paul, Minnesota, by frequency and intensity of interaction

Establishment	Percent of patrons that formed friendships	Intensity of interaction	Frequency of interaction
Hair-cut	33.6%	High	High
Car repair	21.9%	High	Low
Dentist	14.1%	High	Low
Doctor	13.5%	High	Low
Liquor	13.1%	Low	High
Grocery	12.1%	Low	High
Gas station	11.7%	Low	High
Drugstore	10.4%	Low	High
Restaurant	7.8%	High	Low
Hardware	5.3%	Low	Low
Shoes	4.6%	Low	Low
Clothing	4.3%	Low	Low
Furniture	4.1%	Low	Low

Source: Data from Farberman and Weinstein (1970: table 4). Friendships are likely when either intensity or frequency is high.

in hardware, clothing, and furniture stores, friendships were rare. When both were high, as in haircutting establishments—or at least one of them was, as in the less obvious car repair shops—friendships were common. Respondents also often formed friendships at nonobvious establishments, such as dentists and doctor's offices, liquor stores, grocery stores, and gas stations. The accumulation of connections in everyday life may occur in highly unexpected settings, because it turns less on the global purposes or functions of the settings than on the practices taking place within them, in this case, the frequency and intensity of interaction.[4]

Comparing centers to other establishments also suggests that the *strength* of childcare friendships was due to processes not unique to centers. In chapter 4, I proposed that mothers formed standard intimate ties when interaction was both frequent *and* durable—when centers instituted practices that allowed mothers to see each other repeatedly (e.g., at monthly parents association meetings) and for sustained time periods (e.g., at trips to zoos or museums). Consider a recent study of men of advanced age interacting in a neighborhood restaurant. In his study of the Valois restaurant in Chicago, Mitchell Duneier described the institutional practices that made it possible for patrons to interact repeatedly and for extended periods. Prices at Valois were modest, which encouraged repeat patronage. In addition, the managers neither required nor encouraged patrons to leave their tables immediately after eating, instead allowing them to gather at tables for hours.[5] As a result, patrons visiting the restaurant at different hours throughout the day could expect to encounter others sitting at a table long after their meals. This gave rise to "Slim's Table," a table that "for over a decade, [had] been the meeting place of a group of black men who regularly patronize this cafeteria."[6] Since the restaurant allowed extended stays and meals were typically eaten three times daily, the men saw one another often and free from time constraints. Consequently, a collective identity began to develop at Slim's Table. As Duneier explains, "Clearly defined personal activities and repetitive processes are constituents of both individual autonomy and collective solidarity. Collective life among black regulars is therefore characterized by intermittence and recurrence. The same people are usually present at similar times each day or week."[7] The context strengthened relationships dramatically, producing a rich source of supportive social capital. As one patron commented, "These men are like my family now. Because we eat together every day."[8] Men of advanced age differ from mothers of young children as much as diners do from childcare centers. Yet focusing on the context of interaction brings to light elements of the formation of strong ties irreducible to demography, personal motivation, or the uniqueness of childcare centers.

A similar consideration helps understand both the source and usefulness of compartmental intimates. I showed in chapter 4 that mothers formed both standard and compartmentally intimate ties, depending on both their temperaments and the institutional characteristics of the center. The notion that friendships may be *both* compartmental and intimate violates the expectation, by some formal theories, that domain-specific ties are unlikely to be intimate, because they are more difficult to sustain. I argued that organizational contexts intervene to the extent that they present both a focus of orientation and an institutionally mediated setting for regular and predictable interactions with the same patrons.

A study of friendships among older Jewish women frequenting Julie's, a neighborhood beauty shop in a large Midwestern city, bears evidence to this argument. The author, Frida Furman, uncovered a strong sense of community among patrons and employees. Furman insists that this community was not purposive but instead the result of habitual practices centered on the routines of hairdressing: "[C]ommunity at Julie's is of an *unintentional* sort: Without planning or design, Julie's emerges as a group of individuals—a different group depending on which day of the week their appointments fall—who enter into ongoing relations with one another around a shared set of concerns."[9] While unintentional, the ties were nonetheless remarkably *strong*. One client explained, "There's something about that shop that you're never gonna find anywhere. The closeness, you know." Another reported the same ethos of caring we saw in some childcare centers: "And you look forward to seeing the same people, week in and week out. And if you don't see them, you wonder if everything is all right."[10] Furman explains why these relations were important: "As I observe [these] relationships ... I see women as friends, engaged in relationships with one another that involved attention, support, and mutual responsibility—in short, caring. These are significant relationships that clearly provide meaning and value for many women."[11]

Despite their evident strength, these were not standard intimate ties. On the contrary, the relationships were strictly compartmental, sustained only by interactions in the beauty shop. Furman explains, in some detail:

> Some of ... the customers have active friendship networks outside the salon; some have lost most of their friends to moves or to death. In general, women do not socialize with each other outside the salon; their relationships are contained within it ... Beauty-shop friendships ... may be seen as neither better nor worse than other friendships. They are different from other friendships, perhaps, because they are limited to a particular space and time, but the significance of such relationships is not thereby diminished; rather, it is particularlized.[12]

While Furman's language ("particularized") differs from mine ("compartmental"), her discoveries do not: these intimate ties are largely domain specific, sustained, like those in childcare centers, by the institution itself.

The beauty shop also bears evidence to my argument in chapter 4 that compartmentally intimate relations are useful, in part, due to homophily and the ability to discuss common problems. Furman found that their beauty shop relationships helped women discuss personal topics difficult to address in other settings. The patrons of Julie's were mostly women of advanced age. Appropriately, conversation often turned to illness. Furman was "not prepared for the centrality of such a topic in the exchanges ... because speaking about our ailments is not typically acceptable except with close family members. Older people are frequently caricatured about their alleged preoccupations with their ailments; consequently, many are forced into silence about these matters."[13] The beauty shop provided a setting for intimate discourse on topics often not discussed elsewhere. In fact, as the author explains, often "it is the exchange of problems that cements this bond between women, and at Julie's, health issues constitute a primary conduit to intimacy and mutual support."[14]

Chapter 4's arguments on homophily derive a different type of support from a systematic, longitudinal study of friendship formation among students in 10 California elementary schools. Believing that homophily derived not merely from personal preferences but also from institutional factors, Maureen Hallinan and Aage Sorensen explored how friendships responded to ability grouping. They examined students in 32 classrooms where the reading teachers grouped students according to their ability. These groups numbered on average three per class, lasted only about 30 minutes a day, and typically remained stable over the course of the year. The authors uncovered that, net of the students' personal characteristics—such as their race and sex—they were more likely to become and to remain best friends with others assigned to their ability group than with other students in their own classrooms. That is, students developed friendships with others of similar abilities in large part because teachers assigned them to ability-sorted groups. In fact, in a series of studies, Hallinan and her colleagues have found that a number of institutional practices by schools, including assignment to shared tasks, the formation of opportunities for interaction, and the openness of the instructional environment, influence the nature of students' friendships. Their work makes a powerful case that formal properties of networks often thought to result primarily from psychological or rational predispositions can be traced to the influence of organizations.[15]

The dynamics of trust we observed in childcare centers have also been documented in a dramatically different setting. I argued in chapter 5 that Coleman's notion of trust did not accord with the experiences of center mothers, who were willing to trust others with their children (a potentially costly risk) based on little more than intuitive senses gleaned from previous encounters (i.e., rather little information). One might be tempted to attribute their willingness to trust others whose name they did not even know to the context: centers represent a kind of safe space where mothers might be willing to do things they would not in other organizational contexts. There is probably some truth to this idea. Nevertheless, the issue is not the center as a type of entity but, again, the mechanisms at play in a given organization: particularly, that it be a noncompetitive environment in which actors encounter each other repeatedly—even if they do not become friends, interact during their encounters, or speak to one another.

Consider a study of a setting that could not be more different from childcare centers: a U.S. prison. The prison as a whole is a place of confinement, but offices, lobbies for visitors, and other areas in given prisons constitute places where nonprisoners can encounter others, within conditions reflecting different microenvironments. Megan Comfort, a sociologist who had been studying women visiting their spouses in prison, had seen one such woman "multiple times" and "once had helped her find a nearby store where she could buy clothes, since the clothes she was wearing weren't permitted in the prison." One time, the woman went to the prison with her young son, but they were denied entry because the prison "couldn't let him in without his birth certificate." Seeing Comfort there, she asked Comfort to take care of him while she took the bus home to get the certificate, even though she did not know Comfort's name, address, or even business in the prison. A couple of hours later, she returned and went to see her husband:

> When she got into her visit, her husband scolded her because he couldn't believe she had left [their son] with someone she didn't know. "You left my son with some woman and you don't even know her name?" He asked if she had at least written down my driver's license number. [The woman] tried to explain to him, "But she's always there!" and we laughed together about how weak that sounded but how she had known she could trust me.[16]

The predictability engendered by repeated interaction became a kind of resource that, again, the mother accessed because she was in need. This is certainly a type of social capital, but one that is largely generated by institutional processes.

Centers are unique; the mechanisms through which they shape social interaction are not.

Organizational Ties

The brokerage of organizational ties arises from the highly bureaucratic nature of contemporary society, where exchanging goods and resources constitutes much of what businesses, government agencies, and nonprofit organizations do.[17] Childcare centers brokered such connections to the extent that they or their actors had powerful incentives (financial, normative, cognitive) to do so. An important implication of this perspective is that brokerage does not merely derive from the fact that centers are entities with a "service" orientation. Instead, the perspective calls for an appreciation that organizations and their actors respond to multiple interests, regardless of their global purposes.

A study of a business in Berkeley, California, the Steamworks bathhouse, bears evidence to this proposition. In chapters 6 and 7, I made the case that many childcare center staff, because of their professional norms and beliefs, provided information, material goods, and services from other organizations to the patrons of their establishments as the need arose, even when brokering these connections was not required of them. I reported that they brokered these connections through four mechanisms, storage, validation, collaboration, and referrals. Similarly, Melvin Delgado discovered that Steamworks heavily brokered connections for its patrons. The opening of bathhouses has been controversial because they have been blamed in the rapid early spread of HIV/AIDS. Nevertheless, many of the staffers of the business were motivated by a strong belief in the importance of practicing safe sex among members of the gay community. As a result, the bathhouse collaborated actively with outside organizations to provide both information and services through educational sessions and collaborative workshops:

> These [education] sessions [on safer sex] are co-led with the assistance of outside facilitators, some of whom are bilingual (American Sign Language, Chinese, Mandarin, Spanish, and Tagalog). Workshops, in turn, are less verbal and more participatory than the presentations . . . Facilitators for these workshops are found throughout the community . . . These workshops offer 'alternatives to unsafe and unimaginative sex.' They are designed to build self-esteem, improve body image, build trust, support limit-setting, and foster a sense of community. It is believed that after the workshop experience, participants have a 'greater repertoire of truly useful safer sex options.' . . . All workshops are free of charge.[18]

In addition, the bathhouse collaborated with external organizations to provide STD testing: "A local gay health collective offers, through 'Steamworks', bi-monthly, in-house HIV and STD testing and pre-testing counseling."[19]

The bathhouse, like many childcare centers, has also instituted formal referrals and turned itself into a repository for the storage of critical information. From the proceeds of its business, it hired a health educator who, among other duties, "offers referrals and advocacy for all customers" on HIV related issues.[20] The bathhouse also engaged in storage of information and material goods in a number of ways:

> Tables are often set up in the main lobby [where] outside agencies . . . offer brochures, condoms, lubricants, resource referrals and other safe sex information by participating community based organizations . . . Education and prevention materials are available throughout the house: the hallways, congregation areas, and bathrooms. Every room has a notice posting safer sex practices and the house rules regarding this. Across from the Health Education Office there is a large bulletin board with many sheets of information, both social and informative . . . The topics within these materials include: safe sex messages, HIV/STD site locations and issues, medical information on STDs, HIV treatment options, condom usage, substance abuse intervention information, and counseling information.[21]

With respect to its brokerage of organizational ties, the Steamworks bathhouse, a predominantly male business where no children are allowed, resembled many of our childcare centers.

The substantively incongruous yet formally striking similarity between the Steamworks bathhouse and many of our childcare centers illustrates the ability of the perspective to call attention network dynamics often ignored in the study of social inequality. In fact, the four core mechanisms by which centers brokered organizational connections have been reported in several works on inequality in urban contexts. *Referrals* and *collaborations* have been recorded in many other organizations. In recent years, separate studies by Nancy Ammerman, Mark Chaves, and Omar McRoberts have confirmed the prevalence of referrals and collaborations among religious congregations, which tend to maintain resource-rich relationships to food and clothing organizations, policy advocacy groups, health and education organizations, self-help associations, and many others.[22] Urban sociologists such as Robert Chaskin and his colleagues and Nicole Marwell have also shown in recent years that both referral and collaborative relations play much greater roles in the actions of community building organizations than scholars have acknowledged.[23]

In a heavily bureaucratic society, *validation* and *storage* are also common, intuitively understood, and often taken for granted. Validation is the process by which professors in a given private college gain access to the stacks of another university's library by mere presentation of the college's identification card. It is the process by which individuals with a student ID receive discounts for plane tickets, or those with an American Express card receive early notice of a cultural event, or those with membership in a YMCA may enter events in other settings and even in other cities at discounted price. Churches and other religious organizations in urban areas frequently validate people for free health exams once or twice a year.[24] Nonprofit organizations validate their members frequently. Members of the public library in Newton, Massachusetts receive, upon request, free or reduced admission to several of the most popular (and expensive) museums in Massachusetts: the New England Aquarium, the Museum of Fine Arts, the Children's Museum, and the Museum of Science.[25] The passes are free; membership in the library is practically free. Yet acquiring the resource requires working through the organizational connection. Validation may be the simplest means through which organizations reward membership, the source of the popularity of "member benefits."

The idea of storage calls attention to how libraries, schools, childcare centers, community centers, churches, and other organizations serve as repositories of information and resources, an especially important mechanism for those people who are socially isolated or otherwise disadvantaged in their networks. Thousands of people are more likely to use condoms because they can acquire them for free from the bathrooms of their college dorms or the counters of their neighborhood barbershops. Many others only come to learn about facts taken for granted by the middle-class and affluent—from their legal rights in a landlord dispute to their options in cases of domestic violence—from information stored in their routine organizations.

Disadvantages of Organizationally Embedded Ties

I must note that participating in organizationally embedded networks may generate important disadvantages, or what social capital scholars have called "negative social capital." Two are worth mentioning. One potential disadvantage is the reduction of leisure time. Many centers required that mothers surrender much of their time to the organization. This demand exacerbated the guilt that many mothers experienced about the amount of time they devote to their children, intensifying the cultural contradictions of motherhood.[26] The most successful mothers navigated this added burden by multitasking, using their time in the center to fulfill multiple commitments, such as spending quality time with their child, getting out of the city, or socializing with adults. But this approach works only in contexts that allow for multitasking. When the workplace, for example, demands extra hours, these hours must usually be devoted to work, which results in an unqualified burden.

A second disadvantage of organizationally embedded networks can be captured under the rubric of institutional coercion, by which people are forced, for the good of the organization and its members, to forgo at least some rudimentary rights, such as the right to refuse to represent the organization or the right to privacy about their contact information. Fund-raisers could only effectively lower everyone's tuition if all parents could be convinced to participate, to sell, for example, a given amount of cookie dough to others in the center's name. Collective support lists were effective only if all parents could be convinced to give their names and numbers. These cases represent the classic conflict between collective and individual interests.[27] Organizational contexts complicate this conflict by introducing a third party, the organization, whose interests are neither exactly those of the individual nor those of the collective. In fact, organizations often represent their own interests. For example, by creating a support contact list, centers increased their efficiency, cut communication costs during emergencies, and represented themselves before the state or other funders as organized entities. Studies of the organizational embeddedness of networks must take into account both advantages and disadvantages.

Understanding Why Organizations Broker Ties

The perspective advanced in this book assumes that multiple actors and institutions, through multiple mechanisms, may broker social or organizational ties in a given organization. As such, it does not lend itself to easy predictions as to which organizations will broker ties effectively. Nonetheless, I have identified several factors likely to play a role: organizational survival, professional norms and beliefs of practitioners, pressures by powerful external entities, especially the state, and even the neighborhood in which the organization is located. Let me be clear that asking why organizations broker connections is not to ask why they purposely build organizational or social ties, but why they practice acts that have this consequence, sometimes purposely and sometimes not.

A major factor motivating organizations to broker connections is the imperative for organizational survival. Childcare centers often instituted practices that involved parental participation as a way to pool resources or reduce costs. Fund-raisers represent the clearest illustration. The same imperative motivated the use of parents in field trips, since otherwise staff would have to be employed to perform such tasks. Another instance was the use of emergency lists to institute calling chains among parents in the case of an emergency. All these practices, wherein the boundaries between client and employee were blurred, constituted efforts to pull together resources for the survival of the organization.

A different manifestation of the effects of the need to survive is evident among small businesses in poor areas. Based on extensive research across a wide array of local businesses, Delgado has argued that local businesses in poor neighborhoods engage in such practices when local demand compels it:

> Local businesses must cater to the needs of local residents. Retailers still in business tailor their products and services to poor, inner-city residents rather than, as before, to the more affluent population of the entire metropolitan area. Local stores often sell different goods from those sold in the more affluent neighborhoods . . . This resident-driven approach invariably involves provision of services that can be classified as human service related.[28]

For example, food establishments in predominantly Puerto Rican neighborhoods provided translation services and aid in connecting the elderly to government services. Retailers may be forced to form organizational ties to meet the demands of local clients.

Organizational self-interest does not only motivate the brokers; it also often drives those external organizations that *provide* the resources. These organizations hold varied interests, from good publicity to pleasing stockholders to fulfilling a mandate in the organization's charter. An example is the celebrated arrangement by which the Timberland boot company provides funds and free clothing to the City Year inner-city youth leadership program. Every year, a new cohort of thousands of young people in cities throughout the country wear the bright red jackets, baggy khaki pants, and (perhaps most important) popular camel-colored Timberland boots that are the program's signature. The gains to Timberland include positive public relations and the visibility of its brand among urban youth, one of its most important consumer groups. Organizational sociologists have studied the dynamics of similar arrangements in other settings at length.[29]

At least two additional factors help predict which organizations are likely to be effective brokers. As Paul DiMaggio and Walter Powell have argued, "[T]he state and the professions . . . have become the great rationalizers of the second half of the twentieth century."[30] Professions, among other things, disseminate belief systems through training programs, conferences, publications, and the like. The model (in childcare centers) by which "one cannot care for the child without caring for the family" resembles the model (in the San Francisco bathhouse) by which "one must teach safe sex" in the sense that they motivate practitioners to provide access to goods in their respective organizational settings, regardless of their organization's global purposes, including whether the entities are nonprofit institutions or business-oriented firms. Similarly, in her study of case workers in welfare agencies, Celeste Watkins-Hayes uncovered that the workers' beliefs about their role in the community significantly affected how they approached and treated mothers on transitional assistance.[31]

The state remains important. We saw that the Head Start program imposed two sets of mandates on its centers that resulted in the brokerage of ties: it required a parents association, along with other activities likely to build social capital among parents, and it required collaboration with community organizations and resource providers, effectively requiring centers to broker organizational ties for their own patrons. This process highlights the fact that the state can, in fact, create conditions that generate social capital. Some have come to believe that social capital is impossible to shape, structure, or institutionalize, because they have conceived it as a largely informal process. While understanding the nature of informal processes has brought to light the significance of emergent and non-structural conditions, divorcing these processes from formal organizations, including the formal structures of the state, has been a mistake. The perspective advanced in this book suggests that since the state can affect—through the threat of fines, lost funding, or decertification, among other means—what happens in local organizations, it can shape informal networks through observable mechanisms.[32] As such, it argues that state policies, and their anticipated and unanticipated consequences for the institutional practices of childcare centers, schools, community organizations, religious entities, and the host of other local organizations over which states exercise some operational authority, must constitute a core component of a structural theory of the sources and consequences of network inequality.

IMPLICATIONS

This book has offered an approach not merely to personal networks but also to the relationship between networks and inequality in well-being. Like social capital theory, the perspective looks for the roots of inequality in personal ties, but it asks where those ties are embedded—and probes the consequences of this embeddedness. By calling attention to everyday interaction, organizational contexts, and unexpected advantages, the embeddedness perspective brings to light the cumulative effects of small benefits—a free service in one setting, a crucial bit of information in another, a valuable discount in a third, a comforting ear in a fourth—that accrue to those who are effectively embedded. It also brings to light the large benefits sometimes hidden in plain sight, such as the advantage, for someone hoping for a career in banking, of enrolling in a college that organizes recruitment drives by bankers each spring.

The organizational embeddedness perspective links these micro-level processes to the macro-level structures that ultimately affect them. In this respect, it constitutes a *meso-level approach to social inequality*, one that seeks regularities in how people interact, obtain information, trust others, respond to obligations, acquire supportive services, and secure everyday material goods—and probes the organizational mechanisms by which these actions can be tied to state authority, the collaboration between the public and private sectors, and the large organizational networks central to structural inequality. These networks include the cluster of hospitals, HMOs, state agencies, and health businesses that constitute the health care system; the private and public colleges, testing organizations, high schools, and community organizations that constitute the higher education system; and the social service organizations, government agencies, and community building entities that constitute the service-delivery systems of many large cities. Social inequality is generated in part through the actions of these institutions, through how they respond to their own constituencies, how their professionals understand and institute their policies, how they react to state authority, and how their practices generate expected and unexpected consequences for the actors who make use of their services. All of these fields maintain their sets of institutional practices; all carry their own set of professional norms; all bear some relation, or set of relations, to the state. And they all include a set of routine organizations that affect the networks of the mothers and fathers, elderly and young, poor and well-off, who patronize them for their services. In this respect, probing organizational embeddedness will yield, I argue, more powerful insight into contemporary social inequality.

A future book will have to develop the large-scale implications of these arguments. Nevertheless, the present discussion can make clear some of their implications for the currently pressing issues in inequality. Consider, to conclude this book, three questions that currently occupy scholars of social inequality: how people find jobs, how they gain access to health insurance, and how they respond to conditions in their neighborhoods. In all three cases, the embeddedness perspective identifies conditions too often ignored in the public and scholarly discourse on social inequality.

Organizational Embeddedness and Job Finding

One of the most valuable sociological contributions to the study of labor markets has been to document the importance of social ties to people searching for jobs. Mark Granovetter and others have convinced scholars not only to look beyond the skills of the job seeker but also to consider that social ties involve complex dynamics worth studying in their own right. Weak ties, for example, can be more important than strong ties; and, as Sandra Smith has shown, distrust can undermine the usefulness of a social connection to someone looking for a job.[33] Nevertheless, recent studies of job finding among the young have found the need to move a step further and consider the importance of *organizational* ties.

James Rosenbaum and his colleagues have studied the school-to-work transition in many different contexts, asking how and why young men and women find or fail to find formal employment. Some of their most important findings are reported in *Beyond College for All*, which analyses nationally representative data on high school students who graduated in 1982.[34] In his book, Rosenbaum reports two findings consistent with the argument of this book.

First, he found that while social ties help graduates find jobs, organizational ties are more crucial than most researchers have recognized. In fact, for some demographic groups, their use was as common as that of social ties. In chapter 1, I noted that many colleges form and sustain ties to employers who visit campuses every spring to hire graduating seniors. Rosenbaum and his colleagues found that such practices were not uncommon among high schools (though they are more common in Japan and Germany than in the United States). They also uncovered that minority high school students turned to this or other formal organizations much more commonly than did whites. Table 8.3, which reports how U.S. high school graduates in 1982 obtained their first job after graduation, is based on Rosenbaum's work, which reported whether respondents found their jobs through relatives, friends, employment services, their school, applying directly, or other means. The first two of these represent social ties; the third and fourth, organizational ties, as theorized in this book. Table 8.3 collapses the figures into their respective categories.

The first column confirms the importance, documented by Granovetter and many others, of social ties to the job finding process.[35] For most of the

Table 8.3. How U.S. high school graduates in 1982 found their first job (by sex and ethnic background)

	Social ties	Organizational ties	Direct	Other	No answer
Men					
White	38.3%	9.6%	28.3%	13.7%	10.1%
Black	34.7%	13.5%	24.9%	12.7%	14.2%
Latino	38.8%	7.5%	29.4%	11.6%	12.7%
Women					
White	35.4%	15.0%	32.8%	9.6%	7.2%
Black	24.5%	24.0%	36.4%	4.9%	10.2%
Latina	33.7%	16.6%	33.5%	6.3%	9.9%

Source: Data from Rosenbaum (2001:200). Social ties are "friends" or "relatives"; organizational ties are the "school" or "employment service."

demographic categories, more than a third of respondents found their first jobs after high school through social ties. The second column shows that using organizational ties was not uncommon and that it was more prevalent among women than men and much more prevalent among blacks than either whites or Latinos. In fact, black women were almost as likely to find their first job through *social* as through *organizational* connections. Many practitioners, convinced of the importance of informal networks to job finding, have been at a loss when using this information to address unemployment inequality. (How does one get people to find more useful friends?) But Rosenbaum's findings suggest that, for some demographic groups, organizational ties are more promising venues for intervention. They may be especially more promising among poor black women and men if, as Smith has argued, distrust among their social networks undermines the networks' effectiveness in the job search.[36]

In this light, the second of Rosenbaum's findings is relevant: that much of this brokerage in schools was driven by teachers, who acted out of personal and professional motivations, rather than job mandates. Thirty-seven percent of U.S. high schools offered job placement services.[37] In many of these cases, teachers acted "as informal intermediaries for conveying hard-to-assess, relevant, and trusted information between students and employers." Teachers reported active brokerage, vouching for the reliability of students to many employers. According to the authors, "some employers hire[d] applicants they might not have hired otherwise."[38] Additional research would be needed to measure the effectiveness of teacher intervention in the brokerage process. Nevertheless, the work suggests that teachers in schools may represent untapped means for reducing youth unemployment. Policies that, in conjunction with other practices, focused on facilitating organizational brokerage in schools might be more effective than those focused solely on traditional issues such as soft-skills training.

Organizational Embeddedness and Access to Health Insurance

Acquiring health insurance—a health insurance card with a policy attached to it—requires two things: money and the ability to negotiate a bureaucracy. Much has been written about the cost of health insurance, but equally important is the ability to negotiate the bureaucracy, a skill that is relatively scarce. Nevertheless, organizations may mobilize their connections to compensate for this scarcity, helping secure health insurance for their members.

The process by which some mothers in New York City childcare centers acquired health insurance is remarkably similar to that by which I did. As a college professor, my process was made possible by the organizational ties instituted among my employer, the health insurance provider, and a network of clinics and hospitals. I did not require special skills (human capital) to navigate the impenetrable health care system, nor did I resort to my personal social ties (traditional social capital) to find out how to fill out an application, what policies were available, what they would cost, or how the process worked. Instead, my employer provided me a booklet with six options and their costs. After 20 minutes of reading, I checked one of the six boxes, signed my name, and instantly became insured. I acquired health insurance through an institutionalized process neither designed nor determined by me. Through a simple agreement, my employer validated me to the other organizations with which it collaborated for the process, mobilizing a complex set of organizational connections.

Many people may remain uninsured, I suggest, because they are not embedded in such organizational networks. In 2003, 45 million Americans did not have health insurance coverage.[39] Most adults were covered by their employer. The poor, however, are less likely to be employed in jobs that provide full benefits. Among the poor, the most important form of coverage has been Medicaid, which in 2003 provided coverage for 35.6 million. Still, many people who are eligible for Medicaid do not have it. Economist Jonathan Gruber estimated that even though 31% of children were eligible for Medicaid in 1996, only 22.6% had enrolled in it. Stated differently, the take-up rate was only 73%.[40] The millions of Americans who are eligible for but not enrolled in Medicaid, Medicare, or state-sponsored health insurance programs do not lack this resource because of a financial barrier: the resource is free. Instead, one could argue, they lack the organizational capital, if the term is useful, by which to negotiate the process; they lack access to a network of organizations with an institutionalized arrangement by which the government pays hospitals and clinics, the latter receive clients, and the actor receives health coverage.[41] They lack the tie to an organization that, as in my case, provided the informational access to the resource.

A recent natural experiment bears evidence to the argument that when people have access to organizational networks their health coverage increases. As Gruber has written, eligibility for Medicaid is "determined through a complicated set of screens on income, family structure, and in some cases assets."[42] In addition, as a recent *New York Times* article reported, "[F]ederal law generally prohibits anyone but a government employee from working on government enrollments."[43] Therefore, to enroll in Medicaid (or reenroll every year), an individual must either complete the complicated paperwork and documentation at home or speak directly to a Medicaid federal employee. However, the State of New York received an experimental waiver of this rule in 2000 that permitted independent counselors at nonprofit organizations and community-based organizations, such as schools, childcare centers, and places of worship, to enroll individuals.

These organizations could assist with the paperwork, gather the required documents, and even conduct the required face-to-face interview. It is for this reason that when new parents enrolled at Alegre Daycare, the director first determined their Medicaid eligibility and, then, through its parent organization, enrolled families if they were eligible but not insured. This process, referred to as "facilitated enrollment," is effectively a *validation mechanism* by which the local organization can provide access to the resource (health insurance) paid for by the state. In the first six years since the program was instituted, the number of uninsured children in New York dropped by 36%. Supporters attribute facilitated enrollment with increasing New York State Medicaid enrollments by more than one million over a 5-year period, and the state currently boasts one of the highest Medicaid take-up rates in the country.[44]

Organizational Embeddedness and Neighborhood Effects

One of the most important sociological theories in recent years proposed that people living in poor neighborhoods would do better if they lived in nonpoor neighborhoods, since neighborhoods affect people's well-being.[45] Many believe that this "neighborhood effects" hypothesis is obviously correct and even self-evident; others, that it assumes more than has been shown. Skeptics argue that people in poor neighborhoods could do worse not because the neighborhood hurt their lives but because those already destined to do worse are more likely to live in poor neighborhoods.

In the 1990s, a major federally funded study seemed to provide the scientific solution. The Moving to Opportunity (MTO) experiment, run by a large team of social scientists, was fielded among people living in housing projects who were hoping to live elsewhere. Participants who requested housing vouchers and who agreed to participate in the study were assigned at random to different conditions. Some (the control group) were not given a voucher and instead continued to receive their project-based assistance; others (the experimental group) were given a voucher that could be used only in *non*poor neighborhoods.[46] Participants were then tracked over time and asked questions about their employment, education, health, and safety. The experiment was performed in several different cities. Researchers expected that people given the vouchers would exhibit better outcomes, due to their improved neighborhood conditions.

Despite expectations, results have been mixed. For some outcomes in some cities, the experimental group experienced greater well-being; for others, there was no effect.[47] For this reason, many observers have concluded that neighborhood poverty does not, in fact, seriously affect well-being.

But the findings in chapter 7 offer reason to reconsider. Many childcare centers maintained ties to other organizations providing information, services, and goods benefitting mothers and their children. In addition, perhaps ironically, centers in poor neighborhoods maintained more, not fewer, such ties, because local governments and other powerful actors in New York City intervened to this end. Suppose that (a) other urban organizations, such as churches, also maintained similar ties and that (b) those organizations also exhibited *more* ties if they were located in poor neighborhoods. If so, then, all other factors being equal, organizationally embedded people in poor neighborhoods would have easier access to valuable goods than would organizationally embedded people in *non*poor neighborhoods. In such a scenario, people in poor neighborhoods would not always seem to do worse than those in nonpoor neighborhoods, because the negative effects of crime, poor schools, and other factors would be tempered by the positive effects of participating in better connected organizations. That is, even if neighborhood poverty did have negative consequences through other mechanisms, some of these consequences would not register in a controlled experiment that did not take into account organizational connections, such as MTO.

The situation I presented is hypothetical, but by no means far-fetched. Researchers have already documented the rich organizational ties of several types of organizations in high poverty neighborhoods, including beauty salons, botanical shops, and religious organizations.[48] While randomized trials will continue to be important, a more careful assessment of the mechanisms tying neighborhoods to well-being would consider the potentially counteracting effects of organizational connections.

In 1987, William J. Wilson argued that the truly disadvantaged members of American society were the residents of poor inner-city neighborhoods who, as a result of their conditions, had become socially isolated from the networks of mainstream society.[49] An organizational perspective, however, both changes and deepens our understanding of isolation. The most disadvantaged person today may well be the organizational isolate, the one disconnected from childcare centers, religious organizations, political clubs, schools, gyms, neighborhood associations, community centers, and hobby clubs. This person is effectively unplugged not merely from the most reliable way to form and sustain ties in a time-sensitive society but also from the organizational apparatus through which grants, information, consumer goods, discounts, political access, and many other resources are transferred. It is not merely the absence of friends but the absence of contexts in which friends continue to be made; not merely the lack of a tie to the bureaucracy but the lack of access to the numerous resources reserved to the organizational sphere, to the mechanisms by which the goods in that sphere can make up for the goods that friends are unable to provide. In a society increasingly structured around formal organizations, the organizational isolate is the person increasingly guaranteed to be left out.

Appendices

A MULTIMETHOD CASE STUDY

My intention in this book has been to examine and document average tendencies, the variation across them, and the mechanisms underlying all associations. This set of objectives required a careful look at both quantitative and qualitative data, which in turn required making important decisions about approach and epistemology—about how to analyze and present data from such diverse sources while retaining the unity of the whole. Some words on how I approached these decisions are in order.

A project with such diverse data sources can proceed in several different ways. One approach is to give overwhelming primacy to one type of data; an example is a large survey-based book in which interviews are used primarily, and perhaps somewhat sparingly, to illustrate the survey findings or to enrich the discussion. In this approach, the different sources do not complement each other; one (the interview) supplements the other (the survey). Another approach is to truly integrate the different data sources but from a single epistemological perspective. This approach underlies Gary King, Robert Keohane, and Sidney Verba's 1994 *Designing Social Inquiry*, which argues that analyzing qualitative and quantitative data requires the same basic methods, where the objectives are to estimate a central tendency, maximize efficiency, and minimize bias (I critique this perspective in my article "'How Many Cases Do I Need?'" in press in *Ethnography*). A third approach, the one employed in this book, is an epistemological pluralist position, which does not purport that the same basic methods should be employed to analyze every data source, since the analysts can be motivated by numerous types of questions, including not merely those about central tendency but also those about process, dynamic, mechanism, emergence, structure, and other aspects of social life. I assume that different questions require not only different data but also different methodological orientations, and that data sources should be employed to answer only those types of questions (in the case of this book, about averages, about variation, or about mechanisms) for which they are best suited. In the pluralist perspective, integration arises not from the unity of the method but from the complementarity of methods and data sources. This perspective effected

perhaps its greatest consequences in the analysis of the qualitative interviews, where my methods differed substantially from others often employed
in the literature.

Appendices A through C not only reveal the consequences of this general
orientation but also describe, in detail, the procedures used to analyze each
data source. Appendix A unravels the process through which the organizational embeddedness perspective was developed. Appendix B describes the
quantitative data and analysis strategy and produces full tables for all the
statistical regressions reported in the book. Appendix C specifies the data
and analysis strategy for the qualitative methods.

Appendix A

The Process

Many training programs in sociology continue to teach a stylized, and in many ways mythical, model of research, in which the scholar first conjures a hypothesis, then tests it with some form of data, and finally writes up a "report." The finished product, represented as nothing more than the post facto detailing of rationally followed procedures, obscures much of the process, revealing nothing about the role of creativity, mistakes, redefinitions of the questions, or imagination. One of the fruits of the reflexive turn in the social sciences has been the pressure on scholars to increase the transparency of their work. Quantitative researchers in several fields increasingly make their data and programming code available to researchers, and several journals now require this disclosure as a condition of publication. Qualitative researchers, particularly ethnographers, increasingly report the practices by which they entered the field, established rapport, and dealt with the personal dilemmas that arise in the field.[1]

Nevertheless, too many researchers, in both quantitative and qualitative traditions, have quietly but stubbornly resisted calls to engage a discussion of *process*, of how they arrived at a theory, how they came to be convinced of the hypotheses and propositions advanced in their work.[2] Where did the theory come from? Over the last several years, as I have taught courses on field methods and logic of inquiry, I have become increasingly convinced of the importance of reporting the process of theory construction—as a form of measured reflexivity—to the increased transparency of social science research. To this end, I describe the origins of the organizational embeddedness perspective.[3]

This book began as a hunch. Seven or eight years ago, while working as an ethnographer for a project on poor neighborhoods in Boston, I had been entrusted with contacting "neighborhood institutions" to help paint a picture of conditions in urban areas. My strategy, to the extent I had one, was to walk the streets and enter every establishment I saw—restaurants, small clothing stores, churches—and speak to whoever was around about the relationship between the organization and the neighborhood. I walked into a childcare center in a neighborhood that had witnessed a recent surge of immigrants from Latin America. Curious about the provision of services, I asked the social worker with whom I spoke about the childcare curriculum and the afterschool program with which it was associated. But as she related stories of her experiences with clients, it became clear that her center was doing much more than providing childcare. Until 1999, the year before my visit to that center, clients were not required to submit social security numbers to receive subsidized care. Clients, many of them undocumented immigrants, were boldly asking for connections to employers—on anything, washing dishes, cleaning—having heard through the figurative grapevine that the center put people in contact with others who could help. Clients were getting connected to health providers and other institutions in the city. Having neither children nor any prior experience in childcare centers, I was surprised a parent could get anything other than childcare in a center. I wondered how prevalent this was, what kinds of connections people could make in centers, and how useful these connections would turn out to be to them. I suspected that centers might be, as churches had long been taken to be, one of the most important institutions for the sustenance of neighborhood networks. I resolved to pursue the possibility when I moved to New York City in the fall of 2001.

Once in New York, I designed a small pilot study to see whether that childcare center in Boston was a fluke. My research assistant Laura Stark and I visited every center, about 20 in all, in one middle-class and one poor neighborhood in New York City, interviewing directors about their practices. The interviews confirmed my suspicions and piqued my curiosity—there was a lot of networking taking place in childcare centers, much of it in ways I did not anticipate. By nature, I am more driven by questions or puzzles than by a commitment to any particular method. As a result, it was clear early on that conducting this project would require multiple methods and, consequently, a lot of help.

The initial purpose was to use the childcare center as a strategic site to examine how neighborhood organizations shaped the formation of social ties among parents. I wanted to uncover what was common among centers (the average tendency) and what differed from one to the next (the variation). Most important, I wanted to uncover the processes by which parents formed and made use of their new ties (the mechanisms). With some funds provided by my university, I hired Erin Jacobs and Rebekah Massengill, two very bright research assistants, and together we interviewed directors and other staff in 23 new centers in four neighborhoods of different racial and class composition. We complemented these interviews by attending targeted events such as parent meetings, field trips, and events. To learn about tie formation and its consequences from the parents' perspective, we interviewed more than 65 parents, at length, about the ties they formed in centers and their relationships to other patrons and staff. I soon began to be dissatisfied with what we did not know about the distribution of characteristics in the city as a whole. Thus, some time after we had entered the field, I commissioned the Childcare Centers and Families Survey, a survey of nearly 300 randomly sampled childcare centers based on a list of all centers licensed in New York City. By a stroke of luck, one of my colleagues at the time, Sara McLanahan, who was overseeing the Fragile Families survey, a nationally representative survey of urban mothers of newborns, happened to be preparing the questions for the fourth wave of her study, when the children would be about 5 years old. She graciously agreed to let me add a few questions on networks in childcare centers, which allowed to me to assess, on a national scale, the prevalence of what I was observing.

The gradual process of collecting and analyzing data slowly but decidedly began to change my mind about what we were discovering. By now I had confirmed with both qualitative and quantitative evidence that the center I first saw in Boston was not unique: networking was a major component of what took place among mothers in childcare centers. In addition, the networks appeared to be demonstrably useful to the well-being of mothers, decreasing their social isolation and improving their capacity to solve everyday problems and ensure their well-being, such that mothers could be expected to do better when their children were in daycares. But the story I had heard in that Boston center, that some people went to the center *because* they wanted to mobilize the ties they could make there, simply did not hold elsewhere. Mothers, by and large, were not enrolling in or attending centers for the purpose of mobilizing either social or organizational ties. Yes, some of them did, but these women stood out by the instrumental nature of their "networking"; they were the proverbial exceptions that tested the rule. For most mothers, the networks and ensuing resources they acquired were unexpected consequences of their attempt to locate formal childcare. Slowly, I began to change my orientation.

The shift in focus became more radical than I had anticipated. First, it soon became clear that the neighborhood mattered less than the organizational characteristics of the center. In the phrase "neighborhood organization," the adjective had turned into an assumption what should have been an empirical question. Yes, centers were local organizations, but their local nature was not what mattered most about them, except for the fact that what is local is also convenient and therefore likely to be used. What mattered more about them, for the formation of ties and the benefits mothers could gain from these ties, was whether organizational and institutional processes were in place that allowed parents to meet other parents, to contact outside organizations, and to coordinate tasks with center staff. Following current trends in urban sociology (the field in which I was trained), I had always instinctively focused on neighborhoods, believing, like many urban ethnographers and not without reason, that neighborhoods in urban areas played important roles in the formation of ties. The danger was that too much attention on the neighborhood had directed my thinking away from one of the most important aspects of contemporary life: that we are, in Charles Perrow's words, "a society of organizations."[4] As result, I began to think of childcare centers as the one thing I knew they were—organizations—and assessed the role of neighborhoods only to the extent they shaped patrons' social or organizational ties.

Second, I began to think more seriously about process than about types of organizations. Early on, I attempted to determine what types of organizations brokered ties the way centers did: Neighborhood organizations? Service organizations? Community building organizations? As exception piled upon exception, I gradually became convinced of the futility of this exercise. It was also, I came to conclude, the wrong way to think about the case study, a statement reinforced as I reassessed the works of Charles Ragin, Howard Becker, Michael Burawoy, Robert Yin, Peter Hedstrom and Richard Swedberg, and others.[5] What affected the formation of networks was not so much the center as a whole but the presence of specific mechanisms, such as the requirement that people accomplish tasks together or the opportunity to see others repeatedly. The particular combination of mechanisms evident in centers was unique to them, and in this sense there was no other organization like them. In fact, no two centers were alike. On the other hand, the mechanisms themselves were not so unique. Once I identified them, I began to see them everywhere—at work, in law firms, in churches—the way a child, upon learning a new word, seems to suddenly hear or see it everywhere she goes. A veil of sorts was lifted. This cemented my change in orientation toward identifying and understanding mechanisms.

As I observed, wrote, and analyzed, I also studied much of the work on the various issues I believed to be at play. Georg Simmel, Pierre Bourdieu, James Coleman, William J. Wilson, Walter Powell, and Paul DiMaggio were foundational. On well-being, I was heavily invested early on in the work of economist Amartya Sen on capability, and the further elaborations by philosopher Martha Nussbaum; over time, I became less enthusiastic about the potential of the capabilities approach to help unravel what was taking place in childcare centers. The same was true of the work of Ervin Goffman and of Herbert Blumer on interpersonal interaction, though their work, like that of the other two scholars, continued to influence the issues I tended to worry about. More influential were the works of several mid-century sociologists, particularly George Homans, Richard Emerson, Robert Merton, Paul Lazarsfeld, and to lesser extent Theodore Newcomb, all of whom studied one aspect or another of social interaction, social exchange, or network formation. The perspectives of several midcentury anthropologists, particularly Clyde Mitchell and his colleagues and Elizabeth Bott, were also influential. The recent work on exchange theory by Edward Lawler and his colleagues shaped how I understood social interaction and collective tasks; the very sophisticated work of political scientist Russell Hardin on trust, and on rational actor models by Jon Elster, convinced me to take such models much more seriously than I had been. Of the recent work on networks, I especially appreciated the dynamic models of network formation of Tom Snijders and his colleagues and Kathleen Carley and hers, though these researchers' formal approaches were, in the end, too different in orientation from those of my book. Barry Wellman's research on networks and social support played a bigger role. And I appreciated the critiques of networks research by Mustafa Emirbayer and others. Of the work in organizations, Joseph Galaskiewicz, Ron Burt, and Edward Laumann, in addition to the ubiquitous work of Powell and DiMaggio, were most central. And on a substantive level, I paid careful attention to the work of urban sociologists, particularly Sandra Smith, Mitchell Duneier, Robert Chaskin, Gerald Gamm, Mary Pattillo, Melvin Delgado, Barrett Lee, Nicole Marwell, Jennifer Lee, Reuben May, Monica McDermott, Elijah Anderson, Loic Wacquant, and Omar McRoberts, who had studied one or another routine organization specifically in the context of urban inequality. The comprehensive volumes of Katherine Neckerman on social inequality and Sheldon Danziger and his colleagues on poverty were important sources of consultation.[6]

Several theoretical perspectives spoke to what I saw, but none more closely than social capital theory, particularly the foundational texts of Bourdieu and Coleman, and the fully elaborated model of Nan Lin.[7] In my 2004 book *Villa Victoria*, a study of relations in a predominantly Puerto Rican housing complex in Boston, I had written about social capital, but I had used the term largely as shorthand to describe connections among the poor to the middle class and the level of community participation. The closer I probed the foundational literature on social capital, the more I realized that it was missing a lot about how and why people make their connections—and the consequences of these processes. The more I confronted and clarified ambiguities, inconsistencies, and contradictions—in the literature and in my own thinking—the more my critique, and my alternative, increased in sharpness. As I read studies of other organizations, such as bars and beauty shops, and exchanged ideas with several research assistants and many colleagues over several years, I became increasingly convinced. I traveled back and forth from field notes to theory to studies of other organizations, until—many drafts later—the model of organizational embeddedness emerged. I chose to place the model at the start of the book for clarity of exposition. The process to develop it, however, was fully dialectical.

Appendix B

Quantitative Data

The quantitative sources were the Fragile Families and Child Wellbeing Study and the Childcare Centers and Families Survey. The first provided nationally representative data on mothers. The second provided New York City representative data on childcare centers.

SURVEY OF MOTHERS

The Fragile Families survey follows a cohort of nearly 5,000 children born in 20 large U.S. cities between 1998 and 2000. The fourth wave of the study was conducted when the children were approximately 5 years old; the third wave, when they were approximately 3 years old. The principal investigators describe the objectives of the survey as answering four questions: "(1) What are the conditions and capabilities of unmarried parents, especially fathers?; (2) What is the nature of the relationships between unmarried parents?; (3) How do children born into these families fare?; and (4) How do policies and environmental conditions affect families and children?"[1] For the fourth wave of the survey, I submitted a number of questions on the networks that mothers made in centers. Because of cost, many of my questions were cut, but enough were accepted to develop a general sense of tie formation among mothers in centers. All my analyses of Fragile Families data employed statistical weights to account for survey design and attrition. The results are representative of all mothers of 5-year-olds who were newborns in cities with at least 200,000 residents 5 years earlier. (For more detailed information on Fragile Families, see http://www.fragilefamilies.princeton.edu/.)

SURVEY OF CENTERS

The objective of the Childcare Centers and Families Survey, a survey of nearly 300 randomly sampled centers in New York, was to obtain statistically representative data on New York City childcare centers for the variables of interest. I designed the survey based on much of what, by then, my research assistants and I had already learned from the qualitative research. I commissioned the New York survey research firm SRBI to administer the questionnaires. The sample was based on a list, provided by the New York Department of Health, of all licensed centers in the five boroughs of New York City. At the time the survey was conducted (summer and fall of 2004), New York had an estimated 1,683 centers.[2] Because we had conducted the pilot study, in addition to much of the fieldwork, before fielding the survey, we had more information than is often the case about the wording, introduction, and screening that would yield the highest response rates. For example, we knew that the most effective time to contact centers was in the early afternoons, when children typically took naps. At most other times, directors—whose job often involved rushing from class to class and dealing with constant day-to-day crises—would likely be unable to sit at a desk for 25 minutes to answer questions. Therefore, I instructed the firm to conduct the interviews in the early afternoon. We constructed the questionnaire, especially the introductory and screening questions, using language to yield the highest possible response rates. The number of centers interviewed was 293, and the response rate was 60%, a rate that compares favorably to other organizational surveys. For example, on organizational surveys on issues related to childcare, Doug Guthrie and Louise Marie Roth's study of maternity policies in U.S. organizations reports a 57% response rate, and Erin Kelly's study of employer-sponsored childcare reports a 56% response rate.[3] I expected the effects of nonresponse bias to be minor in the statistical regressions. Still, as in all surveys of organizations, results should be interpreted with caution.[4]

The survey consisted of an approximately 25-minute telephone questionnaire with the director. It obtained data on basic organizational structure, services provided other than childcare, referrals to other organizations, ties to other organizations providing services, the characteristics of those organizations, other organizational variables, and center address. We geocoded addresses using ArcView, such that centers were matched to census tracts; tract-level demographic data were then appended from the 2000 Census of Population and Housing, Summary File 3.

An important consideration in the survey was to prevent overreporting in the questions used to measure organizational ties. Based on our prior qualitative research, we developed questions about six specific referral tie resources and five collaborative tie resources, with an additional question for collaborative resources not asked about. Since our concern was active ties, we inquired only about recently accessed ties. We asked respondents, "The next questions are about services (other than childcare) that the center may offer to parents and families, either as referrals or directly by the center. I'm going to start with referrals. In the last 12 months, has the center directly referred parents to a specific agency or organization for any of the following reasons?" We then listed each of the six issues of interest to parents. For each referral, we asked specific questions about the organization, including organization's sector (government, for-profit, or private nonprofit), its name (verbatim), and its location. This helped prevent overreporting of ties, since respondents who reported a false referral would have to lie multiple times to support the false statement. We then asked, "Now I'd like to ask about services the center may provide directly or by bringing in staff from outside organizations. This question does not include referrals. During the last 12 months, did the center provide" each of five different services. As discussed in chapters 6 and 7, we also asked about any other service that we had not included in the questions.

SPECIFIC MODELS

In what follows, I describe the procedure employed in each of the reported statistical regressions. The discussion here summarizes each of the models, by chapter and table or figure number. Additional details are presented in the chapter notes for each model.

Figure 2.3, Predicted Number of Close Friends for a Statistically Average Mother of a 5-Year-Old

This model, based on wave 4 of the Fragile Families survey, estimates the number of close friends a mother has as a function of center enrollment and controls. Traditional ordinary least squares (OLS) models assume a continuous outcome, whereas the outcome variable here indicates a count, the number of close friends. In addition, the variable exhibits overdispersion. Thus, I estimated a negative binomial regression, appropriate for a count outcome that violates the assumptions of the Poisson distribution.[5] (OLS estimates yielded similar results.) This and all models in chapter 2 exhibit the following characteristics: the models control for number of children, age, household income (logged), black, Latina, other race, the number of adults in the household, employment or school enrollment more than 40 hours a week, married, cohabiting, high school graduation, and college graduation, all factors associated with center enrollment. Due to missing data, I imputed income values and included an indicator for whether income had been imputed. The estimates adjust for sampling design. They include robust standard errors adjusted for clustering at the city level and weights to render the results representative to mothers of newborns born 5 years earlier in cities with populations more than 200,000. Full results are given in table B.1. Coefficients in table B.1 indicate the increase in the log number of close friends associated with a one-unit increase in the predictor.

Table B.1. Results for figure 2.3

Predictor	Coefficient
In childcare center	0.290**
	(0.075)
Number of children	0.071*
	(0.035)
Age	−0.004
	(0.009)
Household income, logged	−0.027
	(0.029)
Income was imputed	0.176**
	(0.055)
Black	−0.717**
	(0.214)
Latina	−0.507**
	(0.195)
Other	−0.543**
	(0.124)
Number of adults in household	0.005
	(0.027)
Employed/in school at least 40 hrs	0.131*
	(0.065)
Cohabiting	0.209
	(0.143)
Married	0.153+
	(0.080)
High school graduate	0.408**
	(0.052)
College graduate	0.173+
	(0.102)
Observations	3810
Degrees of freedom	14.00
Log likelihood	−833100.35

+p<0.10   *p<0.05   **p<0.01

Table 2.2, Predicted Probability of Being Socially Isolated: Urban
Mothers of 5-Year-Olds (after controls)

This model, also based on wave 4 of the Fragile Families survey, estimates the
probability of being socially isolated as a function of center enrollment and
controls. Experiencing social isolation was operationalized as reporting no
close friends. Traditional OLS models assume a continuous outcome, whereas the outcome variable is dichotomous. Thus, least squares analysis would
produce inconsistent results. I estimated logit models wherein the log of the

Table B.2. Results for table 2.2

Predictor	Coefficient
In childcare center	−0.297*
	(0.151)
Number of children	0.231**
	(0.056)
Age	0.032**
	(0.011)
Household income, logged	−0.158*
	(0.062)
Income was imputed	0.001
	(0.218)
Black	1.731**
	(0.630)
Latina	1.817**
	(0.523)
Other	1.691*
	(0.802)
Number of adults in household	0.024
	(0.088)
Employed/in school at least 40 hrs	−0.323
	(0.380)
Cohabiting	−0.252
	(0.367)
Married	−0.338
	(0.286)
High school graduate	−0.462*
	(0.199)
College graduate	−0.065
	(0.347)
Observations	3810
Degrees of freedom	14.00
Log likelihood	−943.31

+$p<0.10$ *$p<0.05$ **$p<0.01$

odds that the outcome is positive is said to be a function of a linear combination of predictors.[6] The model includes the controls and survey-design-related specifications described above. Full results reported in table B.2, where coefficients indicate the increase in the log of the odds of being isolated associated with a one-unit increase in the predictor.

Figure 2.4, Predicted Hardship Score: Enrolled Compared to Nonenrolled Mothers

These three models employ waves 3 and 4 of the Fragile Families survey. The models estimate the respondent's (wave 4) material hardship score, which is a count of the number of hardship indicators experienced, as a function of center enrollment and controls, all measured at wave 4. Traditional OLS was inappropriate due to the nature of the outcome variable (overdispersed, count). Thus, I estimated a negative binomial regression. (Alternative specifications of the outcome variable yielded similar results.) The model helps account for selection—for the possibility that unobserved variables are biasing the effect of the covariates on hardship—by including a "lagged" material hardship measure taken at wave 3.[7] I considered several alternatives, but this yielded the most robust results, required the fewest assumptions, and produced the easiest to interpret findings.[8] The first model in figure 2.4 includes all mothers; the other two models are restricted to poor and nonpoor mothers, respectively. The three models include the controls and survey-design-related specifications described above. They also include a control for the total number of friends (logged) a mother has. For full results, see table B.3, where coefficients indicate the increase or decrease in the log hardship score associated with a one-unit increase in the predictor.[9]

Table B.3. Results for figure 2.4

	All mothers	Non-poor mothers	Poor mothers
In center, made no friends	−0.112	0.014	−0.241+
	(0.077)	(0.094)	(0.127)
In center, made friends	−0.453**	−0.525**	−0.236+
	(0.142)	(0.152)	(0.136)
Number of close friends, logged	−0.008	0.019	0.021
	(0.068)	(0.123)	(0.075)
Number of children	−0.018	0.003	−0.052
	(0.039)	(0.060)	(0.037)
Age	−0.015	−0.013	−0.012

(*continued*)

Table B.3. (*continued*)

	All mothers	Non-poor mothers	Poor mothers
	(0.010)	(0.010)	(0.015)
Household income, logged	−0.106**	−0.376*	−0.012
	(0.031)	(0.150)	(0.062)
Income was imputed	−0.432**	−0.521**	−0.357**
	(0.073)	(0.156)	(0.067)
Black	−0.219+	−0.345+	−0.124
	(0.125)	(0.187)	(0.156)
Latina	−0.252	−0.293+	−0.222
	(0.156)	(0.168)	(0.139)
Other	0.001	0.077	0.026
	(0.404)	(0.415)	(0.177)
Number of adults in household	−0.138**	−0.101+	−0.157*
	(0.032)	(0.058)	(0.077)
Employed/in school at least 40 hrs	0.040	−0.172	0.264
	(0.088)	(0.126)	(0.163)
Cohabiting	−0.085	0.039	−0.097
	(0.103)	(0.139)	(0.148)
Married	−0.422**	−0.386**	−0.583**
	(0.094)	(0.125)	(0.172)
High school graduate	−0.277*	0.241	−0.530**
	(0.127)	(0.228)	(0.191)
College graduate	−0.204*	−0.310*	0.348*
	(0.097)	(0.153)	(0.172)
Prior hardship	0.525**	0.625**	0.383**
	(0.047)	(0.064)	(0.039)
Observations	3537	2095	1442
Degrees of freedom	17.00	17.00	17.00
Log likelihood	−283682.18	−149808.97	−127451.68

+$p<0.10$ *$p<0.05$ **$p<0.01$

Table 2.4, Predicted Probability of Experiencing Housing- or Utilities-Related Hardship for a Statistically Average Urban Mother of a 5-Year-Old

The models in table 2.4 employ waves 3 and 4 of the survey. They estimate the respondent's probability of experiencing a housing- or utilities-related hardship at wave 4, as a function of center enrollment, the same hardship measure at wave 3, and all previous controls, including the total number of friends. Adjustments for survey design are identical to those hitherto

Table B.4. Results for table 2.4: Housing-related hardship

Predictor	Coefficient
In center, made no friends	−0.858**
	(0.301)
In center, made friends	−0.842**
	(0.282)
Number of close friends, logged	−0.259*
	(0.122)
Number of children	−0.076
	(0.086)
Age	−0.107**
	(0.038)
Household income, logged	−0.000
	(0.103)
Income was imputed	−1.392**
	(0.380)
Black	0.522
	(0.456)
Latina	−0.079
	(0.390)
Other	0.394
	(0.897)
Number of adults in household	−0.368
	(0.245)
Employed/in school at least 40 hrs	0.509*
	(0.241)
Cohabiting	0.042
	(0.497)
Married	−2.166**
	(0.746)
High school graduate	−0.949**
	(0.348)
College graduate	−0.739+
	(0.421)
Prior housing-related hardship	1.963**
	(0.566)
Observations	1448
Degrees of freedom	17.00
Log likelihood	−453.78

+p<0.10   *p<0.05   **p<0.01

Table B.5. Results for table 2.4: Utilities-related hardship

Predictor	Coefficient
In center, made no friends	−0.128
	(0.183)
In center, made friends	−0.307+
	(0.183)
Number of close friends, logged	0.305+
	(0.170)
Number of children	−0.052
	(0.098)
Age	−0.047*
	(0.023)
Household income, logged	0.048
	(0.057)
Income was imputed	−0.606+
	(0.332)
Black	−0.504
	(0.592)
Latina	−0.123
	(0.569)
Other	−0.337
	(0.593)
Number of adults in household	−0.656**
	(0.239)
Employed/in school at least 40 hrs	0.445*
	(0.186)
Cohabiting	−0.201
	(0.465)
Married	−0.819*
	(0.325)
High school graduate	−0.458+
	(0.237)
College graduate	0.523
	(0.586)
Prior utilities-related hardship	1.585**
	(0.388)
Observations	1446
Degrees of freedom	17.00
Log likelihood	−712.74

+$p<0.10$ *$p<0.05$ **$p<0.01$

employed. Since the outcome variable is dichotomous, I estimated a logit model. Full results are reported in table B.4 for housing-related hardship and table B.5 for utilities-related hardship, where coefficients indicate the increase in the log of the odds that the respondent experienced the hardship associated with a one-unit increase in the predictor.

Figure 2.5, Odds of Being Depressed: Enrolled Compared to Nonenrolled Mothers

This model, which employs waves 3 and 4 of the Families First survey, predicts the probability of experiencing mental hardship during wave 4 as a function of center enrollment, a lagged measure of mental hardship (during wave 3), and all other general controls. Experiencing mental hardship is operationalized as reporting depressive symptoms, following a standard psychological scale (see chapter 2). I estimated a logit model due to the nature of the outcome variable. Models include all adjustments for survey design. For full results, see table B.6. Coefficients indicate the increase or decrease in the log of the odds of being depressed associated with a one-unit increase in the coefficient.

Table B.6. Results for figure 2.5

	Non-poor mother	Poor mother
In center, made no friends	−0.498	−0.162
	(0.464)	(0.305)
In center, made friends	−0.859**	−0.519**
	(0.324)	(0.182)
Number of close friends, logged	0.051	−0.257+
	(0.095)	(0.153)
Number of children	0.058	−0.009
	(0.103)	(0.054)
Age	0.021	−0.042
	(0.027)	(0.042)
Household income, logged	−0.217	−0.054
	(0.256)	(0.066)
Income was imputed	−0.454	−0.333
	(0.289)	(0.274)
Black	−0.355	−1.132*
	(0.326)	(0.510)
Latina	−0.824**	−0.676
	(0.319)	(0.449)
Other	0.104	−2.007
	(0.834)	(1.337)

(continued)

Table B.6. (*continued*)

	Non-poor mother	Poor mother
Number of adults in household	0.004	−0.328
	(0.222)	(0.296)
Employed/in school at least 40 hrs	0.099	0.638*
	(0.168)	(0.317)
Cohabiting	−0.464	−0.166
	(0.556)	(0.280)
Married	0.026	−0.773
	(0.375)	(0.640)
High school graduate	0.894+	−0.132
	(0.515)	(0.288)
College graduate	−0.519	−1.263
	(0.345)	(0.779)
Prior depression	1.565**	2.244**
	(0.355)	(0.362)
Observations	2100	1446
Degrees of freedom	17.00	17.00
Log likelihood	−701.21	−459.11

+$p<0.10$ *$p<0.05$ **$p<0.01$

Figure 3.1, Predicted Probability of Making a Friend in a Center, for Statistically Average Urban Mother of 5-Year-Old Enrolled in a Childcare Center

This model, which is based on wave 4 of the Families First survey and limited to enrolled mothers, predicts the probability that the mother made a friend in the center as a function of whether the center had a parents

Table B.7. Results for figure 3.1

Predictor	Coefficient
Center has Parent's association	0.477**
	(0.119)
Number of close friends, logged	0.833**
	(0.077)
Number of children	0.008
	(0.114)
Age	0.045*

(*continued*)

Table B.7. (*continued*)

Predictor	Coefficient
	(0.018)
Household income, logged	−0.091
	(0.060)
Income was imputed	0.025
	(0.224)
Black	−0.232
	(0.284)
Latina	0.638**
	(0.139)
Other	−0.546**
	(0.178)
Number of adults in household	0.063
	(0.103)
Employed/in school at least 40 hrs	−0.226
	(0.300)
Cohabiting	0.120
	(0.202)
Married	0.710*
	(0.280)
High school graduate	0.256+
	(0.131)
College graduate	0.203
	(0.309)
Observations	2801
Degrees of freedom	15.00
Log likelihood	−1584.51

+p<0.10   *p<0.05   **p<0.01

association, after controls. Since the outcome variable is dichotomous, I estimated a logit model. The model includes the previous design adjustments and controls, including the total number of close friends. Full results are given in table B.7; coefficients indicate the increase in the log of the odds that the mother made a friend in the center associated with a one-unit increase in the predictor.

Table 7.2, Percent Increase in Number of Active Ties Associated with Sector, Need, and Location

This model is based on the Childcare Centers and Families Survey. It predicts the number of active ties a center has as a function of center characteristics and controls. The predictors include government-funded nonprofit status, for-profit status, high percentage of poor children, location in poor neighborhood, and the following neighborhood controls: percent black, percent white, percent Latino, population density (logged), and Bronx, Brooklyn, Queens, or Staten Island location. The controls account for standard factors shown to affect neighborhood conditions in the urban sociological literature.[10] In New York City, boroughs, which have their own presidents, matter for political and sociohistorical reasons, justifying controlling for them. Given the nature of the outcome variable (a count with little overdispersion), a Poisson model was appropriate. The measure of high poverty neighborhood is an indicator variable coded 1 if the center is located in a neighborhood with a poverty rate of 40% or higher. This measure represents the standard yardstick for high poverty status in studies of urban poverty.[11] In the sample, it also represents the cutoff for the highest poverty quintile. Most important, the rate seemed to signal the tracts in the poor neighborhoods (e.g., upper Manhattan and central Brooklyn) that actors such as Kyle, the officer in New York City's education bureaucracy, described in chapter 7, perceived to be those with the "greatest need." The proxy for need in the center is an indicator variable coded 1 if at least 30% of the children in the center were on government vouchers or some type of government subsidy (regardless of the center's location).[12] Thirty-nine percent of centers fell in this category.

Because the sample of centers was comparatively small ($n=293$), I used multiple imputation techniques to account for missing data.[13] The key intuition behind multiple imputation is that an imputed value should not be treated the way a known one is. Thus, for example, rather than imputing a single value for missing profit status for a particular observation, one imputes 10 values, which yields an average value and a standard deviation. Then, 10 regressions are run and the results averaged out, with the standard errors taking into account that some values were imputed and others were not. A special problem emerged in dealing with the data on the networks of centers, since these questions often involved nested subsections. For example, directors were only asked what type of organization (for-profit or nonprofit) they had referred parents to for health issues if the directors first indicated they had made such a referral at least once in the previous 12 months. If they were missing data on the prior question, they would be missing data on both. Researchers at the University of Michigan have released a software package that deals with such designs effectively. I used the software package IVEware when producing the results in table 7.3.[14] Full results are given in table B.8. Coefficients indicate the increase in the log number of active ties associated with a one-unit increase in the predictor.

Table B.8. Results for table 7.2

	Referral ties	Collaborative ties
Center is a government nonprofit	0.402**	1.163**
	(0.157)	(0.242)
Center is a private nonprofit	0.403**	0.437
	(0.619)	(0.277)
Center has a high proportion of poor children	0.421**	0.218**
	(0.109)	(0.154)
Center is located in a poor neighborhood	0.243**	0.368
	(0.123)	(0.164)
Tract percent who lived elsewhere 5 years earlier	0.001	−0.002
	(0.004)	(0.006)
Tract percent black	−0.001	0.008
	(0.004)	(0.006)
Tract percent white	0.000	0.002
	(0.005)	(0.007)
Tract percent Latino	0.007	0.009
	(0.005)	(0.007)
Tract population density logged	0.052	0.043
	(0.045)	(0.069)
Address in Bronx	−0.084	−0.475**
	(0.158)	(0.239)
Address in Brooklyn	−0.246+	−0.186
	(0.138)	(0.199)
Address in Queens	−0.095	0.016
	(0.165)	(0.229)
Address in Staten Island	0.397+	0.170
	(0.211)	(0.350)
Observations	293	293

Poisson regression estimates, 10 imputations.
+$p<0.10$ *$p<0.05$ **$p<0.01$

Table 7.3, Effect of Sector, Need, and Location on the Odds of Having an Active Collaborative Tie Providing a Resource Not Asked About

This model, based on the survey of centers, estimates the probability of having a tie providing an issue not asked about, as a function of the predictors identified in table 7.2. Given the outcome variable, I estimated a logit model. All other model characteristics are identical to those for table 7.2. Full results are reported in table B.9. Coefficients indicate the increase in the log of the odds of having the tie associated with a one-unit increase in the predictor.

Table B.9. Results for table 7.3

Predictor	Coefficient
Center is a government nonprofit	1.148+
	(0.641)
Center is a private nonprofit	0.952
	(0.698)
Center has a high proportion of poor children	−0.790
	(0.497)
Center is located in a poor neighborhood	1.681**
	(0.614)
Tract percent who lived elsewhere 5 years earlier	0.018
	(0.021)
Tract percent black	0.028
	(0.022)
Tract percent white	0.026
	(0.024)
Tract percent Latino	0.009
	(0.028)
Tract population density logged	0.291
	(0.235)
Address in Bronx	−0.988
	(1.031)
Address in Brooklyn	−0.105
	(0.663)
Address in Queens	1.014
	(0.767)
Address in Staten Island	2.183**
	(0.771)
Observations	293

Logistic regression estimates, 10 imputations.

$+p<0.10$ $*p<0.05$ $**p<0.01$

Appendix C

Qualitative Data

The overarching principle governing this book's use of multiple methods was that each method should be deployed to answer the questions for which it is best suited (rather than attempt to force questions, and therefore standards of evidence, into methods for which they are inappropriate).[1] The qualitative portion of this project involved a study of centers and a study of mothers (see chapter 1, table 1.1). If the quantitative studies were used to describe central tendencies, reveal distributions, and uncover associations, then the two sets of case studies were designed to understand the mechanisms underlying the associations and uncover the meaning that actors gave to their actions, relationships, institutional contexts, and circumstances. The following appendix briefly describes the procedures behind the qualitative data collection. It describes first the case study of centers, and then the case study of mothers.

CASE STUDY OF CENTERS

The qualitative study of childcare centers was preceded by the pilot study mentioned briefly in appendix A. For the pilot study, one research assistant and I identified one predominantly poor and one upper-middle-class neighborhood in the city, and visited all centers, about twenty in total, in both neighborhoods. We split the centers in half and visited each center only once, speaking to the director or assistant director anywhere from less than an hour to several hours; taking tours of the facilities; retrieving fliers, posters, and any other available documentation; and assessing the feasibility of a larger study. The centers exhibited the remarkable heterogeneity we later found in the larger study—they were large and small, religious and secular, Head Start and for-profit, state-of-the-art and desperately needing repair. We learned quickly that establishing rapport with directors would be relatively straightforward: even though most centers were high on security and many required buzzing-in for entry, no one turned us away, and most directors provided at least the courtesy of a sit-down meeting with themselves or their assistants. Through the pilot study we learned that the majority of directors, teachers, assistant teachers, and staff were women, regardless of the neighborhood where the center was located. We also came to suspect that our sex or ethnic background, as interviewers, probably would not hinder our ability to establish rapport with the director. While most directors were women, and most had acquired some college education, they varied widely in ethnic background. I am male, of African descent, and born in Panama; my assistant is female, white, and U.S. born; and we uncovered no systematic differences in our ability to quickly establish a comfortable interview.

The pilot study convinced me that parents often formed relations in childcare centers, that they also formed connections to other organizations, and that centers varied dramatically in both respects. But it also showed me that the question was more complex than I initially suspected, and I needed to learn more about how centers differed. For this reason, I designed a qualitative study of centers in which the primary objective with respect to case selection was variability, or range.[2] The project would be larger than I could accomplish on my own. After publishing a paper with my first research assistant, she needed to move on to her dissertation, so I hired two new research assistants who were entering the field with fresh eyes. Together, we identified four neighborhoods with the following characteristics: one predominantly black and poor, one predominantly white and poor, one predominantly Latino and poor, and one upper-middle class. Each neighborhood consisted of three to five census tracts. Census tracts were selected to accord with geographic and social boundaries and to match our income/race criteria. We targeted all 23 centers in those four neighborhoods. Of the 23 centers, 17 served low-income populations; 9 of those were publicly funded, either through New York City's Administration for Children's Services or the national Head Start program. Fourteen offered services either for free or on a sliding scale. The directors were interviewed in person and most centers were observed between one and eight times; when possible, we spoke with a second staff member, such as a parent coordinator or social worker. By the time we had begun to develop preliminary propositions, we spent had spent additional time in a few centers, and much more on these than the rest. After the pilot study, most of my fieldwork took place in the Alegre Daycare and the Standing in Faith center. I came to know several of the staff at Alegre, and I became friends with one member who put me in contact with others throughout the organization. We attended meetings, celebrations, workshops, gatherings, and fieldtrips.[3]

Our interviews and observations gave us a clear sense of what motivated directors and staff to establish interorganizational ties, of the nature of those ties, of the general resources available to parents, and of the opportunities and nature of informal interaction. We developed an understanding of how lobbies, front offices, and classrooms were structured, and how these architectural conditions, in conjunction with rules as to whether and where parents had to wait for their children, shaped interactions among parents. We came to know the many rules and regulations guiding the behavior of teachers, staff, and parents in centers, and how forcefully the influence of state regulations could affect its staff members' preoccupation with parental participation. In one state-funded center, a staff assistant scrambled every year to identify people to run for the four positions required of a parents' association. We came to understand why some mothers described their centers as "warm," and could trace their feelings to a tradition of regular potlucks or an especially effective parents association. We developed a deep sense of the large differences across centers that ostensibly trivial practices produced. It was easy to see, for example, that very lax pick-up and drop-off hours helped explain why, as one director bemoaned, few parents in her center seemed to know any others. And we came to understand how a center's set of organizational ties, at any given time, resulted from both institutional and ad-hoc arrangements. Our comparative design provided clear analytical leverage.

Over many months, we talked, observed, took copious notes, and (sometimes) recorded one-on-one conversations on tape. All interviews and observations were recorded into detailed field notes, which were converted to Atlas.ti primary documents and coded and analyzed using Atlas.ti, a software package that facilitates the storage, sorting, and analysis of qualitative data (http://www.atlasti.com). I trained both research assistants on the particular elements of participant observation, interviewing, and field note writing I found important, such as the use of counterfactual questions when probing the motivations of directors. I read all field notes as they were being completed and met with research assistants weekly or biweekly, to ensure comparability across observations and identify issues to expand on. This resulted in rich, comprehensive notes on a wide range of centers, and comparable data across centers.

I eventually used the data from the 23 centers for an objective different from my original design. At the start of the study, I believed that comparing centers across different neighborhoods would yield rich data on how much neighborhoods mattered, which was a concern consistent with much of the literature on urban neighborhoods.[4] I especially expected that local neighborhood conditions, and even local norms and practices, would shape how parents formed ties in the centers more than would the characteristics of the centers themselves. For example, I expected that Head Start centers in the predominantly black neighborhood would differ from Head Starts in the predominantly white neighborhood and that the former would resemble non-Head Start centers in the black neighborhood. This turned out to be mistaken. While there were many differences across neighborhoods, with respect to my question—how networks were formed, sustained, and mobilized in centers—Head Starts resembled Head Starts, regardless of their location or of the racial composition of their members, because of the pressures of the state regarding their structure, parental participation, and institutional collaboration. Race, in neighborhoods, simply mattered less than I expected. (Of course, race did matter in other respects, which I describe in the book, such as its relationship to homophily and the greater propensity of blacks and Latinas to describe acquaintances as "associates.")

This realization forced me to look more seriously at organizational conditions. I interviewed a half dozen directors or high officers in nonprofit organizations and government agencies that in some capacity brokered relationships among centers and other organizations. These were explicitly key informant interviews, in that their objective was to rely on field experts to describe processes few people understand. These interviews were complemented by archival and documentary data on these organizations and agencies.

CASE STUDY OF MOTHERS

Basic Interview Process

In a subset of seven centers, my research assistants and I interviewed 67 parents in depth about their social networks in centers. The objective was to understand whether and how they had formed ties in the center, how they understood these relations, and under what circumstances they mobilized these ties. All interviews were open ended (within these general topics), but we included questions depicting hypothetical scenarios to understand how parents would deal with everyday problems, such as addressing a child's illness, being unable to retrieve their child from the center, and needing to find a lawyer for a friend. The initial selection strategy called for range (not representativeness), so we first targeted parents who reported knowing many and those who reported knowing few other parents in their center (more on this below). Most of the interviews were conducted by my research assistants; I interviewed about a dozen parents. We interviewed parents in centers, parks, restaurants, sidewalk benches, and buses. We often followed up in person or by telephone. Almost all interviews were recorded, transcribed, and (along with field notes taken during the interviews) stored and analyzed using Atlas.ti software.

The parents were even more diverse than the directors, because the former ranged dramatically in income and education. The vast majority of the parents were mothers, and many of them worked, but they ranged from part-time secretaries and bus drivers to lawyers and specialist doctors, and they were black, white, Asian, and Latino, all of various national origins. I suspected that, contrary to our experience with directors, establishing rapport among parents might be more difficult, particularly because we were interviewing the parents about their own circumstances. Nevertheless, establishing rapport was generally uncomplicated, irrespective of the background of the parent, the background of the interviewer, or the concordance between the two. Both of the main research assistants were white females in their late twenties; a few late interviews were conducted by a white male and a black female, both in their late twenties. I deliberately did not attempt to match interviewer and interviewee, and I was not wrong to do so, for the quality of the interviews depended, above all, on how strong the interviewer was. The best interviews derived from the best interviewers, rather than demographic concordance. (Had the study been focused primarily on sensitive topics such as racial identity or illegal behavior, establishing rapport and conducting effective interviews might have been much more complicated, as others have reported.[5])

In qualitative research on resources among the urban poor, the researcher often faces a dilemma with respect to the boundary between observer and participant. One element of this larger debate concerns whether, when interviewing people about how they deal with poverty, the researcher should also help respondents deal with poverty. The many complex issues involved in this debate could fill another volume. But some researchers believe it is unconscionable to fail to provide aid; others, and I have generally stood in this camp, believe that doing so will often undermine the aims of the project, since one is unable to understand how people truly manage their circumstances. That is, if I had made a practice of helping all my respondents in need, then I would not have learned how the poor gain or fail to acquire resources through their centers; I would have learned how the poor acquire resources when aided by a college professor, a much more limited (and probably less important) set of findings. Nevertheless, as a professor at a major research institute, I had access to a range of social and organizational connections simply unavailable to many of the poorest mothers I was interviewing. During particularly personal interviews—for example, when I interviewed a mother barely rebuilding herself from a prolonged depression, or another struggling to secure health care for her chronically ill child—it was difficult to behave exclusively as an analyst, particularly when a couple of telephone calls on my behalf might make a major difference. I certainly have not resolved the ethical quandary—a few times I helped and others I did not.

But from a scientific perspective, I must note that at least once my intervention undermined my ability to understand the circumstances at play. I interviewed one poor, very isolated, very time-constrained mother whose Medicaid did not cover her child's chronic (but not degenerative) illness. As I met her, her child's condition had taken a slight turn for the worse. It did not take her long to ask me to help her, with very specific issues regarding some complicated matters in the health bureaucracy. I did, and the more I did the more I realized that I had difficulty putting together what she would have done in my absence—there simply was no one of my educational level in her network, and few people who possessed either resources or their own connections. Would she have tried to turn to her center? Would the staff had noticed something with the child, and attempted to mobilize a connection? Would she have turned to some mechanism we did not uncover through our other interviews? I do not know.

Analytical Perspective

My approach to the selection and analysis of interview data differed in important ways from some common practices. I was committed to using the interview data for what they do best, so the strategy for the open-ended interviews was to produce the richest data possible. For this reason, there would be little gain—and some important loss—from attempting to design my in-depth interviews to be "representative" in a way all too common among qualitative research today (by, e.g., selecting a random sample of parents). Even if I had pursued this strategy, the interviews we conducted would not be truly representative of any real population; in addition, I would have produced an inadequate set of cases that failed to deliver on the range of experience required to uncover the full slate of mechanisms through which mothers developed connections. I discuss the epistemological underpinnings of this perspective in detail elsewhere.[6] Here, I provide an outline of the rationale.

The foundation is a distinction that in one way or another has been suggested by several scholars, but most clearly and usefully has been proposed by Robert Yin, in his widely employed handbook on case study methods.[7] Yin argued that there is a fundamental distinction between case study logic and sampling logic.[8] Sampling and case study logic perspectives are distinct and independent ways of approaching data. In a sampling model, the number of cases is predetermined, the sample is (intended to be) representative, all individuals should have equal (or known) probability of selection, and all respondents should be subject to exactly the same questionnaire. Only by following these and other conditions can we draw statistical inferences about the characteristics of the population as a whole based on the sample. Sampling logic, which derives from basic probability theory, is the foundation of survey analysis. A researcher following these criteria can expect the traits of respondents in her sample to match, within a given degree of confidence, those of the population from which it was drawn. Case study logic differs in all important respects. In a case model, the number of cases is unknown until the study is completed; the collection of cases is, by design, not representative; each individual has her or his own probability of selection; and different people have different questionnaires or interviews. A researcher selects a case and uses the knowledge gained from that case to select the next one, and the subsequent one, and so on. A researcher following these criteria cannot expect with any confidence that the traits of respondents in her cases will match those of any wider population. Only sampling logic is appropriate when seeking statistically representative data—that is, when the sample is being used to describe the average characteristics of a wider population (e.g., what percentage is black, or how many friends they make on average in childcare centers). What the case study logic provides, instead, is a clearer procedure for discovering previously unknown practices or processes, and refining one's understanding of the nature of those practices or processes during the conduct of the study. In this respect, case study logic is more powerful, I believe, when seeking to discover *how* and *why* practices or processes take place (for uncovering mechanisms), especially if these are largely unknown—for example, when attempting to understand how people conceive of the closeness of a relationship.[9]

Following case study logic, I have conceived of my interviews as 67 *cases*, not a *sample* of $n = 67$. I make no *statistical* inferences from them, which is why there are no tables or figures indicating the percentage of parents in the in-depth interviews who responded to a question one way or another. Having some statistically representative data (from the Fragile Families survey) allowed me the freedom to push case study logic (rather than sample logic) to its limits, yielding what I found to be the richest interview data.

Thus, my initial approach evolved into what I term "sequential interviewing." My approach was to consider each interview as a case in its own right, a piece of knowledge that should inform future cases.[10] I used the interview to generate expectations about what we would see in the next interview, refining my thinking with each subsequent interview. The objective was that, after enough interviews, we would ultimately attain *saturation* on a given issue. In this respect, the ultimate goal was not representativeness, but saturation. Each subsequent interview was selected to maximize range and to assess whether people with given characteristics would report what we expected them to. Each interview was transcribed and recorded as it was completed. During our weekly or biweekly meetings, the research assistants and I met to discuss what we had learned in our interviews.[11] Then, as some issues emerged that we had not anticipated, we decided to pursue them further in subsequent interviews, so that, in almost Bayesian fashion, future interviews were directly informed by prior ones.

The last interviews were, by design, more subtle on the issues ultimately discussed in the book than were the earlier interviews. In addition, the latter interviews were less concerned with the issues that early on had emerged repeatedly. For example, the early interviews revealed that mothers formed ties through a relatively small number of mechanisms: parent associations, field trips, drop-off and pickup, and a few others. By about the twentieth interview, no new mother we interviewed was reporting any mechanism through which she met others that we had not already discovered—we attained saturation on this particular issue early on. Subsequent interviews spent less time on this issue and more time on issues we had not discovered. Another example illustrates how subsequent interviews evolved from prior ones. During an interview about halfway through the process I discovered, to my surprise, that mothers were willing to trust their children with others they hardly knew. Subsequent questions explicitly asked about this issue, to gain a greater understanding of what later became the basis for chapter 5.

Sequential interviewing is not without its limitations. I cannot use these qualitative interview data to make accurate inferences about the distribution, in the larger population, of the variables for the particular issues I was discovering in the qualitative interviews. For example, I could not state what percentage of parents made compartmentally intimate ties. On the other hand, had I followed the sample logic, I would have had no basis to make such statements, either, because a (biased) sample of 67 people who each received different questionnaires (they were open-ended) would violate many assumptions of basic probability theory. Reporting such percentages would be highly misleading. At best, it would provide the peculiar comfort that comes from placing a statistic, no matter how questionable, next to an idea. In addition, I had already gained a reasonable idea of the distribution of major characteristics (e.g., how many mothers formed ties in centers) from an actual survey, Fragile Families. Finally, I note that other procedures, such as a random sample, would have missed mechanisms that were very rare, a drawback for a project aimed at uncovering processes. My procedure, I believe, made the best use of the interview data for the issues that concerned me. A more thorough discussion of sequential interviewing, and the epistemological foundations sustaining it, can be found elsewhere.[12]

In the end, the multiple data sources, qualitative and quantitative, at the levels of individuals and organizations, served their ultimate purposes, triangulation and saturation. Eventually, when I was convinced I had something worth reporting, I stopped and completed the book.

Notes

CHAPTER 1

1. Becker (1964).
2. Coleman (1988); Bourdieu (1986).
3. Coleman (1990); for a recent review of the sociological and philosophical issues involved in the study of emergent processes, see Sawyer (2001).
4. The term "total institution" was used by Goffman (1961) to describe a system that encompasses and regulates all aspects of a person's life.
5. Few have done more to develop the concept of embeddedness than Mark Granovetter (1985). My use of the term, however, differs from his. Granovetter refers to the embeddedness of people in social networks, which he believes should be taken into account in the study of economic action. This book is concerned with the embeddedness of personal networks in organizational settings, which I believe should inform the study of well-being. While Granovetter argues that we study the embeddedness of people in social ties, I suggest we examine the embeddedness of the ties themselves.
6. Loury (1977); Bourdieu (1986); Coleman (1988); Lin (2001a; 2001b). See also Ronald Burt (2005). Other major researchers examine the social capital not of individuals but of communities and nations. Among these, the most influential are Robert Putnam (2000) and Francis Fukuyama (1995). For a critique, see Alejandro Portes (1998).
7. Bourdieu (1986:248).
8. Bourdieu (1986:249). Despite the fact that social capital might be one of the most important concepts in his oeuvre, Bourdieu spent the least amount of time unpacking it (Bourdieu 1980; 1986). By contrast, he devotes several books to the ideas of the field, habitus, and cultural capital (Bourdieu 1977; 1984; 1990; Bourdieu and Wacquant 1992).
9. Coleman (1990).
10. Coleman (1988:s98).
11. Coleman (1988:s102).
12. Coleman (1988:s104). Coleman believed that norms, to be effective, required closure, such that different actors in the group were tied to one another. Naturally, since the actor is also subject to the norms, this social capital is not unconstrained. "This social capital . . . not only facilitates certain actions; it constrains others" (Coleman 1988:s105).
13. Lin (2001a:29).

14. For example, see Lin, Vaughn, and Ensel (1981); for a review, see Lin (1999a).

15. For reviews, see Portes (1998); Putnam (2000). There is vast body of scholarship on the relationship between social ties and access to resources in urban settings (for reviews, see Small and Newman 2001; Newman and Massengill 2006). These works do not address social capital theory, but cover related issues. Among the most influential is Carol Stack's *All Our Kin* (1974), which found that African-American mothers in the poor urban community she studied did better than expected because their social ties provided everyday support in raising children. Kathryn Edin and Laura Lein (1997) found that more than three-fourths of the poor women they interviewed relied on their social networks to access cash contributions to make ends meet, regardless of whether they were employed. Silvia Domínguez and Celeste Watkins-Hayes (2003) found that the inner-city black and Latina women they interviewed rely heavily on kin and nonkin ties to gain access to social support, cash, and other resources. William J. Wilson (1987) argued that one of the most important reasons that living in concentrated poverty leads to disadvantage is social isolation. By this theory, the residents of poor neighborhoods suffer because many of the most valuable resources—particularly those regarding employment—are contained in the middle class. Other relevant works include Massey and Denton (1993); Anderson (1990, 1999); McRoberts (2003); Pattillo (2007); Pattillo-McCoy (1999); Rankin and Quane (2000); Smith (2007); Kasinitz (2000); Kasinitz and Rosenberg (1996); Klinenberg (2002); Small (2004, 2002); Tigges et al. (1998).

Much of the scholarship has focused on neighborhoods and the resources available to people collectively, such as better police protection. In a series of studies, Robert Sampson and colleagues have shown that neighborhoods with dense social ties and a willingness to cooperate to attain common goals tend to experience lower crime rates, arguably because they are better able to access both formal and informal social control (Sampson, Raudenbush, and Earls 1997; Sampson and Groves 1989; see also Peterson et al. 2000; Kasarda and Janowitz 1974). In a study of a predominantly Puerto Rican poor neighborhood in Boston, I showed that strong ties among neighbors helped create an affordable housing community and obtain several organizational resources, such as a credit union and a recreation center (Small 2004). There are many more studies on these questions (for reviews, see Small and Newman 2001; Sampson, Morenoff, and Gannon-Rowley 2002).

In addition, the immigration literature has produced a number of studies of this question. The literature on ethnic enclaves has made compelling arguments for the importance of dense immigrant networks for the well-being and mobility of immigrants (Portes and Rumbaut 1990; Zhou 1992). Raymond Breton's (1964) concept of "institutional completeness" points to the importance of both social connections and organizational resources in immigrant communities.

16. Social capital theorists might have turned to at least three bodies of work to examine this question. Mid-century social scientists such as Theodore Newcomb (1961), Paul Lazarsfeld and Robert Merton (1954), and later Scott Feld (1981) wrote important works on the friendship formation process. These argued that the key lay in social interaction, a perspective shared by this book. A second literature is the work on "meeting and mating" by standard social network analysts (Verbrugge 1977; Kalmjin and Flap 2001; see also Briggs 2007). More recently, social network analysts have begun to develop dynamic models by which transformations in entire networks (including the

addition or loss of ties) are examined over time. For examples, see the work of Kathleen Carley (1999, 2003) and Tom Snijders (2005) (c.f., Hallinan 1978).

17. Lin (2001a:xi, emphasis added). In his comprehensive exposition of social capital theory, Lin allowed some nuance by granting that noninstrumental motivations could lead to tie formation: "Instrumental actions are those actions taken for the purpose of achieving certain goals. The distinctive feature of this class of actions is that the means and ends are separate and distinct. A typical example is the search for a job or a person. Expressive actions are taken for their own sake: the actions are both means and ends, and are integrated and inseparable. Confiding one's feelings is a typical example" (2001a:58). Yet despite this distinction early in his book, Lin's main theoretical exposition is almost entirely devoted to instrumental actions.

18. Bourdieu (1986:249).

19. Bourdieu (1986:249; emphasis added).

20. Lin (1999b:30). See also Lin (2001b); Spies-Butcher (2002).

21. Bourdieu (1977, 1984); Bourdieu and Wacquant (1992).

22. To be clear, it is certainly the case that Bourdieu argued for a relational sociology organized around fields, in which relations mattered more than individual decisions, and in which dispositions—in the form of habitus or "internalized capital" (Bourdieu 1984:114)—contributed to social inequality in ways actors did not articulate (Bourdieu 1977; 1984). But I do not believe that Bourdieu resolved all of the contradictions in his work on social capital, and this is one of the sources of contradiction. In fact, the cited passage alone suggests that Bourdieu is struggling with the model, since he argues that networks result from "investment strategies" aimed at "usable relationships" but then also adds that these strategies may be "conscious or unconscious." How exactly can a "strategy" be "unconscious"? Bourdieu never answers. One would be forgiven for believing that Bourdieu was trying to have it both ways. It is not surprising that formal modelers (e.g., Lin 2001b; Frank 1992) are more comfortable than sociologists in general and ethnographers in particular with the idea that Bourdieu might be arguing that networks result from deliberate investments, since that seems suspiciously close to a rational actor model.

23. Bourdieu (1986:250). Bourdieu argued:

> The reproduction of social capital presupposes an unceasing effort of sociability, a continuous series of exchanges in which recognition is endlessly affirmed and reaffirmed. This work, which implies expenditure of time and energy and so, directly or indirectly, of economic capital, is not profitable or even conceivable unless one invests in it a specific competence (knowledge of genealogical relationships and of real connections and skill at using them, etc.) and an acquired disposition to acquire and maintain this competence, which are themselves integral parts of this capital. (1986:250)

In an act surprising for an ethnographer, Bourdieu conceived of these relations in the abstract. This resulted from his focus on "the field" and his aim at developing an all encompassing field theory in which forms of capital mattered depending on the field in which they were deployed. The problem is that Bourdieu the theorist got the better part of Bourdieu the participant observer, leading to a theory that neglects that social capital can be reproduced by organizational settings, independent of direct efforts of its beneficiaries.

24. Kadushin (2004).
25. Portes (1998); Burt (2005).
26. Mouw (2003, 2006); see also Granovetter (1974); c.f. Smith (2003, 2005, 2007).
27. Hedstrom and Swedberg (1998).
28. See DeFilippis (2001); see also Wilson (1997).
29. Sampson, Morenoff, and Earls (1999); Sampson et al. (1997).
30. Putnam (2000).
31. A different critique focuses less on social capital theory than on formal social network analysis. Some have argued that social network analysis tends to neglect how people form ties at the expense of studying the nature of network structure or the consequences of networks (Emirbayer and Goodwin 1994). I believe there is merit in this critique. However, scholars such as Carley (1999, 2003) and Snijders (2005) in recent years have been studying network formation within the context of dynamic models.
32. Many traditions in microsociology have focused on routine organizations and the experience of everyday life (Adler, Adler, and Fontana 1987). Erving Goffman's (1959) *The Presentation of Self in Everyday Life* and Harold Garfinkel's (1967) *Studies in Ethnomethodology* represent two of the most prominent traditions in this general line of research. While the model advanced in this book is informed by Goffman's work on the efforts actors make to negotiate interaction, it is not, as will become evident, a treatise strictly in Goffman's dramaturgic tradition. And while it is informed by a situationist approach to interaction, it does not propose the radical situationism of Garfinkel's ethnomethodological tradition, in which "indexicality" is the primary analytical tool.
33. As I discuss in appendix A, I did not develop this model abstractly to subsequently test on childcare centers. On the contrary, much of the model was the result of a recursive, dialectical interaction between theorizing and data analysis that took place over several years and was informed by much of the classic and recent literature on formal network analysis (e.g., Newcomb 1961; Lazarsfeld and Merton 1954; Hallinan 1976, 1979; Carley 1999; Snijders 2005). The reader will note that the model begins with the individual, not the group, as the unit of analysis. Other perspectives on social capital examine group dynamics (Coleman 1990) or national trends (Putnam 2000). As I discuss throughout the chapter, other authors in network analysis have emphasized the importance of organizational context. For examples, see Brass et al. (2004); Popielarz (1999); Hallinan (1976, 1979); Hallinan and Sorenesen (1985).
34. Merton (1936). On purposive action, see Weber (1978); Coleman (1990); Kadushin (2002); Elster (2007). On rational actor theory, see Elster (1986); Green and Shapiro (1994).
35. I recognize that many varieties of rational action theory exist, and that some would incorporate conditions such as altruism into their conception of rational behavior (Elster 1986; Green and Shapiro 1994). I do not find all of these efforts successful, but that debate does not alter this discussion. Certainly, actors sometimes make ties for explicitly rational or instrumental reasons. The point is that they do not always do so.
36. Merton (1936) refers to such acts as "behavior" rather than "conduct." Elster (2007) makes a similar distinction, reserving the term "action" for acts motivated by a purpose. I believe the term "nonpurposive action" is clear enough for this discussion.

37. Lin (2001a).

38. For an interesting discussion of interpersonal dynamics in grocery and convenience stores, see McDermott (2006). McDermott discusses the role of race in complicating these interactions (2006:66ff.).

39. One could argue that the laughter was purposive and that the purpose was to release stress. I suggest the key is that there was no objective separate from the action. If there was a purpose, the action itself was it. Lin (2001a:58) argues that this type of action is also purposive but that the difference between this action and instrumental action is that in the latter the means and ends are separate, while in expressive action the means and ends are the same. I do not find it useful to refer to expressive actions as purposive—one seems to dilute the idea of "purpose" by using it to characterize the laughter that follows a joke, even if the laughter ends up making the person feel better. In the end, this is a semantic distinction, one that would not affect this discussion. (A different way of making this point is to state that I maintain that purposive action should be consequentialist, while Lin does not impose this restriction. See Elster [2007:81ff.].) It will always be difficult for sociologists to ascertain purpose, except at the extremes.

40. Simmel (1971:137).

41. Bourdieu (1977, 1984, 1990).

42. Personal experience inspired this example: when comparing the last two cities in which I have lived, I noticed that Chicagoans cut in front of others—when waiting in line, when crossing the street, when driving—a lot less frequently than do New Yorkers.

43. Certainly, distinguishing purposive from nonpurposive acts may sometimes prove elusive. At times, an actor might have a global purpose but act nonpurposely at the moment she or he encounters others. The lawyer who attended a conference in order to network might, when talking to a particular attendee, be performing a purely expressive action, one in which her prior intentions had been forgotten. In addition, actors do not always know or understand why they act, and even their post facto explanations might amount to little more than rationalizations. In the end, the distinction between purposive and nonpurposive acts is most useful at the extremes, since people sometimes clearly have objectives and other times they clearly do not. Finally, note that by considering both purposive and nonpurposive action, the present model implicitly avoids presenting a single set of motivations for the formation of new ties (but see Kadushin 2002).

44. My general orientation toward social interaction owes something to Goffman (1959, 1967), whose thinking informed an earlier version of the models in several chapters of part II.

45. Lazarsfeld and Merton (1954). See also Newcomb (1961); Huckfeldt (1983); Blau and Schwartz (1997).

46. Blau and Schwartz (1997) probably introduced one of the most systematic propositions, in a study of cross-cutting social circles in contemporary society. The proposition was one of the two basic assumptions guiding their book:

[R]ates of social association depend on opportunities for contact (A-2). It is virtually self-evident that people cannot become friendly unless they have an opportunity to meet. However, the postulate implies more than that. It posits that the extent of contact opportunities governs the probability of associations of people, not merely of casual acquaintances but even of intimate relations, like those of lovers. A clear implication of this assumption, which can serve as a means for testing, is that *spatial propinquity*, because it increases the chances of fortuitous contacts, enhances the probability of friendship and even marriage. (Blau and Schwartz 1997:29)

47. Oldenburg (1989); Hallinan (1979) Wilson (1987). An interesting feature of Hallinan's study is her finding that "open," as opposed to "traditional" classrooms resulted in fewer friendships. Open classrooms presumably provided more opportunities for interaction; however, they also integrated highly heterogeneous students under a single room and instituted other practices that affected social interaction. See Hallinan (1976, 1979); compare to Hallinan and Tuma (1978). Other studies of social relations in restaurants and bars include Duneier (1992); Anderson (1978); May (2001). On the general importance of organizations for tie formation in urban settings, see Fischer (1982); also Taub et al. (1977). On the evidence for Wilson's argument, see Fernandez and Harris (1992); Briggs (2007); Small (2007a); compare Smith (2007).

48. Emerson (1976; 1981); Homans (1950); see also Blau (1986/1964).

49. Lawler (2001); Lawler and Yoon (1993).

50. Duneier (1992). The obvious critique of this proposition is one that dogged Homans after publication of *The Human Group* (1950), that people may like each other *less* the more they encounter each other. For both empirical and theoretical reasons, this critique has held little sway. First, while the critique identifies what could happen, it does not reflect what actually happens. The experimental literature has consistently confirmed that repeated contact increases positive affect and trust, rather than the opposite (Lawler 2001). Second, it is not theoretically difficult to imagine why this would be the case. People assess each other with every subsequent interaction. At early hints of discord or noncompatibility, actors tend to avoid each other. Repeated interaction and, by extension, friendship require the tacit approval of the parties.

51. Feld (1981:1025); see also Feld (1982, 1984). Feld believed that shared relations to a common focus "create positive sentiments indirectly [by generating] positively valued interactions" (1981:1017). In this respect, Feld borrowed heavily from Homans (1961), who maintained that repeated interaction tends to create positive sentiment among members of groups. A similar idea was proposed recently by Randall Collins (2004), who argued that when people perform emotionally charged, ritual acts together, they develop strong bonds among themselves.

52. While Feld's has been one of the most fruitful models of tie formation in network research, the strength of the model is undermined by the slippery nature of the term "focus." In a later paper with William Carter, Feld elaborates on the term; they write, "Foci of activity take varied forms, including families, workplaces, voluntary organizations, and neighborhoods, but all have the common effect of bringing a relatively limited set of individuals together in repeated interactions in and around the focused activities (Feld and Carter 1998:136). The problem with the term "focus" remains, since it conflates a lot of different types of entities under the term "activity," including a neighborhood, a workplace, and even a family. These are not all

organizations, nor are they all places, nor are they all groups of individuals. Since all of these entities must shape the formation of ties through somewhat different mechanisms, the single common mechanism underlying the process remains vague. For the present purposes, the most important limitation is the model's failure to distinguish organizations from other types of entities. Later chapters describe how organizations shape the formation of friendships in specific ways, because they can regulate the frequency of activity, the constitution of the potential friends to be made, the activities they do together, and the like.

53. Oldenburg makes a related point regarding competition when he argues that "third places"—cafes, bars, restaurants—help build community, in part, because they are "levelers," spaces that eschew hierarchy and competition in favor of equality (1989:23). See also Jacobs (1961).

It is important to note, as Simmel (1955) has, that competition and antagonism are not synonymous. Simmel would argue that competition is not so much *against* the opponent as *for* a particular prize, such that conflict, in competition, is indirect. As a result, competition does not necessarily create enemies; in fact, there is such a thing as "friendly competition," and there are multiple social situations where competition and cooperation coexist, such as race car driving in teams of independent drivers, courses were students work in groups but are graded on a curve, or primary presidential elections where candidates must compete against each other but cooperate to overcome the opposing party. The most important element of competition to friendship formation, I argue, lies in the size of the stakes. As the stakes increase, the conflict inherent in competition becomes increasingly direct.

54. Lawler (2001). Lawler termed this process "relational cohesion."

55. Several studies in the social network tradition bear evidence to this point explicitly in the context of friendship or tie formation: Hallinan (1976, 1979); Hallinan and Tuma (1978); Popielarz (1999); see also McPherson, Smith-Lovin, and Cook (2001).

56. Scott (1995).

57. I emphasize that any actor in the organization may shape social interaction, regardless of whether the actor is a client, employee, manager, or any other form of participant—even if, within the formal hierarchy of the organization, these actors do not constitute critical members. Consider how a college student might form social ties: the college's vice president for strategic planning might be less important than the students who organize bimonthly "meet-and-greets," since the latter have greater influence on the student's social interactions.

58. Nee and Ingram (1998:19). See also Nee and Brinton (1998).

59. Meyer and Rowan (1977:341).

60. The work on institutions in the normative sense can be traced to Emile Durkheim (1897/1951), whose perspective focused on the influence of norms on behavior and also influenced Coleman's (1990) functional conception of social capital. The work on institutions in the cognitive sense can probably be traced to Peter Berger and Thomas Luckman (1966), and ultimately Immanuel Kant (1781/1965). On some of the perils of institutional analysis, see Lynne Zucker (1977). The work on institutions is one of the most effective ways to conceive of the role of culture. Readers will note that I have largely avoided the term "culture," even though throughout the book I am effectively discussing cultural practices. The term "culture"

has referred to sufficiently heterogeneous phenomena that the discussion benefits from the clarity of more specific language (Lamont and Small 2008).

61. Meyer and Rowan (1977); Nee and Ingram (1998).

62. The recent *Barbershop* films, centered on the activities at a neighborhood barbershop and starring Ice Cube, make this point explicitly about the role of the barbershop as an institution. See also Delgado (1997; 1998); Furman (1997).

63. Laumann, Galaskiewicz, and Marsden (1978); Levine and White (1961); Galaskiewicz (1979, 1985, 1999); Ebbers (1997); Benson 1975; Small (2006).

64. The Frist Campus Center, a student gathering place at Princeton University, was built under such conditions with funds provided by the Frist family. On authority in inter-organizational relations, see Aldrich (1976); Pfeffer and Salancik (1978).

65. On social interaction and friendship in gyms, see Wacquant (2004). On churches and cooperative action, see Ammerman (2005); Berrien et al. (2000); Chaves (2004); McRoberts (2003); Lichterman (2005). Lichterman emphasizes the importance of what he calls "group customs" for the success of such efforts. An additional issue is worth noting. My discussion of what "other aspects of personal ties" are affected by organizational conditions takes place strictly within the context of *personal* ties, or, at most, what networks scholars would consider dyadic relations. Social network analysts have examined how organizational conditions may affect entire networks structures, including factors such as the number of cliques or the degree of hierarchy. These issues are far beyond scope. For research in that tradition, see Hallinan (1976, 1979); Hallinan and Tuma (1978).

66. Several studies have examined these ties in the context of urban inequality. See Chaskin et al. (2001); Marwell (2007); Small (2006).

67. Lin (2001); Smith (2007); Bourdieu (1980).

68. In a recent study, Smith (2007) has argued that mobilization also depends on the conditions of the dyad, wherein relations characterized by low trust for structural reasons will undermine people's willingness to mobilize their connections when looking for jobs.

69. Portes (1998).

70. On brokerage, see Simmel (1950); Burt (2001, 2005); Chaskin et al. (2001); Pattillo (2007). Burt (2005) has probably written more than anyone in recent years on the concept of brokerage. Burt defines a broker as an actor who occupies a structural hole, that is, the actor lying at the intersection of two or more separate networks. Burt believes, and has shown, that brokers have advantages over other actors, because brokers have access to information and ideas from both networks. My conception of brokerage differs in three important ways. First, we are concerned not with individuals, but with *organizations* as brokers. Specifically, we are concerned with how an organization connects an actor to either another actor or another organization. Second, we are concerned with how brokerage affects the brokered actor, not the broker. At issue is whether an actor has much to gain by being tied to the right organization—that is, to an effective broker. Third, Burt's empirical work takes place in a competitive setting, where some employees are better evaluated than others, and an actor's well-being is, by definition, relative to that of others. We are concerned not with advantages compared to others in the organization with whom an actor competes, but with advantages deriving from organizational membership and participation.

71. Obstfeld and Borgatti (2008) have argued that we should shift from a conception of brokers to one of brokerage, and think of this as a process, not a state. Their perspective is very consistent with that in this book. In social network analysis, the broker is often identified simply as the actor occupying structural holes, with the many implications for her or his relations to others assumed, rather than examined.

72. Delgado and Santiago (1998).

73. Perrow (1984); Vaughan (1996).

74. Festinger, Schachter, and Back (1950).

75. Interestingly, while Coleman said little about how people form ties, he did argue that social capital (by which he meant especially pro-social norms and the presence of trust in a group) often emerged as a result of collective actions perpetrated for other purposes (1990:311ff.). That is, he explicitly incorporated nonpurposive organization into his conception of social capital. However, he did not bring this insight into the study of how individuals form connections, and later researchers such as Lin did not follow through on this work. In the end, his general aim to develop a purposive theory of action might have won out (Coleman 1986).

76. Yin (2003); Small (in press).

77. Bott (1957); Stack (1974); Edin and Lein (1997).

78. U.S. Census Bureau (2008:table 85).

79. Reichman, Teitler, Garfinkel, and McLanahan (2001). The study maintains a website with current information: http://www.fragilefamilies.princeton.edu/.

80. See Small, Jacobs, and Massengill (2008).

81. Hedstrom and Swedberg (1998); Morgan and Winship (2007).

82. One of the best among the recent studies is Ajay Chaudry's (2004) *Putting Children First*. For an economic perspective on childcare, see David Blau's (2001) *The Childcare Problem*. On the relationship between caregiver and employer, see Julia Wrigley's (1995) *Other People's Children*. On the consequences of types of childcare for children, see National Center for Early Development and Learning (2007); NICHD Early Child Care Research Network (2002). There are many others.

CHAPTER 2

1. On its face, the question seems to continue the unfortunate tendency, in commentary on mothers and the workforce, to pit the well-being of the mother against that of the child. Mothers, by one logic, must choose to either selfishly pursue their careers or selflessly devote themselves full-time to their young children, since nothing but the latter constitutes full parenting (Hays 1996). And, in fact, this chapter sets aside one rather obvious consequence, that for a mother to employ childcare increases the number of hours she can work for pay and, thus, the income to which she has access. Nevertheless, the findings in the chapter ultimately undermine the distinction between the interests of the mother and those of the child; they reveal several important and neglected consequences that centers may have on the well-being of the mother, child, and household often in ways parents did not anticipate when they decided to employ formal daycare.

2. Although our primary concern lies more in the differences among centers than in their average effect, finding that centers do, on average, improve well-being would

illustrate the advantages of being embedded in an effective broker. The Fragile Families survey did not have measures of the organizational characteristics of child-care centers that matter to parents' networks. In addition, as shown in later chapters, a different type of survey—a survey of centers, not parents (Childcare Centers and Families Survey)—is required to understand many of these mechanisms.

3. Source: Historical Tables, Table A-2, Census Bureau, http://census.gov/ population/www/socdemo/school.html (accessed 2/7/07). Data are from the Current Population Survey: children are counted as enrolled if they were enrolled at any time during the current school year, full or part time. See "Current Population Survey (CPS)— Definitions and Explanations," Census Bureau, http://census.gov/population/ www/cps/cpsdef.html (accessed 8/15/07).

4. In a study of trends in childcare use over the 1970s and 1980s, Hofferth (1987) found a decrease in the use of nonrelative care and a 60% decrease in the use of babysitters (cited in Hofferth and Wissoker 1992). However, she found an increase over that period of 37% in the use of family care, and of 300% in the use of daycare centers. Only the trend in the use of centers parallels the trends in women's labor force participation.

5. Of course, the decision to work and the choice of care affect each other mutually. For quantitative research on these questions, see Hofferth and Wissoker (1992); Blau (2001). It is worth noting that among single mothers (for whom figures for earlier years are unavailable), labor force participation rose sharply between 1995 and 2000 partly as a result of the passage of the Personal Responsibility and Work Opportunity Reconciliation Act of 1996, which replaced the old welfare system that provided cash assistance indefinitely to needy mothers with a system that imposed lifetime assistance limits and required mothers to work or look for work in order to receive aid.

6. This categorization is not perfect, and the primary *funding* source is not synonymous with the primary entity *operating* the center. For example, Head Start centers in New York are often operated by local community nonprofit organizations based on grants from the federal Head Start program. Thus, Head Starts are funded by the government but run by nonprofit organizations. Such arrangements are not rare (see Smith and Lipsky 1993). In fact, in a study showing the role of the state in the growth of childcare centers, Fuller et al. (2004) found that communities with a greater density of preexisting churches and civic organizations "display a greater capacity to expand and formalize child care centers" in response to state intervention. For research on nonprofit organizations, their relations to state and for-profit orga-nizations, and the strengths and weaknesses of sector distinctions, see also DiMaggio and Anheier (1990) and Powell (1987).

7. On Head Start, see Zigler and Muenchow (1992).

8. "The Children's Aid Society: Financials," Children's Aid Society, http:// www.childrensaidsociety.org/about/financials (accessed 4/21/07).

9. Figures are from the Childcare Centers survey, a random-sample survey of 293 childcare centers in New York City.

10. Hofferth and Wissoker (1992:80). See also Hofferth (1987); Chaudry (2004).

11. Maryland Committee for Children (2003).

12. Hays (1996). See also Hochschild (1989) and Chaudry (2004). The difficulty in deciding among these alternatives was dramatized by the recent outcry following the

publication of a study funded by the National Institute for Child and Health Development, based on a survey of more than 1,300 children, that found that children who had been more exposed to center-based care were reported years later by their elementary-school teachers to exhibit more behavioral problems when dealing with other children (Belsky et al. 2007). Much of the debate rekindled controversies over whether mothers should remain home when their children are young, whether childcare centers are inherently too impersonal for young children, or whether the problem is not necessarily the type of care but the quality within any given type (Carey 2007).

13. For an extended discussion of childcare choices among low-income mothers, see Ajay Chaudry's *Putting Children First* (2004). On satisficing, see Simon (1957:xxiv ff.).

14. To protect the anonymity of respondents, all names of centers, parks, and other venues are pseudonyms. I have changed very minor details unrelated to the substance of the argument that may be used to identify a person. Nevertheless, there are no composites of people, places, or events in this book. Every reported place and organization exists as described, every event occurred as reported, and every statement was uttered as quoted or paraphrased. All sit-down interviews, unless otherwise stated, were tape-recorded. All quotations taken during unobstructed interactions (field trips, meetings, workshops) were taken by hand.

15. Mothers may have other children who may or may not be in centers. All statistical models adjust for the number of children. Since the children are on average about 5 years of age (though some are much younger), many more are in childcare or preschool than would be the case if they were, on average, about 4 or 3 years of age. Therefore, the mothers whose children are not in a center may be more different from other mothers than would be the case a year or two earlier in the children's life course. I employed statistical adjustments to account for this difference.

16. Unfortunately, wave 3 did not contain data on mothers' networks in centers. Though the survey also interviewed fathers, for wave 4 it was unable to locate 36% of the originally sampled fathers (as opposed to 16% of the mothers), which seriously undermines any attempt to examine associations reliably. For this reason, this chapter presents no data on fathers, who, in any case, still spend less time in child-rearing activities, including those associated with centers, than do mothers (Bianchi and Raley 2005).

17. Bromer and Henly (2004).

18. I can only compare mothers with children in centers to all other mothers for two reasons. First, the Fragile Families survey did not ask questions about social networks made through family care providers. Second, the skip patterns in questions regarding childcare did not go as intended. The firm conducting the work first asked parents if they were in childcare, preschool, or kindergarten for 8 or more hours a week and then asked about alternative care only if they were not. The problem with this is that even if a child was in preschool only, say, 2 hours a day, the mother was not asked about alternative forms of care. As a result, only about 50 out of more than 4,000 mothers reported family care, an improbably small number.

19. Most children had more than one childcare arrangement. In addition, people are not consistent in how they define their arrangements, so that one parent might call her center a "daycare center" and another a "preschool." For these two reasons, it

is difficult, if not impossible, to assess the effect of different types of arrangements with any confidence. In addition, there were 242 parents whose children were not in centers but in kindergarten. Given the way the survey was administered, these parents were not asked the questions asked of all parents whose children were in centers, including questions about social networks. By necessity, then, the analysis here excludes those 242 parents from the population of parents with children in centers. (Other parents who initially reported using childcare centers but later clarified their use of kindergarten *were* asked all of the follow-up questions; these are included.) Also note that 14% of the focal children were enrolled in Head Start.

20. Since these are survey data, the standard deviation is an estimate, based on the standard error of the mean and the sample size, of the true standard deviation in the population.

21. The problem is, in fact, even more complicated, given the potential counterfactuals (Morgan and Winship 2007). The data do not permit a more complex analysis.

22. Unfortunately, parents were asked only about their total number of close friends, not their total number of friends. As I show later regarding friends made in childcare centers, this does not seem to make a major difference. Either way, in chapter 4 I show that employing the standard distinction between a friend and a close friend, or between a weak tie and a strong tie, is not an effective way to understand friendships among parents in childcare centers.

23. These models do not account for the amount of time the child is in the center. Seventy-five percent of children are in centers 20 or more hours a week. Examining time in the center is beyond the scope of the present chapter.

24. Jencks and Mayer (1990); Sen (1985, 1999); Iceland and Bauman (2004); Meyer and Sullivan (2003); Conley (2005). There is a debate on whether well-being is best measured through subjective rather than objective indicators (for a recent assessment of subjective indicators, see Krueger and Schkade 2007). Objective indicators measures make comparability feasible; subjective measures capture the inherent relativity of a concept as elusive as well-being. Since the purpose here is assessing whether participation in childcare centers is associated with greater well-being, comparability is critical, and objective measures are more appropriate. Still, later chapters examine how mothers experienced their relationships in childcare centers, yielding insight into subjective well-being with respect to social ties and social isolation.

25. Conley (2005).

26. Mayer and Jencks (1989).

27. There are currently two experimental studies, of Head Start and Early Head Start, that perform a version of the study described, but with a very unrepresentative sample of the population—poor mothers eligible for the program. The studies also only compare Head start/Early Head Start to any alternative, including any other type of childcare center.

28. Hedstrom and Swedberg (1998).

29. Morgan and Winship (2007); Lieberson (1985).

30. Finkel (1995).

31. The basic model takes the general form $Y_t = \beta_1 X_t + \beta_2 Y_{t-1} + U$, whereby outcome Y is a function of covariates X and of Y measured at an earlier time point.

Please note that this method does not take into account time-varying confounding factors. On the other hand, some statisticians argue that the lagged dependent variable Y_{t-1} downwardly biases the estimates of the coefficients for the other independent variables, because of the lagged variable's correlation with the predicted outcome. If so, then the model would constitute a conservative test, and the true effect of being in a center would be center larger than reported.

I also ran versions of the model without the lagged variable and the results were similar, though the center effect was larger. Another solution is to find an instrument for the lagged version of the variable. McManus and DiPrete (2001) estimate a somewhat different dynamic model and use a twice-lagged version of the dependent variable as an instrument for the lagged variable. I tried this strategy, which required estimating a least squares regression, and compared it to an ordinary least squares model with the lagged variable. Results for the variables of interest were similar to each other. However, when compared to the negative binomial regression model, these two models showed a significant effect of friends met at the center (see below) but not a significant effect of being in a childcare center and not making friends there. This may result from the fact that these two models assume a continuous outcome variable that is in fact a categorical count variable. Having said this, there is still debate among statisticians and econometricians about the best way to estimate this model and account for unobserved heterogeneity. In the end, this is still observational, not experimental data.

32. There are two potential problems with this strategy. One is multicollinearity. It is possible that the correlation between the number close friends the mother has and the number of friends made in the center is so high that including the former in the model radically alters the coefficient for the latter. The zero-order correlation between the variables is 0.25, which suggests little reason for concern. An examination of the models also yielded little evidence that multicollinearity was an issue. Multicollinearity many not have been a problem due to a second problem: the variable tapping into friendliness is the number of *close* friends, and friendliness may be better measured by the number of friends, not necessarily only close ones. Unfortunately, the survey did not ask respondents the number of general friends (including nonclose friends) they had. However, it did ask about both friends and close friends met in the center. The estimates for the effects of friendship making in the center were similar whether friends or only close friends were entered, which suggests that the distinction may not be important for the variables of interest. In chapter 4, I show that the term "close friend" may not mean to mothers in centers what it means to social scientists.

33. This is a more logical strategy than performing factor analysis. The items in the scale measure different types of hardship; they are not elements of a single underlying construct. As Mayer and Jencks (1989:98) argue, the "items that compose the hardship measures are not supposed to measure the same underlying construct, so we cannot estimate the measure's reliability from the inter-item correlations, any more than we could estimate the reliability of an income measure from the intercorrelations among various kinds of income."

34. The differences between each condition and the baseline are marginally significant, at the 0.06 level for not making friends in the center versus not being in the center, and at the 0.09 level for making friends there versus not being in a center.

Among enrolled mothers, there is no statistically significant difference between the effects of enrolling while making friends and enrolling while not making friends.

35. Mayer and Jencks (1989).

36. The first four measures in table 2.3 are indicators of housing-related hardship. The first, which asks mothers whether rent or mortgage was paid, is clearly the least pure indicator of hardship. The remaining three are appropriate measures, since they indicate eviction, which is not a person's choice; having to move in with others *because of* financial difficulty; and staying in a shelter, an abandoned building, a car, or some other place not meant for regular housing.

37. The first of these measures has the aforementioned problem: people may have not paid the bill at least once over the previous year for a number of reasons, not merely because they could not afford it. The other two measures, borrowing money in order to pay utility bills and having utilities cut off, more clearly indicate difficulty.

38. Since there was no measure in wave 3 for item 8 (having one's utility cut off), the lagged dependent variable is only for whether the mother borrowed money in order to pay the bills.

39. Mothers may use centers to acquire resources from the state. For example, in New York City, the Home Energy Assistance Program

> assists low-income households with their fuel and/or utility costs. Emergency assistance is also available to HEAP-eligible households that pay directly for heat and are faced with "shut-off" notices. The Department for the Aging also administers the Weatherization, Referral and Packaging Program (WRAP) which provides low-income senior homeowners with free home energy-related services that can lower energy bills and increase the comfort of their homes. For more information or to apply, please call 311. (New York City Department for the Aging, "Frequently Asked Questions," http://home2.nyc.gov/html/dfta/html/faq/faq.shtml, accessed 7/23/06)

40. Kessler et al. (1998). The entire interview is not conducted. Instead, a portion of the interview questions is asked that should be sufficient to assess the probability that the respondent would be categorized as depressed if given the full interview.

CHAPTER 3

1. Of course, mothers may and do employ multiple arrangements (Chaudry 2004). Still, the discussion will show that friendship formation among our respondents had less to do with time than with conditions shaping social interaction.

2. A postscript to this chapter reveals that centers had many motivations, internal and external, institutional and financial, to request mothers' engagement in the activities required to operate; it also explains why some centers had more such requirements than others.

3. Coleman (1990).

4. Children younger than 1 year of age are too young for most field trips.

5. While much of the research on firms sharply distinguishes employees from clients—and therefore considers only the former as "members" of the organizations— the case of childcare center makes clear that the "clients" may well be active members of the functioning and operation of the local organization. In this respect, the center

is less a service organization with a clear distinction between members and clients than a membership organization in which multiple participants with different formal positions still aim for similar goals.

6. Whitebook and Sakai (2003).

7. The process by which church practices inform activities elsewhere is discussed in Pattillo-McCoy (1998).

8. Hochschild (1997); Schor (1991); Bianchi et al. (2006); Jacobs and Gerson (2004).

9. Hochschild (1997:45).

10. Bianchi et al. (2006). See also Bianchi et al. (2005).

11. "Social isolation" has meant different things to scholars of well-being. To some, it refers to the absence of social connections of any type (e.g., McPherson et al. 2006); to others, following Wilson (1987), it refers to the absence of connections to the middle class among residents of poor neighborhoods. In 78% of the centers we surveyed, all or almost all children were residents of the neighborhood, which suggests that centers make friends among other parents who tend to be of the same socioeconomic status. However, as described in later chapters, staff and organizational networks end up connecting parents in poor neighborhoods to the mainstream in ways unanticipated by Wilson's social isolation perspective.

12. Whitebook, Howes, and Phillips (1998); Whitebook and Sakai (2003).

13. The economics of childcare markets is a question best left to an economist. Among the many reasons for the complexity of the market are the fact that centers compete with family care providers, babysitters, and even relatives; that services are sometimes paid and sometimes unpaid; that buyers have heterogeneous motivations, such as education and convenience; and that multiple players are involved, such as parents, providers, the state, and nonprofits. Naturally, this chapter does not argue that economic factors are irrelevant to the motivations behind providers; it argues, instead, that they are insufficient to understand the involvement of parents in concrete tasks conducive to tie formation. The most comprehensive, accessible analysis of childcare from an economic perspective in recent years is David Blau's *The Child Care Problem* (2001).

14. The notion that institutional, not just economic, pressures shape the operation of organizations represents a major contribution of the new institutionalism perspective in sociology (Powell and DiMaggio 1991; Brinton and Nee 2001). This discussion is informed by the work of Paul DiMaggio and Walter Powell (1983), who identified three important pressures: normative pressures, by which actors respond to norms and beliefs held among professionals about the proper conduct of the organization; mimetic pressures, by which they imitate other organizations to attain status, prestige, or acceptance; and coercive pressures, by which they respond to the mandates of more powerful authorities. Their model was an effort to explain what they argued was the increasing isomorphism of organizations over time. While our concern is not isomorphism, the broader insights about the internal and external pressures to which contemporary organizations are subject remain relevant to our question.

15. Austin (2000).

16. Department of Health and Human Services (2005:sec. 1304.50). Several sociologists of organizations have theorized that coercive pressures by external

authorities constitute important factors in the behavior of organizational actors. See Aldrich (1976); Pfeffer and Salancik (1978); DiMaggio and Powell (1983).

17. Department of Health and Human Services (2005:sec. 1304.50).

18. Department of Health and Human Services (2005:sec. 1304.50).

19. Department of Health and Human Services (2005:sec. 1306).

20. The large percentage of privately funded nonprofit centers that involve parents in spring activities may be associated with the economic precariousness of many nonprofit centers that lack the backing of the federal government.

21. Our field observations revealed the presence of such norms and that they were largely universal—in fact, and we found no evidence that childcare centers in different sectors drew staff from different labor pools. This is consistent with findings of the National Childcare Staffing Study, which, based on a survey of center directors throughout the country, reported that the highest paid teachers earned on average only $18,988 in 1997 (Whitebook et al. 1997). Wages at independent nonprofit centers, independent for-profit centers, and church-related nonprofit centers ranged from $6.06 to $6.17 an hour for the lowest paid assistants and from $10.59 to $11.19 an hour for the highest paid teachers. Only for-profit center chains had notably lower wages, with the highest paid teachers earning $7.16. That is, wages for childcare center staff are universally low. (The authors did not report whether for-profit centers that are part of chains provide better benefits. The authors also found that the highest paid teachers at centers accredited by the National Association for the Education of Young Children [NAEYP] earned higher wages, $14.35 an hour on average. Centers voluntarily seek NAEYP accreditation).

CHAPTER 4

1. For an introduction to the analysis of social ties, and to networks more generally, see Wasserman and Faust (1994).

2. Granovetter (1973:1361).

3. Wellman (1979).

4. Granovetter (1973).

5. Granovetter argues: "Weak ties provide people with access to information and resources beyond those available in their own social circle; but strong ties have greater motivation to be of assistance and are typically more easily available" (1983:209). It is important to note that each type of tie carries constraints. While strong ties provide social support, they also tend to come with greater obligations and, since they tend to be inbred, with strongly enforced norms of behavior (Portes 1998). And while weak ties are often sources of new information, an actor who has access only to weak ties will have a difficult time finding help from informal networks in addressing an emergency.

6. Tonnies (1887/1957); Durkheim (1893/1984). See also Fischer (1982); Wellman (1979).

7. Determining whether a social tie is weak or strong can be complicated, since, as suggested by Granovetter's definition quoted above, the "strength" of a tie may refer to various characteristics, such as whether the two parties feel close, whether they provide emotional support for each other, whether they have been tied for a long time, or whether they see each other frequently. In a rigorous evaluation of five

different indicators of tie strength, Peter Marsden and Karen Campbell concluded that "a measure of 'closeness', or the emotional intensity of a relationship, is on balance the best indicator of the concept of tie strength among those available to us" (1984:498). Whether respondents would characterize a person as "close" seems to provide the best clue of whether the tie is, in fact, a strong one.

8. These may or may not be large numbers, depending on how many friends mothers have in general. To assess how large these numbers are, it would be useful to know what percentage of all their close friends the mothers made in the center. Unfortunately, because of the way the variables were coded in the national survey, it is not possible to calculate this figure. (In the survey, while the number of close friends mothers had was recorded as reported, the number of close friends they had *in the center* was coded into four categories [0, 1–2, 3–6, and >6]. Thus, it is not possible to use the latter variable to calculate the percentage of all close friends that come from the center.) Still, as described in chapter 2, mothers in childcare centers had only about five close friends. Since 41% of center mothers made at least one of their close friends in the center, and 14% made at least three close friends, it is clear center-based networks constitute a considerable portion of the mothers' intimate networks. That is, mothers made close friends in childcare centers, and they only had a handful close friends elsewhere.

9. Laumann (1973:114). See also Simmel (1950); Fischer (1982).

10. Wellman (1979).

11. Simmel (1950).

12. Other scholars have made related observations about friendships, but with radically different expectations. In an essay on the nature of secrecy, Simmel wrote that

> differentiated friendships which connect us with one individual in terms of affections, with another, in terms of common intellectual aspects, with a third, in terms of religious impulses, and with a fourth, in terms of common experiences—all these friendships present a very peculiar synthesis in regard to the question of discretion, of reciprocal revelation and concealment. (1950:326)

In his study *Bonds of Pluralism* (1973), Edward Laumann referred to a related idea when he contrasted friendship in radial networks to that in interlocking networks. In interlocking networks, all friends of the focal actor are friends among themselves. By contrast, "[r]adial networks ... may be formed on some more specialized basis (e.g., a common interest in chess, work activities, sports)" (1973:114). Laumann surmised that people whose friendships are radial compartmentalize them around a specific set of issues, such as childcare, sports, law, religion, and work.

These scholars, however, expect compartmental ties to be *weak*. They do so for two reasons. One, these ties are expected to lack the multiple reinforcement of norms produced by interlocking networks. This, for example, is part of the point of Granovetter's (1973) weak-ties argument. If the ties were strong, they probably would not be compartmental, since when two individuals are strongly tied, it is unlikely that one of them but not the other is strongly tied to a third. As Granovetter argues,

> The argument asserts that our acquaintances (*weak ties*) are less likely to be socially involved with one another than are our close friends (*strong ties*). Thus,

the set of people made up of any individual and his or her acquaintances comprises a low-density network (one in which many of the possible relational lines are absent) whereas the set consisting of the same individual and his or her *close* friends will be densely knit (many of the possible lines are present). (1983:201–202)

By this logic, a compartmental tie would only be strong if the actor had no other close friends. Similarly, Laumann argues, "People in radial networks . . . are likely to have a relatively lower affective involvement and commitment to their relations with alters because the set of common interests and concerns is likely to be more severely circumscribed and limited by virtue of the greater likelihood of differing statuses comprising the networks. . . . Consequently, relations in radial structures are likely to be weaker in affective involvement and more functionally specific" (Laumann 1973:114), compared with relations in interlocking networks. The second reason they expect compartmental ties to be weak—and this is implicit when Laumann expects "lower affective involvement"—is that people in compartmental relationships are expected to see each other less frequently than those in noncompartmental relationships. We shall see not only that compartmental relations may be strong, but that organizational contexts facilitate that strength through their effects on sustenance.

13. Blanche, for whom English was a second language, used the term "friend" differently from many other respondents. For her, a "friend" was what others referred to as a "close friend," and an "acquaintance" what others referred to as a "friend." Blanche reserved the phrase "close friend" for a "best friend."

14. Bearman and Parigi (2004).

15. Bearman and Parigi (2004:544).

16. Barry Wellman and Scot Wortley (1990) made a related point about social support: they found that different ties provide different kinds of social support, among five types measured: emotional aid, small services, large services, financial aid, and companionship. There are two things missing from their discussion. First, compartmental intimates differ from other times less in the type than in the *domain* within they provide support. That is, companionship, small services, and emotional aid were fair game among compartmental intimates, provided they were in the same domain. Second, the Wellman and Wortley study still tended to see strong ties as a single type of relationship. For example, they found that "strong ties tend to provide emotional aid, small services, and companionship," while ties to parents among adult children provide financial and emotional aid, larger services, and others (1990:558). In centers, however, it was clear that there were different types of "strong" ties with different implications for the type of support provided.

17. Fathers were no exception to this pattern. David was an Asian scientist in his early forties with salt-and-pepper hair and tortoiseshell glasses whose two daughters were enrolled at the Rainbow Center. Not quite comfortable with the term "close," David made a similar observation when classifying how Beth, whom he met in the center, was a close friend: "Gosh there's so many levels of closeness. . . . But I wouldn't [*unintelligible*] that she and I are so close, but I just mean close in the sense not as a close friend—as in my whole spectrum of friends she's one of my closest friends—but someone who I have talked to about things outside of just seeing her when we drop

off our kids." Ernest was a black male in his late thirties with a bald head and a pencil-thin beard around his chin; at six feet and 250 pounds, he had the build of a football player. His two children were enrolled in Painted Masks, a center in a high-poverty, predominantly black neighborhood. Ernest knew about 15 other parents in the center but did not consider them close friends. As soon as he said this, however, he qualified himself, with a distinction: "I consider friends the people in the [parents association] I would have to say, and a couple of volunteers. I have their phone numbers [and] if there's anything that we need to do we're always in touch that way." Did he ever interact with them outside the center? "No. [*Unintelligible*] we don't call each other and say, 'Hey want to go out for a cup of coffee.' Nah, we don't do that. It's all about the center." He concluded: "This set of friends you sit down and you tell personal things. [Then,] we go over here and we talk about business with this [other] set of friends."

18. The term "associate" in the context of friendships may strike the middle-class ear as peculiar, given its business-like connotations. Yet the adoption of business terms into personal relations has occurred in the middle class, as well. One generation ago, "partner" referred primarily to one engaged in business; today, it is just as commonly used to refer to an intimate relation, especially among middle-class same-sex couples. Similarly, an "associate" among some low-income mothers has come to mean an acquaintance above the basic greeting level but not quite a friend, rather than referring to someone engaged in a business transaction. On trust, friendship, and social capital among African-Americans, see Sandra Smith's *Lone Pursuit* (2007:chap. 4), which also reports on the use of "associates" to denote a type of acquaintance.

19. Hochschild (1997); Schor (1991).

20. Bianchi, Robinson, and Milkie (2006); Jacobs and Gerson (2004); Belkin (2003).

21. Some have read the work of Stack (1974) as a tale specific to low-income black women. It was a case study, however, of support among mothers, and such practices are visible across races and even income groups.

22. The difference was evident even though Naomi was willing to consider Tessie a "good friend," after her interviewer explicitly asked:

She is now. We're on similar schedules with our kids, so I'd walked in and out with her a couple of times and then we bumped into them once on the weekend sort of outside of school. And my husband and I had a good rapport with Tessie and Sam. And when I felt like I knew her well enough I suggested, "Hey do you want to try a baby swap?" and they were open to it and we've done it several times now. Yeah, we're very friendly. In fact last week we took our kids together to . . . a block party at the [park] on the corner.

Tessie and Sam are not "extended family" to Naomi and her husband; they are very good friends when it comes to all things child related.

23. Lazarsfeld and Merton (1954); McPherson, Smith-Lovin, and Cook (2001); Laumann (1973:chap. 5).

24. Maryland Committee for Children (2003).

25. Granovetter (1973:1361).

26. Bourdieu (1986:250).

CHAPTER 5

1. Granovetter (1983).

2. Another way of making the point of this chapter is to argue that, by enrolling in childcare centers, parents enter a generalized exchange system that emerges from repeated interaction, wherein the strength of a tie in any given dyad is unimportant. The literature on generalized and restricted exchange stems from the work of Claude Levi-Strauss and others, who examined the consequences of group exchange systems. This literature examines a set of questions much larger than can be covered in this chapter. In addition, the case of childcare centers has little to add to it. For recent references, see Bearman (1997); Uehara (1990). See also Levi-Strauss (1969).

3. The volumes written on trust by economists, political scientists, sociologists, and psychologists, could fill entire libraries. For reviews of recent work, see Fukuyama (1995); Kramer and Tyler (1996); Cook (2001); Hardin (2002). Much of the literature on trust in organizations examines how trust either among members of an organization or between different organizations helps organizations perform more effectively or reduce transaction costs (Kramer and Cook 2004). Other works examine how institutional rules may help sustain trust by imposing formal sanctions that make transactions possible (Coleman 1990). This chapter briefly examines one element of the relationship between organizations and trust in noncompetitive settings: the relationship between trust and social support, and the role of frequent interaction in this process. For studies of other aspects of trust in organizational settings, see Kramer and Tyler (1996); Kramer and Cook (2004).

4. Coleman (1990:99). Coleman's model assumes that actors make rational calculations when deciding whether to trust others. A more recent, and much more elaborated, version of this general perspective on trust is that of Russell Hardin (2002), who conceives of trust as an "encapsulated interest." Hardin believes that actors trust others because they perceive the others" need to justify their trust.

5. Joseph Wechsberg, *The Merchant Bankers* (1966), cited in Coleman (1990:103).

6. Coleman writes: "Information will have the effect of changing one's estimate of the probability of gain, that is, of moving one's estimate of the probability of gain as far as possible above or below the critical point at which the decision could go either way" (1990:103).

7. The theory of strong ties discussed in chapter 4 would arrive at the same conclusion: not knowing such information is a sign of a weak tie, and actors tend to turn to strong, not weak ties, when they want reliable support.

8. Our hypothetical question is consistent with Russell Hardin's argument that trust is most meaningful when considered as a "three part relation." That is, one asks whether "A trusts B to do X," rather than whether "A trusts B." As he argues: "To say 'I trust you' seems almost always to be elliptical, as though we can assume some such phrase as 'to do X' or 'in matters why.' Only a small child, a lover, Abraham speaking to his god, or a rabid follower of a charismatic leader might be able to say 'I trust you' without implicit modifier" (2002:9).

9. To be clear, some people are simply not very good at recalling names. At issue here is not whether a mother knows a particular piece of information or not but whether Coleman's information-based model needs expansion or revision. I believe it needs both.

10. I recognize that this model prioritizes the context of interaction at the expense of other factors, such as the characteristics of the trustees. A comprehensive theory of trust would have to consider such factors—for example, the ability, benevolence, and integrity of the trustee, as Mayer, Davis, and Schoorman (1995) would argue. In addition, it would examine how these conditions of the trustee interact with the conditions of the context of interaction. An excellent set of chapters on trust in organizational contexts is Kramer and Tyler (1996).

11. Emerson (1976, 1981); Homans (1950); Lawler (2001); Lawler and Yoon (1993).

12. Kollock (1994).

13. For reviews, see Emerson (1976); Lawler and Thye (1999).

14. Coleman (1988). There is a potential problem in the application of this work to the case of childcare centers. It is not obvious that, once outside of the laboratory, recurrent exchange or interaction is a sufficient condition for the formation of trust or commitments of any kind. This problem tormented George Homans, whose early version of the theory—he argued that repeated interaction leads to positive senti- ments, and therefore to interpersonal attachments (1950)—led to an avalanche of complaints based on qualifiers and exceptions (Homans 1961). Sometimes, the more two people interact, the less they like, trust, or rely on each other. Despite this, the experimental data seem to have largely vindicated Homans (e.g., Lawler and Yoon 1993; Lawler, Thye, and Yoon 2000), which is not surprising—people who realize they do not like or trust each other usually find ways of avoiding future interactions.

15. While discussing a new theory of trust, Michael Bacharach and Diego Gambetta insist that what often appears as intuition is, in fact, complex information processing: "We tend to perceive our reactions of this kind as intuition, and therefore as not governed by complex computations. But this is only because we are so good at this activity; it comes naturally to us" (2001:173). In fact, much of the research on trust assumes that either information or rational calculation is at play. However, research on repeated exchange suggests that positive emotion may be at play as well (Lawler and Thye 1999; Lawler 2001, 2002).

16. The independence between tie strength and frequency of their interaction should not be overstated. Certainly, frequent interaction often leads to stronger ties, as with the parents described in preceding chapters who developed close friendships in their centers. But two actors can seldom interact while remaining close, such as many childhood friends, and two actors can interact frequently without strength- ening their tie, such as residents of apartment buildings and their doormen (Bearman 2005). In fact, formal organizational settings often permit what appears implausible in the abstract—frequent encounters in relationships that do not strengthen. If the encounters are short, fleeting, or otherwise very constrained, the familiarity that engenders trust can grow even if no friendship ever does.

17. A full account of this context would examine other elements of the context of interaction, such as the physical conditions of the space, the time of day, the physical appearance of the actors, the familiarity of the actors with each other, their reasons for being in the same location, their previous encounters, and the presence of others.

18. Shapiro, Sheppard, and Cheraskin (1992).

19. There are different versions of this perspective in the literature. Some would call this "noncalculational" as opposed to calculational trust. That is, a form of trust

where rational calculations played little role (Darley 2004). There is a parallel argument in the exchange tradition that repeated exchange improves trust by reducing uncertainty, while others argue it improves trust by increasing positive affect (Lawler 2001; Lawler and Thye 1999).

20. Darley (2004). While much of the research on trust in political science, economics, and some subfields in sociology assume that trust is based on rational decisions, "these assumptions that the motives for trusting are instrumental typically are not empirically tested" (Tyler and Kramer 1996:10). Tyler and Degoey (1996) specifically examined the extent to which trust in authorities can be said to derive from rational calculations and found several conditions under which trust was not supported by instrumental motivations. I believe a model in which actors are assumed to always trust on the basis of either rational or informational processes is less compelling (even if more elegant in a formal sense) than one in which some actors under some circumstances trust on these bases, but others in other settings do not. In this respect, I believe the accounts of mothers in childcare centers disconfirm one of Coleman's propositions and only half-confirm another. First, to the extent they did not require abundant information to take potentially very costly risks, they disconfirm Coleman's basic model. Second, however, to the extent that some mothers resorted to *informational processes* when assessing whether to trust others (as Griselda did), these mothers do confirm his more general orientation, in which information is the principal mechanism. Nevertheless, other, non-informational mechanisms ignored by Coleman clearly seem to be at play among some mothers.

21. On solidarity and norms, see Coleman (1988); Portes (1998). For recent research on the social and economic dynamics underlying gangs, see Venkatesh (2000, 2006); Sánchez-Jankowski (1991); Levitt and Venkatesh (2000).

22. See Department of Health and Human Services (2005:sec. 1304.22):

Health emergency procedures. Grantee and delegate agencies operating center-based programs must establish and implement policies and procedures to respond to medical and dental health emergencies with which all staff are familiar and trained. At a minimum, these policies and procedures must include: . . . (2) Posted locations and telephone numbers of emergency response systems. Up-to-date family contact information and authorization for emergency care for each child. . . . (4) Methods of notifying parents in the event of an emergency involving their child.

23. Portes (1998).

24. We could, as in most surveys, assume that the threshold lies wherever the respondent believes it lies, but whether or not we do this makes no difference to the present discussion. The discussion divides ties into friend and not-friend for clarity, but the argument does not depend on creating dichotomous categories. The probability that an actor will turn to another for social support would be a function of the strength of the relationship (which lies on a continuum) but also, independently, the frequency of contact (which also lies on a continuum).

25. This assumes that each actor can rely on all her friends for emergency support. There are reasons to believe that often this will not be the case, especially among residents of high-poverty urban neighborhoods. Smith (2005) has shown that people often do not recommend jobs to their own friends because they do not trust

them. This is an important point. For our discussion, however, it would simply mean that the expected advantage of B over A is even greater than shown.

26. Walker, Wasserman, and Wellman (1993). The literature on social support is large. Among works relevant to the present study, see Stack (1974); Nelson (2000); Ahmeduzzaman and Roopnarine (1992); Uehara (1990).

27. Wilson (1987).

28. The first "disaster" was the Northeast blackout of 2003, which paralyzed the city.

29. Stack (1974); Edin and Lein (1997). Quote from Nelson (2000:300–301).

30. Levi-Strauss (1969).

CHAPTER 6

1. Earlier versions of Tables 6.1 and 6.2 were previously published in Small (2006). The present chapter, however, is original to the book.

2. The term "cultural capital" refers to both the cultural knowledge and the dispositions that, according to Pierre Bourdieu, privileged social groups possess. The term is rich but also rather elusive, due in part to the fact that Bourdieu employed it in multiple different senses. One important element of cultural capital is the set of natural dispositions, including gestures and ways of speaking and dressing, that actors use to distinguish the elite from others. Another element, more important to the present discussion, is the unstated knowledge about education that the elite possess that is rewarded by but not necessarily taught in the educational system. This would include, for example, the signals that a successful entrance application contains about the applicant's cultivation and worldliness. When Bourdieu wrote theoretically, rather than empirically, he often argued that cultural capital formed part of a field theory of society, in which individuals compete for resources within given "fields," and the possession of some forms of capital (e.g., cultural) are exchangeable for others (e.g., social or economic). This book does not adopt Bourdieu's field theory, or his related concept of "habitus." Nevertheless, the idea of cultural capital can be employed to help understand what a mother such as Destino gained from her organizational connections: access to formal resources that in her case compensated for—but did not, as they could not, replace—her absence of the fundamental knowledge about education that New Yorkers much higher up the socioeconomic ladder possess.

3. No one would argue that accessing resources through these different means represents three versions of the same process. The knowledge accumulated unconsciously through cultural upbringing is more natural than that obtained as an adult from a third party; the information acquired through informal social ties carries different expectations of reciprocity than that acquired from an expert. At issue is whether the substitute mechanism helps the actor attain goals.

4. I am choosing to describe as an "organizational tie" not only the tie to the external organization but also the connection to a person within it, such as the expert, when that person acts as a formal representative of the organization, since the connection is, technically, not to the person but to the position. At issue is the availability of the resources possessed by the external organization. Still, the term "organizational tie" is not perfect. For example, if the expert became a personal friend

of Destino, or provided interpersonal support independent of her capacity as an organizational representative, we would have to consider it as both an organizational and a social tie.

5. Smith (2007).

6. No one has written more on the interorganizational ties of childcare centers than Joel Baum and his colleagues. Baum's work tends to focus on the effect of such ties on legitimation and survival. For example, in a study with Christine Oliver, Baum found that the greater the number of interorganizational ties among childcare centers in an environment, the higher the rates of founding and the lower the failure rates (Baum and Oliver 1992). Other studies in this vein are Baum and Oliver (1991) and Baum and Singh (1994, 1996). While Baum's work examines the importance of organizational ties for centers (or for the entire center industry), the present chapter examines their significance for the individuals who patronize them.

7. DiMaggio (1983); Scott (2003).

8. There are many applications of the idea of a field, some more radically relational than others. Some argue for a relational sociology in which a foundational concept is the field (see Emirbayer 1997; Martin 2003; Bourdieu and Wacquant 1992); in the present chapter, "field" refers to a collection of organizations with some degree of institutionalization. That is, my use of the term is heuristic, not ontological. See Marwell (2007) for an application of field theory in the context of urban organizations. A concept related to the idea of a field is the earlier concept of "interorganizational community," which, as Scott (2003:129) argues, emerged out of the earlier work on urban ecology (e.g., Warren 1978). That concept emerged in reaction to much of the work on organizations, which, using the firm as a starting point, had focused on competition at the neglect of cooperation. Interorganizational community scholars called attention to the way organizations not just competed but also collaborated and exchanged resources. The idea of a "field" emerged later by institutionalists who, influenced by relational models (e.g., Bourdieu 1980), wanted to focus on the nature of the relations between entities, rather than the entities or a system in which participants may or may not evince a sense of community. See Schneiberg and Clemens (2006) for a discussion of the application of the field concept in institutional analysis.

9. See Baum and Oliver (1991, 1992); Baum and Singh (1994, 1996); Scott (2003:129ff.). On the nature of resources exchanged across organizational ties, see Pfeffer and Salancik (1978); Lauman, Galaskiewicz, and Marsden (1978); Warren (1978); Ebbers (1997).

10. Kaufman (2004).

11. See the New York City Human Resources Administration's site, http://www.nyc.gov/html/hra/html/programs/programs.shtml (accessed 1/5/09).

12. Conley (2004).

13. It is possible to separate the brokerage question into two processes, one by which the center forms the tie to the external organization, the other by which it transfers the resource to the patron. Scott (2003:203) refers to the former as "bridging tactics," which is one set of ways organizations manage their environments. This book will have little to say about bridging tactics, simply because our focus has been, and should remain, the level of well-being of the patron. Nevertheless, chapter 7 discuss at length why and how centers developed those particular ties—or, from

Scott's perspective, engaged in those particular bridging strategies—that yielded the resources in which patrons have an interest.

14. In fact, as Burt's (2001, 2005) work has shown, part of the advantage the broker has in competitive settings is control over whom the information is shared with.

15. Scott (2003:201).

16. "About WIC," Special Supplemental Nutritional Program for Women, Infant's, and Children, http://www.fns.usda.gov/wic/aboutwic/mission.htm (accessed 3/20/07).

17. One can make too much of the bits of information stored in childcare centers, but also make too little of them. The information stored on bulletin boards and in newsletter, in fact, addresses issues most likely to be useful to mothers and fathers of young children, because the providers of information anticipate this target audience in the center. For this reason, the storage of information can be seen as one of the many small strands that collectively constitute the institutional support net of the mother in the childcare center.

18. To understand service provision in childcare centers, an important distinction must be made. Sometimes, the childcare center paid for and provided the service: a staff person paid from the center's budget worked in an office on center premises and dispensed the service from this office. Other times, the childcare center had a formal relationship with another organization, which had a staff person who performed the service, either in the center or in a separate office, for example, a government agency or an educational nonprofit entity, or a large business seeking low-skilled labor. From the parent's perspective, it makes no difference. From the organization's perspective, the brokerage process will turn out to be more notable, in part because so few centers have the resources to provide the service directly. Therefore, the majority of the discussion focuses on brokering.

19. The survey included mechanisms to prevent overreporting; see appendix B.

20. For more information, see "Cool Culture," http://www.cool-culture.org (accessed 3/21/07).

21. Pfeffer and Salancik (1978).

22. Lin (1999a,b, 2001a, 2001b).

23. As Lorraine's own comments suggest, this raises a broader issue. Some would argue that by not requiring a mother to exercise self-efficacy, the mechanisms thereby undermine the agency of the mothers. While this process may be conducive to well-being in the short term, it could well undermine it in the long term. For example, inexperienced mothers not forced to negotiate the school system before their children enter it may become ineffective at doing so while their children are in elementary school. In fact, a version of this argument was advanced, during the 1990s, of welfare reform: the former Aid to Families with Dependent Children system, by not requiring that mothers work, discouraged self-efficacy. Could something similar happen among mothers in well-connected centers? This seems unlikely. A center would have to not only broker a *large* number of resources but also broker *most* of them in such a way as to obviate parents' agency for such an effect to be registered. No centers we observed so radically and consistently "held parents' hands," to paraphrase Lorraine. Instead, most centers established a hodgepodge of high- and low-agency mechanisms, none of them persistently enough to turn mothers into institutionally dependent actors. One could compare the center mother to the

parent who works full-time, cooks, cleans the home, and handles household bills, but then, instead of doing her own laundry, has found someone to do it for her. While the aid is certainly beneficial, the fact that she continues to have to conduct so many of her other chores herself means it is unlikely she will lose self-efficacy. Even more substantial assistance for long time periods is unlikely to make a difference, if the case of welfare reform is any indication. After restrictions and time limits were imposed in 1996 (and aided by an enviably robust economy with tight labor markets), mothers, who according to scholars and pundits had become government dependent, swiftly entered the workforce in large numbers.

CHAPTER 7

1. Many of the findings in this chapter were first reported in Small, Jacobs, and Massengill (2008).

2. Wilson (1987); see also Small and Newman (2001).

3. Sampson, Morenoff, and Gannon-Rowley (2002); Small and Newman (2001); Goering and Feins (2003).

4. Park, Burgess, and McKenzie (1925).

5. Sampson (1999); Wilson (1987, 1996).

6. Logan and Molotch (1987).

7. Zigler and Muenchow (1992).

8. Zigler and Styfco (2004).

9. Department of Health and Human Services (2005:sec. 1304).

10. Department of Health and Human Services (2005:sec. 1304).

11. Department of Health and Human Services (2005:sec. 1304).

12. Salamon (1995); Smith and Lipsky (1993).

13. As Salamon (1993) has shown, federal social welfare spending has shifted heavily toward health expenditures and Social Security, dramatically reducing funds for other social services. More generally, the government has retreated from several social service activities, leaving their execution to the private sector.

14. Space constraints prevent us from discussing the factors shaping the resource-transfer activities of larger nonprofit organizations in much depth. Galaskiewicz and Bielefeld (1998) discuss transformations among Minneapolis-St. Paul nonprofit organizations during times of financial uncertainty. Powell's (1987) edited volume presents a comprehensive look at the nonprofit sector from multiple perspectives. See also DiMaggio and Anheier (1990).

15. The names of large nonprofits, and their representatives, are pseudonyms as well.

16. Austin (2000). On the holistic approach to care and the need for parent involvement, see Becher (1989); Fuller and Olsen (1998); Scott (1990); Muller and Kerbow (1993); Levine (1993); Midco Educational Associates (1972).

17. There is a larger question of whether this represents a benign effort at improving the lives of individuals or a more sophisticated form of government social control, by which the state relies on the private nonprofit sector for its bidding. Addressing this question might require its own book (for some of the issues involved, see Smith and Lipsky 1993; Wacquant 2006). Both perspectives, however, would predict rather fluid boundaries among the for-profit, private nonprofit, and government sectors.

18. Meyer and Rowan (1977).

19. Our sample was missing data on number of referral ties (6% missing), number of service ties (11% missing), high proportion of poor children in center (13% missing), and sector (two cases missing). To address the missing data, we employed multiple imputation, where each missing value was imputed 10 times based on random draws from a distribution of possibilities (Rubin 1987). The result was 10 data sets identical on observed values but differing on imputed values. Regression results were averaged across all data sets using IVEware software (to download software, see http://www.isr.umich.edu/src/smp/ive/). Multiple imputation has been shown to produce more reliable results and to rely on more realistic assumptions than single imputation, listwise deletion, or other alternatives (Rubin 1987).

20. See Dobbin et al. (1993).

21. See Frumkin and Galaskiewicz (2004).

22. See Jargowsky (1997); Wilson (1987, 1996). In the sample, the 40% mark also represents the cutoff for the highest poverty quintile.

23. This is the most parsimonious form of the variable given the complex forms in which childcare centers are funded. Most important, in 25% of the centers, 100% of the children received free care. A continuous variable indicating the proportion of children on vouchers would exhibit a skewed and bimodal distribution.

24. The variables percent black, percent white, and percent Latino were included to control for the racial composition of the neighborhood; neighborhood residential instability, which represents the percentage of residents who lived in a different house 5 years before the 2000 Census, was included to account for instability and change; and population density was included to control for total population. I also controlled for the borough in which the center was located (with Manhattan as the omitted category).

25. A higher threshold would have excluded almost all neighborhoods; a neighborhood at the 90th percentile was 46% poor.

26. Wilson (1987); Wacquant and Wilson (1989); Sampson (1999). For critiques focused on organizational density and organizational capacity, see Small (2006, 2007a, 2007b, 2008); Small and McDermott (2006); Small and Stark (2005); Small, Jacobs, and Massengill (2008). For a review of critiques of Chicago School perspectives on urban neighborhoods, see Sampson and Morenoff (1997).

27. Logan and Molotch (1987).

28. As this book was going into production, Martín Sánchez-Jankowski's *Cracks in the Pavement* (2008) was published. Sánchez-Jankowski also calls for an institutional analysis of neighborhood conditions, arguing that one of the primary roles of local organizations is to contribute to the integration and stability of neighborhoods. His focus on integration may be the complement to my focus on personal networks.

CHAPTER 8

1. Women's friendships, for example, have been shown to involve more conversation. For a review of this literature, see Fehr (1996:chap. 5). See also Marsden (1987); Furman (1997).

2. Among urban sociological studies focused on social ties, the study of religious congregations and parishes remains a notable exception to this trend in the literature. Many researchers have examined the multiple tasks in which religious organizations engage, such as community activism, social service, volunteerism, and socialization (Lichterman 2005; Chaves 2004; Ammerman 2005; McRoberts 2003).

3. Farberman and Weinstein (1970).

4. Many commercial transactions operate in contexts that undermine friendship formation. I argued in chapter 1 for the importance of noncompetitive contexts. For example, in a general context of competition or antagonism, frequent interaction may not lead to friendships at all. Lee (2002) has shown that relations between African-American clients and Korean and Jewish store owners in New York City neighborhoods operate under an environment of hostility. Still, the patrons manage an environment of what the author calls "civility."

5. Duneier (1992:35).

6. Duneier (1992:5).

7. Duneier (1992:35).

8. Duneier (1992:55).

9. Furman (1997:22; emphasis original). A notable detail is that Furman reports the same fluidity of the client/employee distinction that I reported in centers, whereby patrons performed tasks otherwise expected of employees. "When the shop phone rings, customers frequently answer it, sometimes providing information, sometimes getting involved in conversations of their own.... On another occasion I see [a customer] emptying out a trash can" (Furman 1997:24).

10. Furman (1997:26).

11. Furman (1997:28).

12. Furman (1997:27).

13. Furman (1997:31).

14. Furman (1997:31).

15. Hallinan and Sorensen (1985). See also Hallinan (1976, 1979); Hallinan and Tuma (1978).

16. I thank Megan Comfort for sharing her field notes with me. Interestingly, after Comfort watched the woman's child, the latter offered to participate in Comfort's study as a way to thank her. See Comfort (2008:204–205). For a study of caregiving, and intimacy in general, that debunks many of the assumptions about the proper context and conditions under which care manifests itself, see Zelizer (2005).

17. Scott (1995). In a recent study, Marwell (2007) has made a strong case for the importance of organizations, and their networks, to conditions in urban neighborhoods.

18. Delgado (1999:95–96).

19. Delgado (1999:96).

20. Delgado (1999:96).

21. Delgado (1999:96–97).

22. Ammerman (2005); Chaves (2004); McRoberts (2003).

23. Chaskin et al. (2001); Marwell (2004, 2007). For additional perspectives from recent studies in this vein, see Saegert, Thompson, and Warren (2001); Doreian and Woodward (1999).

24. There are many studies on the broader relationship between churches and other organizations in the provision of services. See McRoberts (2003); Ammerman (2005); Chaves (2004); Wuthnow (2004).

25. See "Museum Pass Program," http://www.ci.newton.ma.us/Library/museum_ pass/museum_pass.htm (accessed 5'22'08).

26. Hays (1996).

27. Olson (1965).

28. Delgado (1999:113).

29. For reviews, see Scott (2003); Powell (1987).

30. DiMaggio and Powell (1983:147).

31. Watkins-Hayes (forthcoming).

32. For discussion on the potential role of the state in generating social capital in poor neighborhoods, see Saegert et al. (2001).

33. Granovetter (1974); Lin (2001a,b); Smith (2007); Fernandez and Fernandez-Mateo (2006).

34. Rosenbaum (2001). See also Rosenbaum et al. (1999).

35. Granovetter (1974).

36. Smith (2007) found a pattern of "defensive individualism" among black job seekers, and distrust among potential job referrers, that prevents blacks from mobilizing their personal ties effectively to find jobs.

37. Stern et al. (1995), as cited in Rosenbaum (2001).

38. Rosenbaum (2001:218).

39. U.S. Census Bureau. (2006: table 142).

40. Gruber (2003:36). On the problem of take-up rates across a wide array of government programs, see Currie (unpublished manuscript).

41. The term "organizational capital" might not be useful to the extent it reinforces thinking of advantages as rational investments.

42. Gruber (2003:36).

43. Pérez-Peña (2005a).

44. (Children's Defense Fund 2006); Pérez-Peña (2005a,b). A national evaluation of Early Head Start provides experimental evidence consistent with the general idea that people eligible for but not employing resources available to them make greater use of them in broker organizations such as childcare. The study evaluated families eligible for and seeking Earl Head Start and randomly assigned some of them to the program. The authors found that those randomly assigned to Early Head Start were more likely to turn to formal support systems, such as health center programs, family independence agency support, and maternal and infant support services (Early Head Start Research Consortium 2002:93–99).

45. Wilson (1987; 1996).

46. Neighborhoods could be no more than 10% poor. The experiments also involved a third group, which was given a voucher with no geographic restrictions. See Goering, Feins, and Richardson (2003:7).

47. For a review see Goering and Feins (2003). See also Ellen and Turner (2003).

48. Delgado (1997; 1998; 1999); Ammerman (2005); McRoberts (2003); Chaskin et al. (2001).

49. Wilson (1987).

APPENDIX A

1. For very different models, see Duneier (1999); Wacquant (2004). Some anthropologists have turned authors themselves into objects of inquiry, pushing self-reflection to one of its logical conclusions (see Clifford and Marcus 1986). I do not believe we must refocus analysis from the object to the scientist in order to produce valuable research. On the other hand, I concur with the proposition that transparency about process helps assess and interpret the utility of a theory.

2. Grounded theory was founded in this spirit and remains the strongest advocate of this position (Glaser and Strauss 1967).

3. To be clear, I do not claim that introducing a description of the process improves the quality of the theory. In the end, the sophistication of a theory depends less on the process required to arrive at it than on the cogency, beauty, or—in the best of them—clear-eyed simplicity of its core insights. The most compelling theories manage not only to convince the reader but also to render it impossible to conceive the world independently of their categories. (In fact, as Aristotle wrote in *On Rhetoric*, the most effective communicators manage to convince the reader that the author's conclusions were the reader's own, as if the latter had always understood the world a given way but had not yet realized it [Aristotle 1991].) Nevertheless, some transparency about process serves an important function: describing the origins of theories may bring to light many of the ambiguities lost deep in the all-too-common jargon of the social science specialist. For example, I suspect many of the debates surrounding Pierre Bourdieu's work would have been resolved had he described more explicitly the personal and practical origins of the theories.

4. Perrow (1991). In her recent book, Nicole Marwell (2007) makes a similar point about the importance of organizations in urban contexts, adopting a perspective in which organizations are said to operate within specific fields.

5. Ragin (1997, 2008); Ragin and Becker (1992); Burawoy (1998); Burawoy et al (1991; 2000) Yin (2003); Hedstrom and Swedberg (1998). By contrast, I did not find compelling the approach to case studies in King, Keohane, and Verba (1994), partly for the reasons offered by Campbell and Stanley (1963:6). See appendix C; also, Small (in press).

6. Simmel (1950, 1955, 1971); Bourdieu (1974, 1980, 1984, 1986, 1990); Coleman (1986, 1988, 1990, 1991); Wilson (1987, 1996); DiMaggio and Powell (1983); Powell (1987); Powell and DiMaggio (1991); Sen (1995, 1999); Goffman (1959, 1961, 1967, 1983); Homans (1950, 1961); Emerson (1976, 1981); Lazarsfeld and Merton (1954); Newcomb (1961); Mitchell (1969); Bott (1957); Lawler (2001, 2002); Lawler and Thye (1999); Lawler and Yoon (1993); Lawler et al. (2000); Hardin (2002); Elster (1986, 2007); Snijders (2005); Carley (1999, 2003); Wellman (1979, 1999); Wellman and Wortley (1990); Emirbayer and Goodwin (1994); Galaskiewicz (1979, 1985, 1999); Galaskiewicz and Bielefield (1998); Galaskiewicz and Wasserman (1989); Burt (1992, 2001, 2005); Laumann (1973) Laumann et al. (1978); Powell and DiMaggio (1991); Smith (2003, 2005, 2007); Duneier (1992, 1999); Duneier and Molotch (1999); Chaskin et al. (2001); Gamm (1999); Pattillo (2007); Pattillo-McCoy (1998, 1999); Delgado (1997, 1998, 1999); Delgado and Santiago (1998); Lee et al. (1984); Marwell (2004, 2007); Marwell and McInerney (2005); Lee (2002); May (2001); McDermott

(2006); Anderson (1978); Wacquant (2004, 2006); McRoberts (2003); Neckerman (2004); Danziger and Haveman (2002); Danziger et al (1994).

7. Lin (1999b, 2001a, 2001b).

APPENDIX B

1. From the Fragile Families and Child Wellbeing Study homepage, http://crcw.princeton.edu/ff.asp (accessed 6/4/07).

2. Because of the frequency with which centers open and close or fail to apply for license renewals, the exact number of centers in the city at any given time is always an estimate. For the study, the unit sampled was the establishment, not the organization. Thus, if a large organization operated three centers in different locations, each center had a probability of being selected equal to that of any other center in the sample. All three could have been interviewed, and they would constitute three responses, not one. Sampling the establishment was appropriate to my question here, since I was concerned with access to ties from the parent's perspective.

3. Guthrie and Roth (1999); Kelly (2003). On organizational sampling frames, see Kalleberg et al. (1990).

4. The response rate was calculated as the number of completes over the number of eligible targeted centers. The category "eligible" includes centers for which eligibility could not be determined (e.g., because of a wrong phone number); thus, this is a conservative calculation of the response rate. Raw numbers follow: 555 total centers were randomly sampled; 68 were determined to be ineligible during interview (e.g., no longer in business); 44 were refusals; 293 were completed; and, for 150, eligibility could not be determined. I expect bias from nonresponse to be minor. The sampling list contained limited information on the characteristics of centers. However, it contained general information on main funding source. Government-funded centers had somewhat higher completion rates (60%) than nongovernment funded centers (49%); both types had refusal rates of 8%. Eligibility was not determined in 27% of originally sampled centers that were government funded and in 21% of those that were not government funded. If completion rates are positively correlated with connectedness, then the positive effect of government funding would be somewhat upwardly biased.

5. Long (1997:230ff.).

6. Long (1997:34ff.).

7. Finkel (1995).

8. Future studies can explore the possibility of estimating this and other models from a counterfactual perspective, wherein predictor variables are conceived as "treatments" and the estimate of interest is the average treatment effect. See Morgan and Winship (2007).

9. A different way to estimate this model is to include a dummy variable for whether the mother is in a center, and another dummy (or an interaction variable) for whether she made friends. This approach distinguishes mothers who made friends from mothers who were in centers but did not make friends, while the approach presented distinguishes both types of mothers from a baseline of not being in a center. This does not affect either the coefficients and standard errors of other variables or the overall model fit; it simply provides an additional comparison

point. The case where the point of comparison made a difference is noted in the text in chapter 2.

10. Small and Newman (2001).

11. Jargowsky (1997); Wilson (1987; 1996).

12. This is the most parsimonious form of the variable given the complex ways in which childcare centers are funded. Most important, in 25% of the centers, 100% of the children receive free care. A continuous variable indicating the percentage of children on vouchers would exhibit a skewed and bimodal distribution.

13. The sample was missing data on number of referral ties (6% missing), number of service ties (11% missing), high percentage of poor children in center (13% missing), and sector (two cases missing). On multiple imputation, see Rubin (1987).

14. For details, see http://www.isr.umich.edu/src/smp/ive/ (accessed 5/28/08).

APPENDIX C

1. This is an epistemological pluralist position, which argues that different questions require different methods and that different methods require different perspectives. An essentially pragmatist orientation, the epistemological pluralist selects a method and, by extension, the standards of evidence only after the question is determined. By contrast, several recent scholars believe that a single, unifying set of standards apply for all methods, quantitative or qualitative (King, Keohane, and Verba 1994). To be clear, I believe that most empirical methods generally seek the same ends: that claims are supported by evidence and that findings can in theory be repeated. At issue, however, is that the means for attaining these general goals differ dramatically, from my perspective, from method to method. See Small (in press); Yin (2003).

2. On sampling for range, see Weiss (1994).

3. We interviewed six of seven center directors in the low-income black neighborhood, six of eight center directors in the low-income Latino neighborhood, 6 of 14 centers in the low-income white neighborhood, and five of six centers in the upper middle-class neighborhood. The low-income white neighborhood's large number of childcare centers was due to its much larger population. We stopped after six centers to retain comparability across neighborhoods.

4. Wilson (1987, 1996); Sampson and Groves (1989); Sampson et al (1997); Sampson (1999); Small and Newman (2001).

5. For some examples, among the many in existence, see Venkatesh (2000, 2006); Duneier (1999).

6. Small (in press).

7. Yin (2003). Whereas Yin distinguishes one type of "logic" from another, others distinguish among types of "inference." Clyde Mitchell (1983) distinguishes "statistical" from what he variously calls "logical," "causal," or "scientific inference." In one of the first modern discussions, Znaniecky (1934) distinguishes "enumerative" from "analytical deductions." While these distinctions refer to somewhat different issues and procedures, they all aim to distinguish the types of inferences made when dealing with survey (or otherwise large-n) data from those made when dealing with case study data.

8. Some of the most comprehensive books on the issues involved in case studies are Feagin, Orum, and Sjoberg (1991), Ragin (1987, 2008), and Ragin and Becker (1992), and Yin (2003).

9. All too often, qualitative interview studies pursue an awkward mix of both types of logic. For example, a study might conduct open-ended interviews that differ from person to person but then select respondents at random from the phone book in an attempt to ensure the sample is "representative." That approach violates several assumptions of sample-based logic: not all respondents are subject to the same interview (it is open-ended), the probability of selection is not known, the final respondents are especially likely to be a biased sample (since the average person rarely agrees to two-hour open-ended interviews on personal questions), and the sample is likely to be too small a sample to make confident inferences about the average characteristics of any major population. I do not believe we should continue calling such studies "representative." By the standards of basic probability theory that inspires them, they are no such thing. In addition, this orientation shifts focus away from the true strengths of interview-based research.

10. To see the logic, consider a stylized model from the case of psychology, based very loosely on the actual research of Steele and Aronson (1995). (This discussion is based on Small [in press].) Consider that most psychological experiments are conducted on small and highly unrepresentative samples of college students at large research universities. This is not an issue for psychologists because they do not expect to settle an issue on one experiment; they expect multiple experiments over time to provide (the external validity that accompanies) *saturation* on a topic. Suppose that Alfonse conducts an experiment in which one group of black and white students at Berkeley is told they will receive an IQ test and another is told nothing. Both complete the same test, and blacks in the first group do much worse than whites, while those in the second do as well as whites in their group. Alfonse concludes that the fear of fulfilling a stereotype about low IQs among blacks is at play. He then does performs two tasks, literal and theoretical replication (Yin 2003). With a colleague at Duke, he repeats the experiment among Duke undergraduates (literal replication); back at Berkeley, he repeats it, but using men and women instead of blacks and whites (theoretical replication). If the theory is right, it should work for any groups, not just blacks and whites, in which a stereotype is at play. Some results confirm his findings; others do not. Then he tries it among Asians and whites, and among issues other than IQ, and on more campuses, and with high school students and seniors, and on an on. Slowly, as the number of experiments increases, his confidence that his theory is right begins to increase. Eventually, every new experiment contributes very little new knowledge, such that the 89th experiment, with immigrant Asians and Russians in a low-income high school, shows exactly what he expected. At this point, he has attained saturation. The same logic can be applied to interviews, wherein each interview is considered in its own right. It is resembles an experiment not in the sense of any random assignment but in the sense that it yields clear predictions about the conditions under which it should be replicable literally or theoretically.

11. The interviews and their field notes were also entered into Atlas.ti and coded. We then extracted and sorted quotations in multiple ways over a few years and analyzed them for content. Atlas.ti, in this project, was largely a storage and basic sorting program. After the first or open coding, I printed reams of pages of quotations and analyzed everything personally by hand. After the first time I did this, I returned to the literature, pursued new works (e.g., the exchange theory tradition or

Laumann's work on radial networks), and then returned to recode the field notes and interviews. Throughout this process, we were also conducting interviews, so I sometimes used my newfound knowledge to inform future interviews. This dialectical process took several years, and it continued until I found patterns about which I was convinced.

    12. Small (in press).

References

Adler, Patricia A., Peter Adler, and Andrea Fontana. 1987. "Everyday Life Sociology." *Annual Review of Sociology* 13:217–235.

Ahmeduzzaman, Mohammad, and Jaipaul L. Roopnarine. 1992. "Sociodemographic Factors, Functioning Style, Social Support, and Fathers' Involvement with Preschoolers in African-American Families." *Journal of Marriage and the Family* 54:699–707.

Aldrich, Howard E. 1976. "Resource Dependence and Interorganizational Relations: Local Employment Service Offices and Social Services Sector Organizations." *Administration and Society* 7:419–454.

Ammerman, Nancy Tatom. 2005. *Pillars of Faith: American Congregations and Their Partners.* Berkeley: University of California Press.

Anderson, Elijah. 1978. *A Place on the Corner.* Chicago: University of Chicago Press.

———. 1990. *Streetwise: Race, Class, and Change in an Urban Community.* Chicago: University of Chicago Press.

———. 1999. *Code of the Street: Decency, Violence, and the Moral Life of the Inner City.* New York: W. W. Norton.

Aristotle. 1991. *On Rhetoric: A Theory of Civic Discourse*, translated by George A. Kennedy. New York: Oxford University Press.

Austin, James E. 2000. "Strategic Collaboration between Nonprofits and Businesses." *Nonprofit and Voluntary Sector Quarterly* 29:69–67.

Bacharach, Michael, and Diego Gambetta. 2001. "Trust in Signs." Pp. 148–184 in *Trust in Society*, edited by Karen Cook. New York: Russell Sage Foundation.

Baum, Joel A. C., and Christine Oliver. 1991. "Institutional Linkages and Organizational Mortality." *Administrative Science Quarterly* 36(2):187–218.

———. 1992. "Institutional Embeddedness and the Dynamics of Organizational Populations." *American Sociological Review* 57(4):540–559.

Baum, Joel A. C., and Jitendra V. Singh. 1994. "Organizational Niches and the Dymanics of Organizational Founding." *Organization Science* 5(4):483–501.

———. 1996. "Dynamics of Organizational Responses to Competition." *Social Forces* 74(4):1261–1297.

Bearman, Peter S. 1997. "Generalized Exchange." *American Journal of Sociology* 102(5):1383–1415.

———. 2005. *Doormen.* Chicago: University of Chicago Press.

Bearman, Peter S., and Paolo Parigi. 2004. "Cloning Headless Frogs and Other Important Matters: Conversation Topics and Network Structure." *Social Forces* 83(2):535–557.

Becher, R. 1989. *Parent Involvement: A Review of Research and Principles of Successful Practice.* Washington, DC: National Institute of Education.

Becker, Gary S. 1964. *Human Capital: A Theoretical and Empirical Analysis with Special Reference to Education.* New York: Columbia University Press.

Belkin, Lisa. 2003, October 26. "The Opt-Out Revolution." *New York Times Magazine,* 42, 44–46, 85–86.

Belsky, Jay, Deborah Lowe Vandell, Margaret Burchinal, K. Alison Clarke-Stewart, Kathleen McCartney, Margaret Tresch Owen, and the NICHD Early Child Care Research Network. 2007. "Are There Long-Term Effects of Early Child Care?" *Child Development* 78(2):681–701.

Benson, Kenneth J. 1975. "The Interorganizational Network as a Political Economy." *Administrative Science Quarterly* 20:229–249.

Berger, Peter L., and Thomas Luckmann. 1966. *The Social Construction of Reality: A Treatise in the Sociology of Knowledge.* Garden City, NJ: Doubleday.

Berrien, Jenny, Omar McRoberts, and Christopher Winship. 2000. "Religion and the Boston Miracle: The Effect of Black Ministry on Youth Violence." Pp. 266–285 in *Who Will Provide? The Changing Role of Religion in Social Welfare,* edited by Mary Jo Bane, Brent Coffin, and Ronald Thieman. Boulder, CO: Westview Press.

Bianchi, Suzanne M., Lynne M. Casper, and Rosalind Berkowitz King. 2005. *Work, Family, Health, and Well-being.* Mahwah, NJ: Lawrence Erlbaum Associates.

Bianchi, Suzanne M., and Sara B. Raley. 2005. "Time Allocation in Families." Pp. 21–42 in *Work, Family, Health, and Well-being,* edited by Suzanne M. Bianchi, Lynne M. Casper, and Rosalind Berkowitz King. Mahwah, NJ: Lawrence, Erlbaum Associates.

Bianchi, Suzanne M., John P. Robinson, and Melissa A. Milkie. 2006. *Changing Rhythms of American Life.* New York: Russell Sage Foundation.

Blau, David M. 2001. *The Child Care Problem.* New York: Russell Sage Foundation.

Blau, Peter M. 1986 [1964]. *Exchange and Power in Social Life.* New Brunswick, NJ: Transaction Publishers.

Blau, Peter M., and Joseph Schwartz. 1997. *Crosscutting Social Circles: Testing a Macrostructural Theory of Intergroup Relations.* New Brunswick, NJ: Transaction Publishers.

Blumer, Herbert. 1969. *Symbolic Interactionism: Perspective and Method.* Berkeley: University of California Press.

Bott, Elizabeth. 1957. *Family and Social Network.* London: Tavistock Publications.

Bourdieu, Pierre. 1977. *Outline of a Theory of Practice.* Cambridge: Cambridge University Press.

———. 1980, January. "Le Capital Social." *Actes de la Recherche en Sciences Sociales* 31:2–3.

———. 1984. *Distinction: A Social Critique of the Judgment of Taste.* Cambridge, MA: Harvard University Press.

———. 1986. "The Forms of Capital." Pp. 241–258 in *Handbook of Theory and Research for the Sociology of Education,* edited by J. G. Richardson. New York: Greenwood.

———. 1990. *The Logic of Practice.* Palo Alto, CA: Stanford University Press.

Bourdieu, Pierre, and Loic Wacquant. 1992. *An Invitation to Reflexive Sociology.* Chicago: University of Chicago Press.

Brass, Daniel J., Joseph Galaskiewicz, Henrich R. Greve, and Wenpin Tsai. 2004. "Taking Stock of Networks and Organizations: A Multilevel Perspective." *Academy of Management Journal* 47(6):795–817.

Breton, Raymond. 1964. "Institutional Completeness of Ethnic Communities and the Personal Relations of Immigrants." *American Journal of Sociology* 70:193–205.

Briggs, Xavier de Souza. 2007. "'Some of My Best Friends Are . . .': Interracial Friendships, Class, and Segregation in America." *City and Community* 6 (4):263–290.

Brinton, Mary C., and Victor Nee (Eds.). 2001. *The New Institutionalism in Sociology.* New York: Russell Sage Foundation.

Bromer, Juliet, and Julia R. Henly. 2004. "Child Care as Family Support: Caregiving Practices across Child Care Providers." *Children and Youth Services Review* 26:941–964.

Burawoy, Michael. 1998. "The Extended Case Method." *Sociological Theory* 16(1):4–33.

Burawoy, Michael, Joseph A. Blum, Sheba George, Zsuszsa Gille, Teresa Gowan, Lynne Haney, Maren Klawiter, Steven H. Lopez, Sean O Riain, and Millie Thayer. 2000. *Global Ethnography: Forces, Connections, and Imaginations in a Postmodern World.* Berkeley: University of California Press.

Burawoy, Michael, Alice Burton, Ann Arnett Ferguson, Kathryn J. Fox, Joshua Gamson, Nadine Gartrell, Leslie Hurst, Charles Kurzman, Leslie Salzinger, Josepha Schiffman, and Shiori Ui. 1991. *Ethnography Unbound: Power and Resistance in the Modern Metropolis.* Berkeley: University of California Press.

Burt, Ronald S. 1992. *Structural Holes: The Social Structure of Competition.* Cambridge, MA: Harvard University Press.

———. 2001. "Structural Holes versus Network Closure as Social Capital." Pp. 31–56 in *Social Capital: Theory and Research,* edited by Nan Lin, Karen Cook, and Ronald S. Burt. New York: Aldine de Gruyter.

———. 2005. *Brokerage and Closure: An Introduction to Social Capital.* Oxford: Oxford University Press.

Campbell, Donald T., and Julian C. Stanley. 1963. *Experimental and Quasi-Experimental Designs for Research.* Boston: Houghton Mifflin Company.

Carey, Benedict. 2007, March 26. "Poor Behavior Is Linked to Time in Day Care." *New York Times.* Available at http://www.nytimes.com/2007/03/26/us/26center.html (accessed 1/7/09).

Carley, Kathleen M. 1999. "On the Evolution of Social and Organizational Networks." Pp. 3–30 in *Research in the Sociology of Organizations: Networks in and around Organizations,* edited by Steven B. Andrews and David Knoke. Stamford, CT: JAI Press.

———. 2003. "Dynamic Network Analysis." Pp. 133–145 in *Dynamic Social Network Modeling and Analysis: Workshop Summary and Papers,* edited by Ron Breiger, Kathleen Carley, and P. Pattison. Washington, DC: Committee on Human Factors, National Research Council.

Chaskin, Robert J., Prudence Brown, Sudhir A. Venkatesh, and Avis Vidal. 2001. *Building Community Capacity.* New York: Aldine de Gruyter.

Chaudry, Ajay. 2004. *Putting Children First: How Low-Wage Working Mothers Manage Child Care.* New York: Russell Sage Foundation.

Chaves, Mark. 2004. *Congregations in America*. Cambridge, MA: Harvard University Press.

Children's Defense Fund. 2006. *Outreach Strategies for Medicaid and SCHIP: An Overview of Effective Strategies and Activities*. Kaiser Family Foundation. Available at http://www.childrensdefense.org/site/DocServer/OutreachStrategies MedicaidCHIP.pdf (accessed 12/30/08).

Clifford, James, and George E. Marcus (Eds.). 1986. *Writing Culture: The Poetics and Politics of Ethnography*. Berkeley: University of California Press.

Coleman, James S. 1986. "Social Theory, Social Research, and a Theory of Action." *American Journal of Sociology* 91(6):1309–1335.

——. 1988. "Social Capital in the Creation of Human Capital." *American Journal of Sociology* 94:s95–s120.

——. 1990. *Foundations of Social Theory*. Cambridge, MA: Belknap.

——. 1991. *Parental Involvement in Education*. Washington, DC: U.S. Department of Education, Office of Educational Research and Improvement, Programs for the Improvement of Practice.

Collins, Randall. 2004. *Interaction Ritual Chains*. Princeton, NJ: Princeton University Press.

Comfort, Megan. 2008. *Doing Time Together: Love and Family in the Shadow of the Prison*. Chicago: University of Chicago Press.

Conley, Dalton. 2004. *The Pecking Order: Which Siblings Succeed and Why*. New York: Pantheon Books.

——. 2005. "Poverty and Life Chances: The Conceptualization and Study of the Poor." Pp. 327–344 in *The Sage Handbook of Sociology*, edited by Craig Calhoun, Chris Rojek, and Brian S. Turner. Thousand Oaks, CA: Sage.

Cook, Karen S., ed. 2001. *Trust in Society*. New York: Russell Sage Foundation.

Currie, Janet. "The Take-up of Social Benefits." Unpublished manuscript, Princeton University.

Danziger, Sheldon H., and Robert H. Haveman. 2002. *Understanding Poverty*. New York: Russell Sage Foundation.

Danziger, Sheldon H., Gary Sandefur, and Daniel Weinberg. 1994. *Confronting Poverty*. Cambridge, MA: Harvard University Press.

Darley, John M. 2004. "Commitment, Trust, and Worker Effort Expenditure in Organizations." Pp. 127–151 in *Trust and Distrust in Organizations: Dilemmas and Approaches*, edited by Roderick M. Kramer and Karen S. Cook. New York: Russell Sage Foundation.

DeFilippis, James. 2001. "The Myth of Social Capital in Community Development." *Housing Policy Debate* 12(4):781–806.

Delgado, Melvin. 1997. "Role of Latina-Owned Beauty Parlors in a Latino Community." *Social Work* 42:445–453.

——. 1998. "Puerto Rican Elders and Merchant Establishments: Natural Caregiving Systems or Simply Businesses?" *Journal of Gerontological Social Work* 30:33–45.

——. 1999. *Social Work Practice in Nontraditional Urban Settings*. Oxford: Oxford University Press.

Delgado, Melvin, and Jorge Santiago. 1998. "HIV/AIDS in a Puerto Rican/Dominican Community: A Collaborative Project with a Botanical Shop." *Social Work* 43:183–187.

Department of Health and Human Services. 2005. Part 1304—Program Performance Standards for the Operation of Head Start Programs by Grantee and Delegate Agencies. Available at http://www.access.gpo.gov/nara/cfr/waisidx_05/45cfr1304_05.html (accessed 1/27/07).

DiMaggio, Paul J. 1983. "State Expansion and Organizational Fields." Pp. 147-161 in *Organizational Theory and Public Policy*, edited by Richard H. Hall and Robert E. Quinn. Berverly Hills: Sage Publications.

DiMaggio, Paul J., and Helmut Anheier. 1990. "The Sociology of Nonprofit Organizations and Sectors." *Annual Review of Sociology* 16:137-159.

DiMaggio, Paul J., and Walter W. Powell. 1983. "The Iron Cage Revisited: Institutional Isomorphism and Collective Rationality." *American Sociological Review* 48:147-160.

Dobbin, Frank, John R. Sutton, John W. Meyer, and Richard W. Scott. 1993. "Equal Opportunity Law and the Construction of Internal Labor Markets." *American Journal of Sociology* 99:396-427.

Domínguez, Silvia, and Celeste Watkins. 2003. "Creating Networks for Survival and Mobility: Social Capital among African-American and Latin-American Low-Income Mothers." *Social Problems* 50:111-135.

Doreian, Patrick and Katherine L. Woodward. 1999. "Local and Global Institutional Processes." *Research in the Sociology of Organizations* 16:59-83.

Duneier, Mitchell. 1992. *Slim's Table: Race, Respectability, and Masculinity*. Chicago: University of Chicago Press.

———. 1999. *Sidewalk*. New York: Farrar Straus and Giroux.

Duneier, Mitchell, and Harvey Molotch. 1999. "Talking City Trouble: Interactional Vandalism, Social Inequality, and the 'Urban Interaction Problem.'" *American Journal of Sociology* 104:1263-1295.

Durkheim, Emile. 1951 [1897]. *Suicide: A Study in Sociology*, translated by John A. Spaulding and George Simpson. New York: Free Press.

Durkheim, Emile. 1984 [1893]. *Durkheim: The Division of Labor in Society*. New York: Free Press.

Early Head Start Research Consortium. 2002. *Making a Difference in the Lives of Infants and Toddlers and Their Families: The Impacts of Early Head Start*. Vol. 3. *Local Contributions to Understanding the Programs and Their Impacts*. Washington, DC: U.S. Department of Health and Human Services.

Ebbers, Mark (Ed.). 1997. *The Formation of Inter-organizational Networks*. Oxford: Oxford University Press.

Edin, Kathryn, and Laura Lein. 1997. *Making Ends Meet: How Single Mothers Survive Welfare and Low-Wage Work*. New York: Russell Sage Foundation.

Ellen, Ingrid Gould, and Margery Austin Turner. 2003. "Do Neighborhoods Matter and Why?" Pp. 313-338 in *Choosing a Better Life?* edited by John Goering and Judith D. Feins. Washington, DC: Urban Institute Press.

Elster, John (Ed.). 1986. *Rational Choice: Readings in Social and Political Theory*. New York: New York University Press.

———. 2007. *Explaining Social Behavior: More Nuts and Bolts for the Social Sciences*. Cambridge: Cambridge University Press.

Emerson, Richard M. 1976. "Social Exchange Theory." *Annual Review of Sociology* 2:335-362.

——. 1990. "Social Exchange Theory." Pp. 30–65 in *Social Psychology: Sociological Perspectives*, edited by Morris Rosenberg and Ralph H. Turner. New Brunswick: Transaction Books.

Emirbayer, Mustafa. 1997. "Manifesto for a Relational Sociology." *American Journal of Sociology* 103(2):281–317.

Emirbayer, Mustafa, and Jeff Goodwin. 1994. "Network Analysis, Culture, and Agency." *American Journal of Sociology* 99:1411–1454.

Farberman, Harvey A., and Eugene A. Weinstein. 1970. "Personalization in Lower Class Consumer Interaction." *Social Problems* 17(4):449–457.

Feagin, Joe R., Anthony M. Orum, and Gideon Sjoberg (Eds.). 1991. *A Case for the Case Study*. Chapel Hill: University of North Carolina Press.

Fehr, Beverley. 1996. *Friendship Processes*. Thousand Oaks, CA: Sage Publications.

Feld, Scott L. 1981. "The Focused Organization of Social Ties." *American Journal of Sociology* 86:1015–1035.

——. 1982. "Social Structural Determinants of Similarity among Associates." *American Sociological Review* 47(6):797–801.

——. 1984. "The Structured Use of Personal Associates." *Social Forces* 62(3):640–652.

Feld, Scott L., and William C. Carter. 1998. "Foci of Activity as Changing Contexts for Friendship." Pp. 136–152 in *Placing Friendship in Context*, edited by Rebecca G. Adams and Graham Allan. Cambridge: Cambridge University Press.

Fernandez, Roberto, and Isabel Fernandez-Mateo. 2006. "Networks, Race, and Hiring." *American Sociological Review* 71(1):42–71.

Fernandez, Roberto, and David Harris. 1992. "Social Isolation and the Underclass." Pp. 257–293 in *Drugs, Crime, and Social Isolation: Barriers to Urban Opportunity*, edited by Adele Harrell and George Peterson. Washington, DC: Urban Institute Press.

Festinger, Leon, Stanley Schachter, and Kurt Back. 1950. *Social Pressures in Informal Groups: A Study of Human Factors in Housing*. Stanford, CA: Stanford University Press.

Finkel, Steven E. 1995. *Causal Analysis with Panel Data*. Newbury Park, CA: Sage Publications.

Fischer, Claude. 1982. *To Dwell among Friends: Personal Networks in Town and City*. Chicago: University of Chicago Press.

Frank, Robert H. 1992. "Melding Sociology and Economics: James Coleman's Foundations of Social Theory." *Journal of Economic Literature* 30(1):147–170.

Frumkin, Peter, and Joseph Galaskiewicz. 2004. "Institutional Isomorphism and Public Sector Organizations." *Journal of Public Administration Research and Theory* 14:283–307.

Fukuyama, Francis. 1995. *Trust: Social Virtues and the Creation of Prosperity*. New York: Free Press.

Fuller, Bruce, Susanna Loeb, Annelie Strath, and Bidemi Abioseh Carrol. 2004. "State Formation of the Childcare Sector: Family Demand and Policy Action." *Sociology of Education* 77(4):337–358.

Fuller, Mary Lou, and Glenn Olsen. 1998. *Home-School Relations: Working Successfully with Parents and Families*. Boston: Allyn and Bacon.

Furman, Frida Kerner. 1997. *Facing the Mirror: Older Women and Beauty Shop Culture*. New York: Routledge.

Galaskiewicz, Joseph. 1979. "Structure of Community Organizational Networks." *Social Forces* 57:1346–1364.

——. 1985. "Interorganizational Relations." *Annual Review of Sociology* 11:281–304.

——. 1999. "The Formation of Inter-organizational Networks." *Contemporary Sociology* 28:55–56.

Galaskiewicz, Joseph, and Wolfgang Bielefeld. 1998. *Nonprofit Organizations in an Age of Uncertainty: A Study of Growth and Decline*. New York: Aldine de Gruyter.

Galaskiewicz, Joseph, and Stanley Wasserman. 1989. "Mimetic Processes within an Interorganizational Field: An Empirical-Test." *Administrative Science Quarterly* 34:454–479.

Gamm, Gerald H. 1999. *Urban Exodus: Why The Jews Left Boston and the Catholics Stayed*. Cambridge, MA: Harvard University Press.

Garfinkel, Harold. 1967. *Studies in Ethnomethodology*. Cambridge: Polity Press.

Glaser, Barney G., and Anselm L. Strauss. 1967. *The Discovery of Grounded Theory: Strategies for Qualitative Research*. Chicago: Aldine.

Goering, John, and Judith D. Feins, eds. 2003. *Choosing a Better Life? Evaluating the Moving to Opportunity Social Experiment*. Washington, DC: Urban Institute Press.

Goering, John, Judith D. Feins, and Todd M. Richardson. 2003. "What Have We Learned about Housing Mobility and Poverty Deconcentration?" Pp. 3–36 in *Choosing a Better Life? Evaluating the Moving to Opportunity Social Experiment*, edited by John Goering and Judith D. Feins. Washington, DC: Urban Institute Press.

Goffman, Erving. 1959. *The Presentation of Self in Everyday Life*. New York: Doubleday Anchor Books.

——. 1961. *Asylums: Essays on the Social Situation of Mental Patients and Other Inmates*. New York: Anchor Books.

——. 1967. *Interaction Ritual: Essays in Face-to-Face Behavior*. Chicago: Aldine.

——. 1983. "The Interaction Order." *American Sociological Review* 48:1–17.

Granovetter, Mark. 1973. "The Strength of Weak Ties." *American Journal of Sociology* 78:1360–1380.

——. 1974. *Getting a Job: A Study of Contacts and Careers*. Cambridge, MA: Harvard University Press.

——. 1983. "The Strength of Weak Ties: A Network Theory Revisited." *Sociological Theory* 1:201–233.

——. 1985. "Economic Action and Social Structure: The Problem of Embeddedness." *American Journal of Sociology* 91(3):481–210.

Green, Donald P., and Ian Shapiro. 1994. *Pathologies of Rational Choice Theory: A Critique of Applications in Political Science*. New Haven, CT: Yale University Press.

Gruber, Jonathan. 2003. "Medicaid." Pp. 15–77 in *Means Tested Transfer Programs in the U.S.*, edited by Robert Moffitt. Chicago: University of Chicago Press.

Guthrie, Doug, and Louise Marie Roth. 1999. "The State, Courts, and Maternity Policies in U.S. Organizations: Specifying Institutional Mechanisms." *American Sociological Review* 64:41–63.

Hallinan, Maureen T. 1976. "Friendship Patterns in Open and Traditional Classrooms." *Sociology of Education* 50:273–289.

——. 1978. "The Process of Friendship Formation." *Social Networks* 1(2):193–210.

——. 1979. "Structural Effects on Children's Friendships and Cliques." *Social Psychology Quarterly* 42(1):43–54.

Hallinan, Maureen T., and Aage B. Sorenesen. 1985. "Ability Grouping and Student Friendships." *American Educational Research Journal* 22(4):485–499.

Hallinan, Maureen T., and Nancy B. Tuma. 1978. "Classroom Effects on Change in Children's Friendships." *Sociology of Education* 51(4):270–282.

Hardin, Russell. 2002. *Trust and Trustworthiness*. New York: Russell Sage Foundation.

Hays, Sharon. 1996. *The Cultural Contradictions of Motherhood*. New Haven, CT: Yale University Press.

Hedstrom, Peter, and Richard Swedberg (Eds.). 1998. *Social Mechanisms: An Analytical Approach to Social Theory*. Cambridge: Cambridge University Press.

Hochschild, Arlie. 1989. *The Second Shift*. New York: Avon Books.

——. 1997. *The Time Bind: When Work Becomes Home and Home Becomes Work*. New York: Metropolitan Books.

Hofferth, Sandra L. 1987. "Child Care in the U.S." Testimony before the Select Committee on Children, Youth, and Families, U.S. House of Representatives. Pp. 163–187 in *American Families in Tomorrow's Economy*, released by the United States Congress, House, Select Committee on Children, Youth, and Families. Washington, DC: Goverment Printing Office.

Hofferth, Sandra L., and Douglas A. Wissoker. 1992. "Price, Quality, and Income in Child Care Choice." *Journal of Human Resources* 27(1):70–111.

Homans, George Caspar. 1950. *The Human Group*. New York: Harcourt, Brace.

——. 1961. *Social Behavior: Its Elementary Forms*. New York: Harcourt, Brace and World.

Huckfeldt, R. Robert. 1983. "Social Contexts, Social Networks, and Urban Neighborhoods: Environmental Constraints on Friendship Choice." *American Journal of Sociology* 89(3):651–669.

Iceland, John, and Kurt Bauman. 2004. "Income Poverty and Material Hardship: How Strong Is the Association?" National Poverty Center Working Paper Series. Ann Arbor: University of Michigan.

Inzerilli, Giorgio. 1979. "The Organization-Client Relationship as an Aspect of Interorganizational Analysis." *Human Relations* 32:419–437.

Jacobs, Jane. 1961. *The Death and Life of Great American Cities*. New York: Vintage.

Jacobs, Jerry, and Kathleen Gerson. 2004. *The Time Divide: Work, Family, and Gender Inequality*. Cambridge, MA: Harvard University Press.

Jargowsky, Paul. 1997. *Poverty and Place: Ghettos, Barrios, and the American City*. New York: Russell Sage Foundation.

Jencks, Christopher, and Susan Mayer. 1990. "The Social Consequences of Growing Up in a Poor Neighborhood." Pp. 111–186 in *Inner-City Poverty in the United States*, edited by Laurence E. Lynn and Michael G. H. McGeary. Washington, DC: National Academy Press.

Kadushin, Charles. 2002. "The Motivational Foundation of Social Networks." *Social Networks* 24:77–91.

——. 2004. "Too Much Investment in Social Capital?" *Connections* 26:75–90.

Kalleber, Arne L., Peter V. Marsden, Howard E. Aldrich, and James Cassell. 1990. "Comparing Organizational Sampling Frames." *Administrative Science Quarterly* 35(4):658–688.

Kalmjin, Matthijs, and Henk Flap. 2001. "Organized Meeting and Mating: Unintended Consequences of Organized Settings for Partner Choices." *Social Forces* 79(4):1289–1312.

Kant, Immanuel. 1965 [1781]. *Critique of Pure Reason*, translated by Norman Kemp Smith. New York: St. Martin's Press.

Kasarda, John D., and Morris Janowitz. 1974. "Community attachment in mass society." *American Sociological Review* 39:328–339.

Kasinitz, Philip. 2000. "Red Hook: The Paradoxes of Poverty and Place in Brooklyn." *Research in Urban Sociology* 5:253–274.

Kasinitz, Philip, and Jan Rosenberg. 1996. "Missing the Connection: Social Isolation and Employment on the Brooklyn Waterfront." *Social Problems* 43:180–196.

Kaufman, Leslie. 2004, June 10. "As Workers Strike, Parents Spend Day with Child in Tow." *New York Times*. Available at http://query.nytimes.com/gst/fullpage.html?res=9F04E2DE1430F933A25755C0A9629C8B63 (accessed 1/7/09).

Kelly, Erin L. 2003. "The Strange History of Employer-Sponsored Child Care: Interested Actors, Uncertainty, and the Transformation of Law in Organizational Fields." *American Journal of Sociology* 109:606–649.

Kessler, Ronald C., Hans-Ulrich Wittchen, Jamie M. Abelson, Katherine Mcgonagle, Norbert Schwarz, Kenneth S. Kendler, Barbel Knauper, and Shangyang Zhao. 1998. "Methodological Studies of the Composite International Diagnostic Interview in the US National Comorbidity Survey." *International Journal of Methods in Psychiatric Research* 7(1):33–55.

King, Gary, Robert O. Keohane, and Sidney Verba. 1994. *Designing Social Inquiry: Scientific Inference in Qualitative Research*. Princeton, NJ: Princeton University Press.

Klinenberg, Eric. 2002. *Heat Wave: A Social Autopsy of Disaster in Chicago*. Chicago: University of Chicago Press.

Kollock, Peter. 1994. "The Emergence of Exchange Structures: An Experimental Study of Uncertainty, Commitment, and Trust." *American Journal of Sociology* 100(2):313–345.

Kramer, Roderick M., and Karen S. Cook (Eds.). 2004. *Trust and Distrust in Organizations: Dilemmas and Approaches*. New York: Russell Sage Foundation.

Kramer, Roderick M., and Tom R. Tyler. 1996. *Trust in Organizations: Frontiers of Theory and Research*. Thousand Oaks, CA: Sage Publications.

Krueger, Alan B., and David A. Schkade. 2007. "The Reliability of Subjective Well-being Measures." *Journal of Public Economics* 92(8–9):1833–1845.

Lamont, Michele, and Mario Small. 2008. "How Culture Matters: Enriching Our Understanding of Poverty." Pp. 76–102 in David Harris and Ann Lin, (eds.), *The Colors of Poverty: Why Racial and Ethnic Disparities Persist*. New York, NY: Russell Sage Foundation.

Laumann, Edward O. 1973. *Bonds of Pluralism: The Form and Substance of Urban Social Networks*. New York: Wiley Interscience.

Laumann, Edward O., Joseph Galaskiewicz, and Peter V. Marsden. 1978. "Community Structures as Interorganizational Linkages." *Annual Review of Sociology* 4:445–484.

Lawler, Edward J. 2001. "An Affect Theory of Social Exchange." *American Journal of Sociology* 107:321–352.

——. 2002. "Micro Social Orders." *Social Psychology Quarterly* 65(1):4–17.

Lawler, Edward J., and Shane R. Thye. 1999. "Bringing Emotions into Social Exchange Theory." *Annual Review of Sociology* 25:217–244.

Lawler, Edward J., Shane R. Thye, and Jeongkoo Yoon. 2000. "Emotion and Group Cohesion in Productive Exchange." *American Journal of Sociology* 106(3):616–657.

Lawler, Edward J., and Jeongkoo Yoon. 1993. "Power and the Emergence of Commitment Behavior in Negotiated Exchange." *American Sociological Review* 58:465–481.

Lazarsfeld, Paul F., and Robert K. Merton. 1954. "Friendship as Social Process: A Substantive and Methodological Analysis." Pp. 18–66 in *Freedom and Control in Modern Society*, edited by Morroe Berger, Theodore Abel, and Charles Page. New York: Van Nostrand.

Lee, Barrett A., R. S. Oropesa, Barbara J. Metch, and Avery M. Guest. 1984. "Testing the Decline-of-Community Thesis: Neighborhood Organizations in Seattle, 1929 and 1979." *American Journal of Sociology* 89:1161–1188.

Lee, Jennifer. 2002. *Civility in the City: Blacks, Jews, and Koreans in Urban America.* Cambridge, MA: Harvard University Press.

Levine, James A. 1993. "Involving Fathers in Head Start: A Framework for Public Policy and Program Development." *Families in Society* 74:4–21.

Levine, Sol, and Paul E. White. 1961. "Exchange as a Conceptual Framework for the Study of Interorganizational Relationships." *Administrative Science Quarterly* 5:583–601.

Levi-Strauss, Claude. 1969. *The Elementary Structures of Kinship*, translated by J. Bell von Sturmer and R. Needham. Boston: Beacon Press.

Levitt, Steven D., and Sudhir A. Venkatesh. 2000. "An Economic Analysis of a Drug-Selling Gang's Finances." *Quarterly Journal of Economics* 20:755–789.

Lichterman, Paul. 2005. *Elusive Togetherness: Church Groups Trying to Bridge America's Divisions.* Princeton, NJ: Princeton University Press.

Lieberson, Stanley. 1985. *Making It Count: The Improvement of Social Research and Theory.* Berkeley, CA: University of California Press.

Lin, Nan. 1999a. "Social Networks and Status Attainment." *Annual Review of Sociology* 25:467–487.

——. 1999b. "Building a Network Theory of Social Capital." *Connections* 22(1):28–51.

——. 2001a. *Social Capital: A Theory of Structure and Action.* Cambridge: Cambridge University Press.

——. 2001b. "Building a Network Theory of Social Capital." Pp. 3–30 in *Social Capital Theory and Research*, edited by N. Lin, K. Cook, and R. Burt. New York: Aldine de Gruyter.

Lin, Nan, John C. Vaughn, and Walter M. Ensel. 1981. "Social Resources and Occupational Status Attainment." *Social Forces* 59:1163–1181.

Logan, John R., and Harvey L. Molotch. 1987. *Urban Fortunes. The Political Economy of Place.* Berkeley: University of California Press.

Long, J. Scott. 1997. *Regression Models for Categorical and Limited Dependent Variables.* Thousand Oaks, CA: Sage.

Loury, Glenn C. 1977. "A Dynamic Theory of Racial Income Difference." Pp. 153–186 in *Women, Minorities and Employment Discrimination*, edited by P. Wallace and A. LaMont. Lexington, MA: Lexington Books.

Marsden, Peter V. 1987. "Core Discussion Networks of Americans." *American Sociological Review* 52:122–131.

Marsden, Peter V., and Karen E. Campbell. 1984. "Measuring Tie Strength." *Social Forces* 83:482–501.

Martin, John Levy. 2003. "What Is Field Theory?" *American Journal of Sociology* 109:1–49.

Marwell, Nicole P. 2004. "Privatizing the Welfare State: Nonprofit Community-Based Organizations as Political Actors." *American Sociological Review* 69:265–291.

———. 2007. *Bargaining for Brooklyn: Community Organizations in the Entrepreneurial City*. Chicago: University of Chicago Press.

Marwell, Nicole P., and Paul-Brian McInerney. 2005. "The Nonprofit/For-Profit Continuum: Theorizing the Dynamics of Mixed-Form Markets." *Nonprofit and Voluntary Sector Quarterly* 34:7–28.

Maryland Committee for Children. 2003. "Child Care Demographics 2003: Maryland Report." Baltimore: Maryland Committee for Children.

Massey, Douglas, and Nancy Denton. 1993. *American Apartheid: Segregation and the Making of the Underclass*. Cambridge, MA: Harvard University Press.

May, Reuben. 2001. *Talking at Trena's: Everyday Conversations at an African-American Tavern*. New York: New York University Press.

Mayer, Roger C., James H. Davis, and F. David Schoorman. 1995. "An Integrative Model of Organizational Trust." *Academy of Management Journal* 20(3):709–734.

Mayer, Susan E., and Christopher Jencks. 1989. "Poverty and the Distribution of Material Hardship." *Journal of Human Resources* 24(1):88–114.

McDermott, Monica. 2006. *Working Class White: The Making and Unmaking of Race Relations*. Berkeley: University of California Press.

McManus, Patricia A., and Thomas A. DiPrete. 2001. "Losers and Winners: The Financial Consequences of Separation and Divorce for Men." *American Sociological Review* 66(2):246–268.

McPherson, Miller, Lynn Smith-Lovin, and Matthew E. Brashears. 2006. "Social Isolation in America: Changes in Core Discussion Networks over Two Decades." *American Sociological Review* 71:353–375.

McPherson, Miller, Lynn Smith-Lovin, and James M. Cook. 2001. "Birds of a Feather: Homophily in Social Networks." *Annual Review of Sociology* 27:415–444.

McRoberts, Omar. 2003. *Streets of Glory: Church and Community in a Black Urban Neighborhood*. Chicago: University of Chicago Press.

Merton, Robert. 1936. "The Unanticipated Consequences of Purposive Social Action." *American Sociological Review* 1(6):894–904.

Meyer, Bruce D., and James X. Sullivan. 2003. "Measuring the Well-being of the Poor Using Income and Consumption." *Journal of Human Resources* 38:1180–1220.

Meyer, John W., and Brian Rowan. 1977. "Institutionalized Organizations: Formal Structure as Myth and Ceremony." *American Journal of Sociology* 83:340–363.

Midco Educational Associates (Denver, CO). 1972. "Perspectives on Parent Participation in Project Head Start." Document HEW-OS-72-45. Washington, DC: Department of Health, Education and Welfare, Office of Child Development.

Morgan, Stephen L., and Christopher Winship. 2007. *Counterfactuals and Causal Inference: Methods and Principles for Social Research*. Cambridge: Cambridge University Press.

Mouw, Ted. 2003. "Social Capital and Finding a Job: Do Contacts Matter?" *American Sociological Review* 68:868–898.

———. 2006. "Estimating the Causal Effect of Social Capital: A Review of Recent Research." *Annual Review of Sociology* 32:79–102.

Muller, Chandra, and David Kerbow. 1993. "Parental Involvement in the Home, School and Community." Pp. 13–42 in *Parents, Their Children and Schools*, edited by Barbara Schneider and James S. Coleman. Boulder, CO: Westview.

National Center for Early Development and Learning. 2007. "Cost, Quality, and Outcomes Study." Available at http://www.fpg.unc.edu/~ncedl/pages/cq.cfm (accessed 1/7/09).

Neckerman, Kathryn. 2004. *Social Inequality*. New York: Russell Sage Foundation.

Nee, Victor, and Mary C. Brinton (Eds.). 1998. *The New Institutionalism in Sociology*. New York: Russell Sage Foundation.

Nee, Victor, and Paul Ingram. 1998. "Embeddedness and Beyond: Institutions, Exchange, and Social Structure." Pp. 19–45 in *The New Institutionalism in Sociology*, edited by Mary C. Brinton and Victor Nee. Palo Alto, CA: Stanford University Press.

Nelson, Margaret K. 2000. "Single Mothers and Social Support: The Commitment to, and Retreat from, Reciprocity." *Qualitative Sociology* 23:291–317.

Newcomb, Theodore M. 1961. *The Acquaintance Process*. New York: Holt, Rinehart, and Winston.

Newman, Katherine, and Rebekah Peeples Massengill. 2006. "The Texture of Hardship: Qualitative Sociology on Poverty 1995–2005." *Annual Review of Sociology* 32(18):1–24.

NICHD Early Child Care Research Network. 2002. "Early Child Care and Children's Development Prior to School Entry: Results from the NICHD Study of Early Child Care." *American Educational Research Journal* 39(1):133–164.

Nussbaum, Martha, and Amartya Sen (Eds). 1993. *The Quality of Life*. Oxford: Clarendon Press.

Obstfeld, David, and Steve Borgatti. 2008. "Brokerage Is a Process, Not a Structure: A Clarification of Social Network Language." Paper presented at Sunbelt XXVIII, International Sunbelt Social Network Conference.

Oldenburg, Ray. 1989. *The Great Good Place: Cafes, Coffeeshops, Bookstores, Bars, Hair Salons, and Other Hangouts at the Heart of a Community*. New York: Paragon House.

Olson, Mancur. 1965. *The Logic of Collective Action*. Cambridge, MA: Harvard University Press.

Park, Robert, Ernest W. Burgess, and Roderick D. McKenzie. 1925. *The City*. Chicago: University of Chicago Press.

Pattillo, Mary. 2007. *Black on the Block: The Politics of Race and Class in the City*. Chicago: University of Chicago Press.

Pattillo-McCoy, Mary. 1998. "Church Culture as a Strategy of Action in the Black Community." *American Sociological Review* 63:767–784.

———. 1999. *Black Picket Fences: Privilege and Peril among the Black Middle Class*. Chicago: University of Chicago Press.

Pérez-Peña, Richard. 2005a (November 21). "For Medicaid Clients, New Hurdle Looms." *The New York Times*. Available at http://www.nytimes.com/2005/11/21/nyregion/21medicaid.html (accessed 1/7/09).

——. 2005b (December 6). "State Seeks Renewal of Medicaid Exemption." *The New York Times*. Available at http://www.nytimes.com/2005/12/06/nyregion/06medicaid.html (accessed 1/7/09).

Perrow, Charles. 1984. *Normal Accidents: Living with High-Risk Technologies*. New York: Basic Books.

Peterson, Ruth D., Lauren J. Krivo, and Mark A. Harris. 2000. "Disadvantage and Neighborhood Violent Crime: Do Local Institutions Matter?" *Journal of Research in Crime and Delinquency* 37:31–63.

Pfeffer, Jeffery, and Gerald R. Salancik. 1978. *The External Control of Organizations: A Resource Dependence Perspective*. New York: Harper and Row.

Popielarz, Pamela A. 1999. "Organizational Constraints on Personal Network Formation." Pp. 263–281 in *Research in the Sociology of Organizations: Networks in and around Organizations*, edited by Steven B. Andrews and David Knoke. Stamford, CT: JAI Press.

Portes, Alejandro. 1998. "Social Capital: Its Origins and Applications in Modern Sociology." *Annual Review of Sociology* 24:1–24.

Portes, Alejandro, and Ruben G. Rumbaut. 1990. *Immigrant America: A Portrait*. Berkeley: University of California Press.

Powell, Walter W. (Ed.) 1987. The Nonprofit Sector: A Research Handbook. New Haven, CT: Yale University Press.

Powell, Walter W., and Paul J. DiMaggio (Eds.). 1991. *The New Institutionalism in Organizational Analysis*. Chicago: University of Chicago Press.

Putnam, Robert D. 2000. *Bowling Alone: The Collapse and Revival of American Community*. New York: Simon and Schuster.

Ragin, Charles C. 1987. *The Comparative Method: Moving Beyond Qualitative and Quantitative Strategies*. Berkeley: University of California Press.

——. 2008. *Redesigning Social Inquiry: Fuzzy Sets and Beyond*. Chicago: University of Chicago Press.

Ragin, Charles C., and Howard S. Becker. 1992. *What Is a Case? Exploring the Foundations of Social Inquiry*. Cambridge: Cambridge University Press.

Rankin, Bruce, and James Quane. 2000. "Neighborhood Poverty and the Social Isolation of Inner-City African American Families." *Social Forces* 79:139–164.

Reichman, Nancy E., Julien O. Teitler, Irwin Garfinkel, and Sara McLanahan. 2001. "Fragile Families: Sample and Design." *Children and Youth Services Review* 23(4/5):303–326.

Rosenbaum, James E. 2001. *Beyond College for All: Career Paths for the Forgotten Half*. New York: Russell Sage Foundation.

Rosenbaum, James E., Stephanie DeLuca, Shazia R. Miller, and Kevin Roy. 1999. "Pathways into Work: Short- and Long-Term Effects of Personal and Institutional Ties." *Sociology of Education* 72:179–196.

Rubin, Donald B. 1987. *Multiple Imputation for Nonresponse in Surveys*. New York: J. Wiley and Sons.

Saegert, Susan, J. Phillip Thompson, and Mark R. Warren. 2001. *Social Capital in Poor Communities*. New York: Russell Sage Foundation.

Salamon, Lester M. 1993. "The Marketization of Welfare: Changing Nonprofit and For-Profit Roles in the American Welfare State." *Social Service Review* 67(1):17–39.

———. 1995. *Partners in Public Service: Government-Nonprofit Relations in the Modern Welfare State*. Baltimore, MD: Johns Hopkins University Press.

Sampson, Robert J. 1999. "What Community Supplies." Pp. 241–292 in *Urban Problems and Community Development*, edited by Ronald Ferguson and William Dickens. Washington, DC: Brookings Institution.

Sampson, Robert J., and W. Byron Groves. 1989. "Community Structure and Crime: Testing Social Disorganization Theory." *American Journal of Sociology* 94(4):774.

Sampson, Robert, and Jeffrey D. Morenoff. 1997. "Ecological Perspectives on the Neighborhood Context of Urban Poverty: Past and Present." Pp. 1–22 in *Neighborhood Poverty*. Vol. 2: *Policy Implications in Studying Neighborhoods*. New York: Russell Sage Foundation.

Sampson, Robert J., Jeffrey D. Morenoff, and Felton Earls. 1999. "Beyond Social Capital: Spatial Dynamics of Collective Efficacy for Children." *American Sociological Review* 64:633–660.

Sampson, Robert J., Jeffrey D. Morenoff, and Thomas Gannon-Rowley. 2002. "Assessing 'Neighborhood Effects': Social Processes and New Directions in Research." *Annual Review of Sociology* 28:443–478.

Sampson, Robert J., Stephen Raudenbush, and Felton Earls. 1997. "Neighborhoods and Violent Crime: A Multilevel Study of Collective Efficacy." *Science* 227:918–924.

Sawyer, R. Keith. 2001. "Emergence in Sociology: Contemporary Philosophy of Mind and Some Implications for Sociological Theory." *American Journal of Sociology* 109(3):551–585.

Sánchez-Jankowski, Martín. 1991. *Islands in the Street: Gangs and American Urban Society*. Berkekely: University of California Press.

———. 2008. *Cracks in the Pavement: Social Change and Resilience in Poor Neighborhoods*. Berkeley: University of California Press.

Schneiberg, Marc, and Elisabeth S. Clemens. 2006. "The Typical Tools for the Job: Research Strategies in Institutional Analysis." *Sociological Theory* 24(3):195–227.

Schor, Juliet B. 1991. *The Overworked American: The Unexpected Decline of Leisure*. New York: Basic Books.

Scott, Gill. 1990. "Parents and Preschool Services: Issues of Parental Involvement." *International Journal of Sociology and Social Policy* 10:1–13.

Scott, W. Richard. 1995. *Institutions and Organizations*. Thousand Oaks, CA: Sage.

———. 2003. *Organizations: Rational, Natural, and Open Systems*. Upper Saddle River, NJ: Prentice Hall.

Sen, Amartya. 1985. *Commodities and Capabilities*. New York: Elsevier Science.

———. 1999. *Development as Freedom*. New York: Knopf.

Shapiro, Debra L., Blair H. Sheppard, and Lisa Cheraskin. 1992. "Business on a Handshake." *Negotiation Journal* 8(4):365–377.

Simmel, Georg. 1950. *The Sociology of Georg Simmel*, translated and edited by Kurt H. Wolff. New York: Free Press.

———. 1955. *Conflict and the Web of Group-Affiliations*. New York: Free Press.

———. 1971. *Georg Simmel: On Individuality and Social Forms*, edited by Donald H. Levine. Chicago: University of Chicago Press.

Simon, Herbert. 1957. *Administrative Behavior: A Study of Decision-Making Processes in Administrative Organization*, 2nd ed. New York: Macmillan.

Small, Mario L. 2002. "Culture, Cohorts, and Social Organization Theory: Understanding Local Participation in a Latino Housing Project." *American Journal of Sociology* 108:1–54.

———. 2004. *Villa Victoria: The Transformation of Social Capital in a Boston Barrio.* Chicago: University of Chicago Press.

———. 2006. "Neighborhood Institutions as Resource Brokers: Childcare Centers, Inter-organizational Ties, and Resource Access among the Poor." *Social Problems* 53:274–292.

———. 2007a. "Racial Differences in Networks: Do Neighborhood Conditions Matter?" *Social Science Quarterly* 88(2):320–343.

———. 2007b. "Is There Such a Thing as 'The Ghetto'? The Perils of Assuming that the South Side of Chicago Represents Poor Black Neighborhoods." *City* 11(3):413–421.

———. 2008. "Four Reasons to Abandon the Idea of the Ghetto." *City and Community* 7(4):389–398.

———. In Press. " 'How Many Cases Do I Need?' On Science and the Logic of Case Selection in Field-Based Research." *Ethnography.*

Small, Mario L., Erin Jacobs, and Rebekah Peeples Massengill. 2008. "Why Organizational Ties Matter for Neighborhood Effects: A Study of Resource Access through Childcare Centers." *Social Forces* 87(1):387–414.

Small, Mario L., and Katherine Newman. 2001. "Urban Poverty after *The Truly Disadvantaged*: The Rediscovery of the Family, the Neighborhood, and Culture." *Annual Review of Sociology* 27:23–45.

Small, Mario L., and Laura Stark. 2005. "Are Poor Neighborhoods Resource-Deprived? A Case Study of Childcare Centers in New York." *Social Science Quarterly* 86:10113–10136.

Smith, Sandra. 2003. "Social Capital and the Urban Poor: Extending the Scholarly Tradition of William Julius Wilson." *Ethnic and Racial Studies* 26:1029–1045.

———. 2005. "'Don't Put My Name on It': (Dis)Trust and Job-Finding Assistance among the Black Urban Poor." *Amercan Journal of Sociology* 111(1):1–57.

———. 2007. *Lone Pursuit: Distrust and Defensive Individualism among the Black Poor.* New York: Russell Sage Foundation.

Smith, Steven Rathgeb, and Michael Lipsky. 1993. *Nonprofits for Hire: The Welfare State in the Age of Contracting.* Cambridge, MA: Harvard University Press.

Snijders, Tom A. B. 2005. "Models for Longitudinal Network Data." Pp. 215–247 in *Models and Methods in Social Network Analysis*, edited by Peter J. Carrington, John Scott, and Stanley Wasserman. Cambridge: Cambridge University Press.

Spies-Butcher, Ben. 2002. "Tracing the Rational Choice Origins of Social Capital: Is Social Capital a Neo-liberal 'Trojan Horse'?" *Australian Journal of Social Issues* 37:173–192.

Stack, Carol B. 1974. *All Our Kin: Strategies for Survival in a Black Community.* New York: Harper and Row.

Steele, Claude M. and Joshua Aronson. 1995. "Stereotype Threat and the Intellectual Test Performance of African Americans." *Journal of Personality and Social Psychology* 69(5):797–811.

Taub, Richard P., George P. Surgeon, Sara Lindholm, Phyllis Betts Otti, and Amy Bridges. 1977. "Urban Voluntary Associations: Locally Based, Externally Induced." *American Journal of Sociology* 83:425–442.

Tigges, Leann M., Irene Browne, and Gary P. Green. 1998. "Social Isolation of the Urban Poor: Race, Class, and Neighborhood Effects on Social Resources." *Sociological Quarterly* 39:53–77.

Tonnies, Ferdinand. 1957 [1887]. *Community and Society*. New York: Harper Torchbooks.

Tyler, Tom R., and P. Degoey. 1996. "Trust in Organizational Authorities: The Influence of Motive Attributions on Willingness to Accept Decisions." Pp. 331–356 in *Trust in Organizations: Frontiers of Theory and Research*, edited by Roderick M. Kramer and Tom R. Tyler. Thousand Oaks, CA: Sage Publications.

Tyler, Tom R., and Roderick M. Kramer. 1996. "Whither Trust?" Pp. 1–16 in *Trust in Organizations: Frontiers of Theory and Research*, edited by Roderick M. Kramer and Tom R. Tyler. Thousand Oaks, CA: Sage.

Uehara, Edwina. 1990. "Dual Exchange Theory, Social Network Analysis and Informal Social Support." *American Journal of Sociology* 96(3):521–557.

U.S. Census Bureau. 2006. *Statistical Abstract of the United States*. Washington, DC: U.S. Department of Commerce, Economics, and Statistics Administration, Bureau of the Census.

———. 2008. *Statistical Abstract of the United States*. Washington, DC: U.S. Department of Commerce, Economics, and Statistics Administration, Bureau of the Census.

Vaughan, Diane. 1996. *The Challenger Launch Decision: Risky Technology, Culture, and Deviance at NASA*. Chicago: University of Chicago Press.

Venkatesh, Sudhir A. 2000. *American Project: The Rise and Fall of a Modern Ghetto*. Cambridge, MA: Harvard University Press.

———. 2006. *Off the Books: The Underground Economy of the Urban Poor*. Chicago: University of Chicago Press.

Verbrugge, Lois M. 1977. "The Structure of Adult Friendship Choices." *Social Forces* 56(2):576–597.

Wacquant, Loïc J. D. 2004. *Body and Soul: Notebooks of an Apprentice Boxer*. Oxford: Oxford University Press.

———. 2006. *Urban Outcasts: A Comparative Sociology of Advanced Marginality*. Cambridge: Polity.

Wacquant, Loïc J. D., and William J. Wilson. 1989. "The Cost of Racial and Class Exclusion in the Inner City." *Annals of the American Academy of Political and Social Science* 501:8–25.

Walker, Michael, Stanley Wasserman, and Barry Wellman. 1993. "Statistical Models for Social Support Networks." *Sociological Methods and Research* 21:71–98.

Warren, Roland L. 1978. *The Community in America*. Chicago: Rand McNally College.

Wasserman, Stanley, and Katherine Faust. 1994. *Social Network Analysis: Methods and Applications*. Cambridge: Cambridge University Press.

Watkins-Hayes, Celeste. Forthcoming. *The New Welfare Bureaucrats: Entanglements of Race, Class, and Policy Reform*. Chicago: University of Chicago Press.

Weber, Max. 1978. *Economy and Society: An Outline of Interpretive Sociology*, edited by Guenther Ross and Claus Wittich. Berkeley: University of California Press.

Weiss, Robert Stuart. 1994. *Learning from Strangers: The Art and Method of Qualitative Interview Studies.* New York: Free Press.

Wellman, Barry. 1979. "The Community Question." *American Journal of Sociology: The Intimate Networks of East Yorkers* 84:1201–1231.

———, (Ed.). 1999. *Networks in the Global Village: Life in Contemporary Communities.* Boulder, CO: Westview Press.

Wellman, Barry, and Scot Wortley. 1990. "Different Strokes from Different Folks: Community Ties and Social Support." *American Journal of Sociology* 96:558–588.

Whitebook, Marcy, Carollee Howes, and Deborah Phillips. 1997. *Worthy Work, Unlivable Wages: The National Childcare Staffing Study, 1988-1997.* Washington, DC: Center for Childcare Workforce. Available at http://www.ccw.org/pubs/worthywork.pdf (accessed 8/15/07).

Whitebook, Marcy, and Laura Sakai. 2003. *By a Thread: How Child Care Centers Hold on to Teachers.* Kalamazoo, MI: W. E. Upjohn Institute for Employment Research.

Wilson, Patricia. 1997. "Building Social Capital: A Learning Agenda for the Twenty-first Century." *Urban Studies* 34:745–760.

Wilson, William J. 1987. *The Truly Disadvantaged: The Inner City, the Underclass, and Public Policy.* Chicago: University of Chicago Press.

———. 1996. *When Work Disappears: The World of the New Urban Poor.* New York: Knopf.

Wrigley, Julia. 1995. *Other People's Children: An Intimate Account of the Dilemmas Facing Middle-Class Parents and the Women They Hire to Raise Their Children.* New York: Basic Books.

Wuthnow, Robert. 2004. *Saving America? Faith-Based Services and the Future of Society:* Princeton, NJ: Princeton University Press.

Yin, Robert K. 2003. *Case Study Research: Design and Methods.* Thousand Oaks, CA: Sage Publications.

Zelizer, Viviana. 2005. *The Purchase of Intimacy.* Princeton: Princeton University Press.

Zhou, Minh. 1992. *New York's Chinatown: The Socioeconomic Potential of an Urban Enclave.* Philadelphia: Temple University Press.

Zigler, Edward, and Susan Muenchow. 1992. *Head Start: The Inside Story of America's Most Successful Educational Experiment.* New York: BasicBooks.

Zigler, Edward, and Sally J. Styfco (Eds.). 2004. *The Head Start Debates.* Baltimore: Brookes Publishing Company.

Znaniecky, Florian. 1934. *The Method of Sociology.* New York: Farrar & Rinehart.

Zucker, Lynne G. 1977. "The Role of Institutionalization in Cultural Persistence." *American Sociological Review* 42:726–743.

Index

Page numbers in bold indicate figures or tables.